Temples
of
Chance

David Johnston

Temples
of
Chance

*How America Inc.
Bought Out Murder Inc.
to Win Control of the
Casino Business*

Doubleday
New York   London   Toronto   Sydney   Auckland

PUBLISHED BY DOUBLEDAY
a division of Bantam Doubleday Dell Publishing Group, Inc.
666 Fifth Avenue, New York, New York 10103

DOUBLEDAY and the portrayal of an anchor with a dolphin are
trademarks of Doubleday, a division of Bantam Doubleday Dell
Publishing Group, Inc.

Book design by Patrice Fodero

Library of Congress Cataloging-in-Publication Data
Johnston, David, 1948–
Temples of chance / David Johnston. — 1st ed.
p.   cm.
Includes index.
1. Casinos—Economic aspects—United States.   I. Title.
HV6711.J64   1992
338.4'7795'0973—dc20   92-8727
CIP

ISBN 0-385-41920-1

October 1992

First Edition

1   3   5   7   9   10   8   6   4   2

For
Wallace Turner,
Edwin O. Guthman
and
Eugene L. Roberts, Jr.

Contents

Contents

1

Trump Beaches a Whale

Donald Trump couldn't sleep. He was so nervous that he insisted Al Glasgow call him every thirty minutes until right before dawn, when his three Atlantic City casinos closed.

Glasgow, a gravel-voiced concrete contractor who used to drink mob lawyers under the table in the days before he became one of Trump's closest advisers, stepped from behind the low black marble wall that separated the high-roller tables from the rest of Trump Plaza Hotel & Casino. He rang the boss.

"He's up four point two," Glasgow said, not needing to add the word *million*.

"Make it four point four," Sonny Nathans whispered to Glasgow, who passed the number on from his post on the floor at Trump Plaza, the mighty cash machine that powered the Trump empire, throwing off more than $80 million in 1988.

What had kept Trump up all night was a Japanese businessman with a serene smile, a white shirt open at the collar and gray wool slacks with pockets as big as bank vaults.

Akio Kashiwagi was one of the world's five biggest gamblers, literally a one-in-a-billion customer, who at this very moment in May 1990 was sitting at a green-felt table at Trump Plaza calmly wagering $14

1

million an hour. He had been there for nearly a week. Glasgow called him The Warrior.

For three and a half years Trump Plaza had been trying to lure Kashi-wagi from his mansion near the foot of Mount Fuji, a house known locally as Kashiwagi Palace, to this low-lying island on the New Jersey shore where the South Bronx meets Las-Vegas-by-the-Sea. When Trump flew to Japan in his own Boeing 727 for the Mike Tyson–Buster Douglas world heavyweight championship fight he presented this fellow real estate speculator with an autographed copy of his myth-making autobiography *The Art of the Deal*, a gift Trump would later regret.

Casino executives in London, Las Vegas and down under in Darwin all pursued Kashiwagi, one of that rare breed of gamblers known as *whales* because they are willing to risk $1 million or more during each casino visit. Kashiwagi was, by far, the biggest whale beached in Atlantic City since legal gambling began there in 1978.

There were others who came and lost big, their names and gambling habits kept secret by the corporate priests who minister in the temples of chance. All of the whales led lives as mysterious as the real denizens of the deep.

The most mysterious of them all was Farayala Janna, an Arabic-speaking Colombian national who liked blackjack, was good for a million dollars–plus of credit at Caesars—Trump's arch rival—and for much, much more credit than that at the Aruba Concorde, a little casino in the Caribbean. Janna was also in deep with the Medellín drug cartel, moving cash in and out of one of its most important money-laundering accounts in Miami, passing it through the Aruba Concorde and then on to accounts at the notorious Bank of Credit and Commerce International, or as some wags called it, the Bank of Cocaine and Conspiracies International.

Richard Hartman, another whale, was the lawyer who ran the New York City Patrolmen's Benevolent Association. Hartman claimed he made $6 million a year, all paid to him in cash, and he dropped millions all over Atlantic City. Sometimes Hartman, who was later disbarred, bought his chips with checks cops had written as down payments on homes in deals Hartman was handling.

Philadelphia trucking magnate Leonard Tose lost millions and eventually had to sell his football team, the Philadelphia Eagles.

But the biggest loser of them all was Robert Libutti, who blew $12 million in more than three hundred trips to the craps tables, mostly at Trump Plaza. Once Trump Plaza had emptied his wallet, the casino regulators took their turn at making Libutti's life miserable and ultimately banned him from the casinos.

But none of these men gambled on the scale of Kashiwagi, who drew hushed crowds to the black marble wall, crowds that watched and tried to imagine betting in a few minutes more money than they would earn in a lifetime. So impressive was Kashiwagi's play that, at the baccarat table to his right, hardly anyone noticed an elderly Hong Kong businessman with more than a million dollars at risk.

Kashiwagi began with a huge pile of baked white clay discs flecked with red and blue. The chips cost five thousand dollars each and covered a large portion of the baccarat table. He arranged them twenty in a stack, seven stacks to a row, each row worth seven hundred thousand dollars. There were seventeen of these rows plus one extra stack of chips —$12 million total.

That day, in all of the dozen Atlantic City casinos, all other players together would lose only two-thirds the amount of money sitting on this one table. The $8 million the casinos would rake in would represent the losses of nearly one hundred thousand visitors to this seaside slum that calls itself the Queen of Resorts.

Kashiwagi took a final puff on his Marlboro Light and set it down in the clean ashtray. Instantly, the most voluptuous cocktail waitress in the casino appeared at his side. She bent low in her tiny black velvet suit, which was cut to resemble a merry widow, exchanged the ashtray for a clean one and handed him a moist towel hot from a microwave placed on a table nearby just for him. The fifty-three-year-old real estate baron cleansed his face, returned the towel and with a subtle nod signaled the female dealer to begin.

Like Ian Fleming's James Bond, Kashiwagi favored baccarat. The object is to get nine points. Face cards and tens count as zero, aces count as one. There is no skill involved. Gamblers make only one basic decision: whether to bet for or against the bank. The game's fascination lies in the speed with which money changes hands, which explains why the French call their version chemin de fer or "the railroad."

For six days Kashiwagi had been steaming down this track, betting

3

two hundred thousand dollars on each hand at the rate of seventy hands an hour. His bet never varied from the moment Trump Plaza's casino opened at ten in the morning until it closed just before dawn, a legal requirement in New Jersey at that time. The intention was to give gamblers a chance to get a grip on their pocketbooks before the casinos picked them clean. Kashiwagi had no such concerns. He left the table only for meals, accompanied by his own aides and a squad of casino security guards, and to visit a nearby restroom that had been closed to all other patrons with an "out of order" sign on the handle of a mop stuck in a bucket outside the door.

Kashiwagi told Ernie Cheung, Trump's specialist in Asian marketing, that he was on a round-the-world gambling spree during which he was willing to risk $50 million. Other casinos desperately wanted a piece of that action. Caesars Atlantic City Hotel-Casino, which vied with Trump Plaza as the top money-winner on the Boardwalk, had invited Kashiwagi to drop in. Steve Wynn, the golden boy of Las Vegas gaming, wanted Kashiwagi to visit the Strip and try his luck at the brand-new Mirage, a giant ivory-trimmed gold box featuring a volcano out front, white tigers just off the casino floor and, lest anyone forget its elemental purpose, a huge aquarium behind the registration desk where sharks lurked. But at this moment it was Trump who had Kashiwagi's action—and all the risks that go with it.

The Warrior had visited Trump Plaza once before, twelve weeks earlier, when he beat Trump for $6.4 million in ten hours. Two months before that Kashiwagi had flown to Darwin, where he had won the Australian equivalent of $19 million at the Diamond Beach Casino, bankrupting it.

Trump figured it was now his turn to win. But just to make sure, he paid five thousand dollars to secure the advice of a man who knew as much about baccarat and the numbers that rule the gaming business as anyone else on earth. Hardly a soul besides the executives at the high-roller houses in Atlantic City and Las Vegas has ever heard of Jess Marcum. An owlish little man who in his youth had helped invent radar, he was a founder of the RAND Corporation, the Air Force think tank, and later worked on the neutron bomb. The casino executives all trusted his mathematical genius. Stories abounded among the small circle who

4

knew him of how he would glance down a page filled with numbers and spot one minor error.

Ever since a friend had drawn him from his think-tank office in Santa Monica to see the horses at Hollywood Park in 1953, Marcum had been hooked on gaming theory. He quit RAND and started placing bets in Las Vegas. Within two years he had become wealthy. He was also banned from every betting parlor in town simply because he hardly ever seemed to lose. He managed a casino once, but that was thirty years ago when he was young and foolish enough to think a great mathematical mind made for a great casino operator.

Now Marcum lived in a Reno hotel, placing ice hockey bets based on a complex formula designed to exploit anomalies in the wagering patterns of other players. And he was a consultant with some of the casinos. Marcum had endeared himself to the industry by inventing a new baccarat bet, the tie, that was lucrative beyond even the greedy imaginings of casino owners.

Gamblers who bet that the bank and the player will get the same score have a chance to win seven dollars for each dollar they risk. But the odds of a tie are eight to one, giving the house a whopping 14.4 percent advantage on each tie bet. At Caesars Palace in Las Vegas, where gamblers buy more than $500 million worth of chips each year, tie bets account for just 3 percent of the money wagered at the baccarat tables, but provide 10 percent of what the house rakes in. It is a sucker's bet, Marcum said. It was one bet Kashiwagi never made.

Kashiwagi and his entourage had arrived in Atlantic City on a Thursday. The next day he began demonstrating that he understood that the art of the deal in high stakes casino gaming occurs in the casino cage, the gambling hall's financial office, where players buy their chips. He had told Cheung when he arrived that he wanted to gamble $22 million at Trump Plaza. He was told to bring checks that could be verified easily and cleared through the banks. Instead Kashiwagi brought a $6 million check drawn on a Singapore bank and a $4 million instrument that could be cashed only in Japan. He asked for $12 million in credit.

Mike Mullen, the Trump Plaza cage manager, confirmed that the $6 million Singapore check was good. He sent it to Manufacturers Hanover in New York, which would send it on to Asia. But Mullen rejected the $4 million instrument, one of many that Kashiwagi had brought in a brief-case, because it was cashable only in person at a particular bank in Japan. The casino authorized a $6 million line of credit, which when added to the Singapore check provided $12 million for chips.

The maximum bet was set at two hundred thousand dollars per hand, double what anyone else in Atlantic City had ever been allowed to wager.

Kashiwagi was ready. The Warrior strolled across the bold red-and-gold Trump Plaza carpet to the high-roller area. An aide carried the fortune in chips in boxes under his arms, uniformed security guards making sure the path was clear and that others saw how royally big players were treated.

Most gamblers vary their bets. They believe in streaks. When they feel lucky, they double their bets; when they feel the cards are running against them, they cut back. Marcum thought this was all hokum at baccarat, where only probability, but no skill, is involved.

"There are no such things as lucky streaks," Marcum said, "but all gamblers believe in them." Well, almost all. Kashiwagi liked to make the same flat bet with every hand, firing as many bullets—as he called his chips—as he could each time. Marcum knew this was the smartest way to bet. It was math, pure math. But while the casino executives paid Marcum for his knowledge, he knew that in their hearts they were all believers in that great and fickle goddess, Lady Luck. In that respect, Marcum was an atheist.

Marcum, in a confidential written report to Trump, calculated that even with Kashiwagi's bold and smart betting style, the odds were five-to-one that the high roller would lose his bankroll before doubling it. That meant if Kashiwagi made six visits and bought $12 million in chips each time, Trump could expect to win five times, collecting $60 million, and lose once, leaving Trump with a net win of $48 million.

Each time Kashiwagi made a bet the odds favored the house, but only by a tiny margin. The only decision in baccarat is to bet with the player or the bank. Because of a dozen subtle rules, the odds on a "player" bet favor the house by 1.36 percent while a "banker" bet gives the house a 1.17 percent advantage. But the house also takes as its fee, or *vigorish,* 5 percent of any winning banker bet. Kashiwagi switched from player to banker bets at random.

Those statistical slivers grow in importance as the play continues, eroding the player's remaining bankroll. The house advantage works like the reverse of compound interest, which makes a dollar saved grow over time. After 10,000 hands, Marcum's calculations showed, Trump could expect to win 5,125 bets to Kashiwagi's 4,875. At that point Kashiwagi theoretically would be out $50 million. In reality his $12 million stake would have been lost long before them.

"Probability is like a wave," Marcum explained, running his hand up and down across an imaginary line on which player and casino are even. "Because of the house advantage, over time the player dips lower and lower until he stops crossing the midpoint and ultimately loses all his money, unless he quits first."

The problem for the casino is that a player may quit at the top of the curve. That's what Kashiwagi had done in February. He quit while he was ahead. Marcum's pages of handwritten numbers showed that after seventy hands, about one hour of play at baccarat, there was a 46 percent chance that Kashiwagi would be ahead. But after seventy hours of play, the likelihood that Kashiwagi would be winning would have shriveled to just 15 percent.

On the second day of Kashiwagi's marathon play in May, however, his curve remained well above the line.

Trump flew down from Manhattan that Saturday accompanied by arms merchant Adnan Khashoggi, four vivacious blondes and an Arab prince. Khashoggi was well known in gambling circles, especially for all the unpaid markers he had left behind at the Sands in Las Vegas, which its chief executive blamed for that casino's collapse in 1983.

The deal artist, the arms merchant and the Arab prince checked into Trump Castle and that evening limoed over to Trump Plaza. Trump introduced Khashoggi to Kashiwagi, saying they must have met because they traveled in the same circles. They had not.

Khashoggi sat down at the high-limit blackjack table next to Kashiwagi's baccarat table and began to play.

Trump hung around, pumping hands and cocking his ears to hear how great he was. Some saw Trump's behavior as nervous pacing, rather than his usual glad-handing. Casino owners, favored by the odds, are not supposed to begrudge lucky players their winnings, are not supposed to "sweat the action." And if they do sweat, they should do it from their executive offices, watching on a remote television screen, their anxiety hidden from the player. Within a quarter hour, Trump had grown restless and left.

Soon Kashiwagi was ahead $6.8 million. Together with the $12 million in chips he had bought, his pot had grown to $18.6 million. His 3,720 chips could not be stacked on the table neatly, so rows of chips were arranged on the floor next to him. Crowds gathered along the low black marble wall just to stare at all the money. Kashiwagi seemed oblivious, continuing to wager steadily.

Finally Trump panicked. He wanted the game stopped. Now. He could stop the game at any time by lowering the maximum bet that the house would accept. Glasgow and everyone else involved knew that lowering the limit would be an insult, that Kashiwagi would almost certainly storm out and probably never return—and he would be leaving with all that money.

And they knew word would get around that Donald Trump was not a worthy opponent but a coward. This was an extremely sensitive subject with Trump. While he gloried in his image as a fearless capitalist, he surrounded himself with bodyguards. And while he sponsored heavyweight fights, he had also acknowledged that he could not imagine a physical blow and recoiled from the thought of being struck. That Trump's image could descend from all powerful into fancy-pants wimp vexed some of his executives and advisers.

Glasgow put Marcum on the phone to Trump.

"He's on a winning streak," Trump insisted, his voice gathering force for one of his frequent temperamental storms. Is Kashiwagi cheating? he asked. No, Marcum said, Kashiwagi is no cheat.

"Be patient," Marcum counseled. "He wants to keep playing, and soon the wave will run the other way." Trump said he would let the game go on a bit longer, but he wanted to know at once if Kashiwagi's pot continued to grow.

The game was less than half over. But before it ended, some of the most interesting action would take place away from the baccarat table.

2

America Inc. Buys Out Murder Inc.

Since the dashing Bugsy Siegel built America's first gambling resort, the Flamingo, in 1946, mobsters and murder have shaped the desolate stretch of asphalt known as South Las Vegas Boulevard into the pulsating neon forest known around the world as the Strip. The idea that Las Vegas is a Mafia-run playground, and that Atlantic City is the Mafia's empire in the East, contains powerful romantic appeal. *The Godfather* and a thousand other movies, novels and television shows have burned into the public consciousness the image of casino gambling as a mob business.

That image no longer reflects reality.

Today the Flamingo is owned by Hilton Hotels Corporation, a Fortune Service 500 company traded on the New York Stock Exchange (NYSE). Next door, at the corner of the Strip and Dunes Boulevard, stands the Barbary Coast, whose investors include Richard Crane, former chief of the U. S. Justice Department Organized Crime Strike Force in Los Angeles, which prosecutes Vegas mobsters. Across Dunes Boulevard from the Barbary Coast is Bally's Las Vegas. It opened as the MGM Grand and then, after a disastrous 1980 fire that killed eighty-four people, was acquired by Bally Manufacturing, another NYSE company. Catty-corner from Bally's Las Vegas and across the Strip from the Fla-

9

mingo, Roman statuary guards a grand oval reflecting pool bordered by streams of cool water cascading into the desert air. This ancient imperial setting encompasses Caesars Palace, the casino most associated with mobsters in films. Money from the then-mob-dominated Teamsters union built this pleasure dome in 1966, but today its stock also trades on the NYSE. Its chief executive's office, a dice throw from Beverly Hills, has not been occupied by a mob associate for more than a decade.

Next to Caesars, behind a tropical lagoon dotted with palm trees and a volcano that shoots steam and flames into the night air, stands the most ostentatious gambling palace of them all, Steve Wynn's Mirage, which opened on Thanksgiving weekend 1989. Mirage Resorts' stock trades on the Big Board, too. Across the street from the Mirage, next to Hilton's Flamingo, sits the giant riverboat facade of Harrah's (until recently called the Holiday casino). It was once owned by a company that became a household name by catering to middle-class American families on vacation, the Holiday Inn chain based in Memphis, Tennessee. The stock of Holiday and its successor firm, the Promus Companies, also trade on the NYSE.

Ramada Inn bought the Tropicana in 1979—twenty-two years after that casino opened as a mob joint.

Across the Strip from the Trop a gargantuan white version of a medieval castle with bright red-and-blue spires rose in 1990. The Excalibur is the world's largest hotel, with four thousand budget rooms and a two-and-a-half-acre casino designed on a Knights of the Round Table theme. Excalibur is owned by Circus Circus, a New York Stock Exchange company so well-managed that every third dollar in revenues flows directly into its treasury.

On the third corner at South Las Vegas and Tropicana boulevards, investors are backing the building of an even larger casino resort, the five-thousand-room MGM, which will adjoin a theme park filled with rides and amusements inspired by the classic 1939 MGM film *The Wizard of Oz*. The fourth corner is owned by a Japanese firm that builds slot machines. In time another giant casino is sure to rise from this sand-swept place.

Fly east to Atlantic City and the story is similar. Hilton, Holiday and Ramada all came here, although Hilton had to sell out to Donald Trump when it was refused a New Jersey casino license in 1985 because of past

10

mob ties that the company refused to confess. (Hilton tried again and easily won a New Jersey license in 1991.)

Caesars is in Atlantic City, too. Bally has two Boardwalk casinos, one of them purchased from Steve Wynn's company at a fantastically inflated price when he retreated to the desert to create his Mirage.

The Atlantic City market is dominated, though, by Donald Trump. He owns three of the area's twelve casinos and controlled Resorts, the first Boardwalk gambling hall, until Merv Griffin bought it in a hostile takeover that grew from stock market manipulation. Shares of two Trump casinos and Resorts trade on the American Stock Exchange, as do the bonds of all four casinos.

Of the dozen casinos in Atlantic City all but one has publicly traded stock or bonds. A complex partnership owns the exception, the Claridge, which until 1989 had been the property of a publicly traded company with an interesting tie to the history of modern Las Vegas: the old owner was the Del E. Webb Corp., which built the Flamingo for Bugsy Siegel.

The individual gamblers and their underworld backers who built Las Vegas, and who escaped both jail and hitmen, began selling out two decades ago, replaced by a new generation of owners: corporations specializing in the business of risk. In the casino industry, America Inc. bought out Murder Inc.

Brand name hotel chains—Hilton, Holiday, Ramada—moved into the gambling business in the seventies. Meanwhile, New Jersey casino regulators forced men tainted by dealings with mobsters to resign as the chief executives of Bally Manufacturing and Caesars. These five firms, plus Wynn's Mirage, Circus Circus and Trump dominate the casino business in America today.

The gambling boom that rebuilt the Atlantic City Boardwalk and launched a new era on the Strip in Las Vegas was not limited to America, but was part of a global phenomenon. From Moscow to Sidney, from Saipan to Warsaw, and from Cairo to Aruba investors poured money into new temples of chance designed to attract the prospering multitudes to their games.

Just as Bugsy Siegel saw the potential for Las Vegas in the prosperity that was sure to follow the Second World War, in the seventies and eighties the corporate executives who ran the megacasinos in Nevada and New Jersey began envisioning the potential for a global gambling market. Their most intensive missionary work was reserved for those who had access to millions or even tens of millions of dollars and were driven by the desire to advance into the realm of high rollers.

Australia, whose government envied the growing riches of Japan (where casino wagering is forbidden) started casinos aimed at Asian tourists and invited Harrah's, Pratt Hotel and others to bid for licenses. In Canada entrepreneurs devised the most ambitious gambling plan ever, a global lottery whose prize was an annuity that would pay out $1 billion, an idea whose success awaits only government approvals. Carnival Cruise Lines showed its competitors how to fatten profit margins by adding a few blackjack and roulette tables and some slot machines to help vacationers while away the hours just as passengers had on Mississippi paddle wheelers a century and a half earlier.

During the eighties corporate gamblers applied mass merchandising techniques to give betting a new image, although the underlying reality remained unchanged. The basic human desires that make gambling appealing to most people still stir the blood, but with help from master advertising men—one of whom went on to mold President Bush's image in the White House—these gaming corporations successfully repackaged the popular view of gambling, selling it as just another form of recreation by making it appear to be free of either moral or financial worries.

Their success selling gambling as entertainment, as a fun way to pass an evening or a week, holds important consequences for the nation's economic future because it ignores the potential for ruin and how the casinos encourage that outcome. Casino marketers direct attention away from the psychological pull that makes some players into compulsive gamblers who will steal to play and many more into obsessives who plunk every spare quarter into the slots. Unlike cocaine or Disneyland, which can be consumed only until exhaustion sets in, there is no limit to how much a gambler can lose in a single sitting.

The level of betting practiced regularly by high rollers today was never allowed when mobsters controlled the casino business in Nevada. The mob lacked the bankroll to pay out winnings that might reach a million bucks in five minutes. Then casinos were run by men who learned casino management on the streets and who relied on the crude

12

method of skimming casino winnings in the count room to make their operations worthwhile.

They have been succeeded by college graduates expert at handling money. Today's casino companies are run by graduates of Harvard, Cornell and Penn's Wharton School of Finance. These executives earn extraordinary sums even in the context of the bloated salaries of corporate America. Former stockbroker Richard Gillman, who runs Bally's four casinos, earned a base pay of $4 million for years and in 1988 was paid more than $10 million. (His name did not appear in the business magazine lists of well paid CEOs, however, because he only ran Bally's casino unit.) Dennis Gomes was paid $1.2 million in his first year as president of Donald Trump's Taj Mahal Casino Resort, more than the chief executive of the Ford Motor Company earned. David P. Hanlon earned more than $2 million cash in 1991 to head Merv Griffin's struggling Resorts casinos.

These giant paychecks are possible because the modern hotel-mega-casino generates a torrent of cash, a torrent so huge that it can allow even abysmally managed companies to survive year after disastrous year. A hotel with a casino can net more money *each week* than a plain hotel of similar size might net in a year or even two. Hilton's four Nevada casinos bring it more than twice the revenues of its 264 franchised hotels combined.

Nowhere was the fantastic profitability of well-managed casinos more evident than at the Holiday Corporation. In 1989 there were 1,589 Holiday Inns scattered across the land, yet the Holiday Corporation that year earned twenty-eight cents of each dollar's profit from a single building in a marsh along the New Jersey shore—Harrah's Marina Hotel Casino in Atlantic City. The lure of such phenomenal profits from gambling prompted Holiday management to sell its namesake business in January 1990 to Bass Ale, the British brewers, and to create a new firm devoted to becoming the leading gaming concern in the world. Because it promised to make shareholders and management rich in the nineties and beyond, this new firm was named the Promus Companies.

Ramada quickly followed suit, selling its lodging chain and emerging as a new firm with three big casinos, but saddled with inept management. Barron Hilton tried the same move, but couldn't get a high enough price for the hotel side of the Hilton Hotel Corporation.

13

These corporate gamblers and others are now investing in lavish fantasy gambling resorts that combine flamboyant design with what the Disney folks—frequent advisers to the casino industry—call *imagineering.* Their aim is to bedazzle customers, creating must-see attractions that will draw millions of new players and keep the old ones coming back.

But fantasy costs money. Wynn's Mirage features the only man-made volcano on earth, a fifty-four-foot cone belching fire and steam every quarter hour after dark. Behind this desert resort dolphins frolic in a seaquarium. The Mirage cost $630 million to build. Circus Circus' Excalibur, with its indoor dinner theater built around a giant dirt ring where knights joust twice nightly, was a comparatively low-budget affair costing $290 million. When completed the new MGM in Las Vegas, with its Oz theme park, will have cost about $1 billion.

Such megacasino projects require access to capital on a scale that the Mafia could not produce even with its influence over the Teamsters union and its profits from drugs, loan-sharking and sweetheart government contracts. The corporate gamblers' friend who made these fantasy palaces possible was Michael Milken of the now bankrupt Drexel Burnham Lambert securities firm. For years Wynn boasted that Golden Nugget was the first investment banking client Milken brought to Drexel, a boast that lost some of its value after Milken admitted to six felonies and took up residence at the Club Fed an hour's drive from San Francisco.

Milken addicted casino executives to junk, not the kind heroin addicts shoot into their veins in the burned-out buildings a block from the Boardwalk casinos, but the kind companies inject onto their books. Junk bonds catapulted Steve Wynn from a mere millionaire to a fortune two hundred times that size, commanding a company with a billion dollars in annual revenue. Hilton, Holiday, Ramada, Circus Circus and Merv Griffin all loaded up on Drexel debt while Donald Trump and others relied on junk sold by Drexel's imitators. Casino companies sold more than $5 billion worth of junk bonds in the eighties, some of which was never paid back despite the supposedly intense regulation of modern casinos by the states of New Jersey and Nevada.

The need for these enormous pools of money to finance megacasinos required the major gaming companies to issue stock and bonds. Today anyone can own part of a casino, occasionally for less money per share than it takes to activate some slot machines. That prosaic fact is not the concept that the casinos want to project, however, to players looking for excitement. The casino companies continue to foster the fiction that mobsters run the joints because an aura of criminality is good for business, appealing to people who would like to rub shoulders with one of John Gotti's henchmen, albeit in a secure environment. Bob Stupak, sole owner of Vegas World (where the Strip begins), believes corporate-owned casinos are bad for business because boring corporate bureaucrats run them. Characters like Benny Binion, who bragged of killing those who crossed him, and Bill Harrah, who in his sixties drag-raced teens at Reno traffic lights, are what the casinos need, he says. Except for himself and Steve Wynn, though, the colorful characters are mostly gone. "What this town needs," Stupak said one night after beating the competing Aladdin casino's craps table for twenty-four thousand dollars in five minutes, "is that scent of vice, a little sin, to stir that desire to come to Las Vegas."

The godfathers and the wise guys did not just disappear from the casinos when Wall Street arrived. Like many founders leaving a business, they were smart enough to figure out ways to continue getting paid. Mob-connected firms still arrange many gambling junkets, provide buses and limousines, and handle headliners in the showrooms. The result of the continuing involvement of mob figures in lucrative supporting roles is a dangerous mix of legitimacy and illegitimacy that without aggressive regulation invites scandal, political upheaval and corruption. Casinos remain attractive places to launder illicit cash from cocaine smuggling and insider trading on Wall Street. The mob has discovered rich opportunities in manipulating casino securities.

Today the brand-name companies and others that control the casino industry are busy increasing their market and expanding commercial gambling across the country. Their goal is to make gambling a routine leisure activity for most Americans, as it has become for 28 percent of metropolitan Philadelphia residents—from gritty South Philadelphia row houses as well as the mansions of the Main Line. Among their strategies is encouraging young adults to gamble often—and on credit—as the beer and cigarette companies aim to make customers for life of people just entering adulthood. With their new attractions, from caged tigers to strolling court jesters to a theme park filled with rides, Wynn,

15

Circus Circus and others are leading a movement to market Las Vegas as a family vacation center, a move that will acquaint legions of little children with the excitement of Las Vegas.

When Nevada had a monopoly on legal American casinos, the social and economic problems posed by gambling had a limited impact. Then, in 1978, Atlantic City brought legal casinos to the East Coast; suddenly one in four Americans lived within a six-hour drive of a blackjack table. A decade later South Dakota voters approved gambling in Deadwood. Play started there in 1990, setting off an explosion of casino gambling. Since then Colorado, Illinois, Iowa, Louisiana and Mississippi have legalized casinos, while gambling halls run by Indians flourish in California, Connecticut, Michigan, Minnesota, Nebraska and Wisconsin.

Indian-owned casinos are likely soon in Florida, Kansas, Nevada, Oklahoma, South Dakota and Washington state. Steve Wynn's Mirage and other experienced casino companies are signing contracts to manage these casinos. The mob has also tried to muscle in on some Indian gaming and at least one Indian leader who spoke out against such involvement was murdered.

Just as significant, and perhaps more so, video slot machines are proliferating, and many in the industry believe they will be a standard feature in nearly every neighborhood tavern in America within a few years. They are already legal along Maryland's Eastern Shore and in Montana, Oregon, South Dakota and West Virginia. Bills to legalize video poker in bars are being pushed aggressively in state capitals across the land, backed not only by the manufacturers, but by public officials who contend that the government cannot adequately police illegal slot machines—so it should license them and share in the profits as a way to ease the burdens of taxpayers.

So completely, and quietly, has the trend toward universal casino gambling swept the nation that few people realize that Minnesota now has more casinos than New Jersey. Significantly, one of those is run under an agreement with the city of Duluth, which receives nearly a quarter of the profits from the casino that's housed in an old Sears store. State lottery officials around the nation have closely followed this trend, which started in Canada, and West Virginia has already joined it. More

16

casinos managed or owned by state and local governments are a virtual certainty.

Gambling interests are aggressively pushing for legalization of casino games in a variety of states, including Indiana, Missouri, New York, Pennsylvania and Washington. By 1992, every state but two, Utah and Hawaii, had laws making legal at least one form of commercial gambling: lotteries, casinos, dog or horse racing, jai alai, bingo, sports betting or charity "Las Vegas Nights."

Achieving the gambling industry's goals depends on cooperation from politicians, who must pass laws granting the corporate gamblers exemptions from the criminal statutes governing gambling. In many states approval of gambling occurred only after corporate gamblers and lawmakers joined in promising to funnel the government's cut to specific constituencies, usually senior citizens or public schools.

By the turn of the century half of the states or more will probably have casinos, in part because of a 1987 U.S. Supreme Court decision that recognized the right of Indian tribes to offer any gambling games on their reservations that are allowed in the state where the reservation is located. Thirty-one states allow charities to raise funds through so-called Las Vegas Nights, and fourteen of these states have recognized Indian reservations.

Just outside the little seaport of Mystic, Connecticut, the Mashantucket Pequot Indian tribe's Foxwoods High Stakes Bingo and Casino offers craps, poker, blackjack and other table games, but not slot machines. Within a month of opening, the table drop at Foxwoods—the amount of chips sold—exceeded that at Trump Plaza in Atlantic City. The Pequots plan to add hotels, restaurants and other amenities. Other Indian nations from Nebraska to California are moving to copy all or part of this format, some with professional management.

The gambling companies successfully sold riverboat casinos as the way to polish up Rust Belt centers like Davenport, Iowa, even though they will create few new jobs and may worsen the woes of retailers, as dollars that would have gone to buy toasters and cars, and into a nest egg to supplement pensions, instead are lost at floating craps tables. Some hospitality business chains envision franchising hotels in Old West towns like Deadwood, which before gambling were too small to

17

warrant their attention. In theory gambling is supposed to revive Deadwood as a historic town, the place where Wild Bill Hickok died with two pair, aces and eights, in his hand and a bullet in the back.

Small distant towns like Cripple Creek, Colorado, or even Iowa riverports, are not the main interest of the billion-dollar gambling companies like Promus and Mirage Resorts. They want to manage casinos near larger cities like Denver and Omaha. The corporate gamblers also want casinos in the first-class Manhattan hotels, at historic Penn's Landing in Philadelphia, along Pittsburgh's three rivers, in downtown Detroit, and on the lakefront sites of abandoned steel mills in Gary, Indiana, a short drive from the Chicago Loop. In St. Louis and New Orleans and in every other city seeking economic revival, the gambling companies promise new jobs if only legislators will exempt them from laws that make commercial gambling a crime.

As well-paying industrial jobs have begun to dry up in America, the children of the blue-collar workers who once fit truck cabs to frames or cabinets to television sets or, if they were skilled, machined parts on a lathe, are finding gambling tables the nineties' equivalent of the assembly lines where their parents labored. Like their parents they perform repetitive tasks that require little education, such as shuffling cards and passing the dice after a player craps out. The new jobs mean coming home with clean fingernails. They also mean less money, often less than half what their parents made with fewer benefits, little individual job security and no sense that their labor is building anything tangible or enduring. In Atlantic City a side effect has been rising juvenile delinquency, even in the suburbs, with few parents available for weekend activities from organized soccer to church visits.

Casinos were supposed to be the catalyst to rebuild Atlantic City. The promise has never been fulfilled, however, because the law worked against redevelopment by requiring that each temple of chance in Atlantic City be a self-contained city. The main purpose is gambling, but within the temple walls people can dine, drink, exercise, make love and sleep. To tempt those who quit the games while they were ahead, and to keep their winnings from leaving the temple, pricey boutiques offer an array of fancy raiment as well as Tiffany diamonds, Leroy Neiman prints and Kron chocolates.

The casinos are to Atlantic City as factories are to a Third World country, thrown up at a distant location, served by a highway designed primarily to obtain raw materials and ship out finished products. The raw materials coming down the Atlantic City Expressway are wallets and pocketbooks, which are cleaned of their paper and plastic and then sent back up the highway to be filled again for another trip.

Making full-blown casinos, on land or afloat, easily available to most Americans is just one part of the corporate plan to profit by infecting America with an incurable case of gambling fever. Another gambling company, International Game Technology of Reno, wants to create a vast new market for its video poker machines, which allow gamblers to play cards with a computer. IGT wants its high-tech slot machines in every neighborhood bar. But knowing that the term *slot machines* might arouse opposition, the firm relies on the sort of polished sleight of hand long employed by Madison Avenue.

IGT president Charles Mathewson believes there is a market for several hundred thousand of these machines, which differ from casino slots only in that instead of the plink, plink, plink of quarters falling into a metal tray, winners get a slip of paper that the bartender will trade for cash or another shot of bourbon. Because the machines pay winners in scrip, not coin, the gambling industry calls them Video Lottery Terminals or VLTs. The one-armed bandits of the cashless society.

As the nineties began, bills to make slot machines legal began popping up in statehouses like crab grass in spring. "I simply cannot keep track of them all," lamented William R. Eadington, a University of Nevada–Reno economics professor who has been a leader in examining the rise of corporate-owned casinos and the spread of gambling beyond the Silver and Garden states. Sponsors of these slot machine bills argued that the mob earns growing profits from illegal slot machines in bars, many of them fitted with switches so their video screens can change instantly to resemble lawful arcade games.

E. E. "Butch" Brian, the West Virginia lottery director, contends that residents pump $280 million into mob-owned video poker machines, depriving his impoverished Appalachian state of vital revenues. He wants the state government to take over this business, saying it would ease the burdens on taxpayers. In 1990, at Mountaineer Race Track, the West Virginia lottery installed banks of Video Lottery Terminals. After nine months this government-sponsored gambling parlor was produc-

19

ing profits for one of the poorest states in the country at an annual rate of nearly seven thousand dollars per machine. South Dakota's lottery licensed the same kind of modified slot machines in bars, prompting an immediate 51 percent jump in its lottery revenues.

Some state lottery directors want to go even further than running government-sponsored slot machine parlors. Many of them are looking north to Canada, where in December 1989, the Manitoba Lottery Foundation opened a casino in Winnipeg, a city of six hundred thousand that is just sixty miles north of the Minnesota border. Despite limits on betting it won nearly $20 million from its patrons in the following year.

Eugene Martin Christiansen, a leading gambling industry consultant, watched all the activity taking place to legalize and expand gambling as the nineties began and concluded that "there is a general move toward legal casino-type games. It is part of a fundamental change that is irreversible at this point because the country is changing with fewer people going to church, more older people with time and money on their hands and, especially, with state lottery advertising campaigns that make it seem that buying lottery tickets is almost a patriotic duty."

During the Reagan years Las Vegas shamelessly wrapped itself in the flag, selling itself through national television commercials as "The American Way to Play." Sig Rogich, the veteran Strip publicity agent who coined that phrase, moved on to George Bush's 1988 presidential campaign and then into the White House. President Bush put Rogich in charge of remaking his image from wimp into the brave leader of a New World Order.

As America approaches the dawn of a new millennium, its industrial might withering, the business of chance prospers. The automobile, steel and electronics industries are in shambles, while legal gambling is one of the country's fastest-growing businesses, touted by politicians as the way to revive dying towns and create jobs. That casinos create no new wealth, that they act to take money from many people and funnel it to the few lucky enough to hold a casino license, seems of little consequence to the growing number of politicians urging more gambling on the public.

Christiansen predicts that between 1989 and 1995 the amount of money Americans lose in casinos will grow by two thirds, from $9 billion to $15 billion. Expand the measure of gambling to include state lotteries—the biggest gambling game of them all—plus horse racing, dog tracks, bingo run by churches and Native Americans as well as legal sports betting, and the total Americans lost gambling legally in 1989 came to $24 billion. Christensen expects that will increase to $40 billion by 1995. Few industries in an era of slow growth or retrenchment can imagine such phenomenal growth, especially for a multibillion-dollar industry whose basic offering is almost as old as mankind's ability to count.

One argument for casinos is that the wise guys continue to shoot the dice at the craps tables. In a perverse way casinos help recycle mob dollars from extortion, loan-sharking and drugs back into the legitimate economy. High rollers generally do not play with money legitimately earned and already taxed by the government. They play with unreported or underreported dollars and in time many of them come to financial ruin or an early death because of their profligacy. Casino owners, too, can run wild with all the cash that comes their way, squandering it instead of using it to expand their businesses or branch out into other economic activities. (Christiansen and others who have studied the industry understand that the financial troubles of Donald Trump's and Merv Griffin's casinos result from borrowing binges and poor management, not from any fundamental weakness in the business of risk.)

Many leaders in the gambling business consider Christensen's projections conservative, in part because he foresees less government sponsorship than others predict. Flayed by citizens who want additional services from lower taxes, governments now look upon gambling as an easy street for raising money. Pressure to create jobs in areas hardest hit by white-collar layoffs, factory closings and economic decline is spurring more states to approve casinos. Thomas D. Carver, president of the New Jersey Casino Association, believes that the future will include more legal gambling in more places because "government is engaged in a desperate search for ways to raise revenues without raising taxes, and it sees gambling as a painless way to raise money."

Casinos are also engaged in a desperate search for states and cities that will give them just enough regulation to protect them from extortion by organized crime. They want to be otherwise free to run their businesses as they please, to push liquor on a suddenly rich man until he signs away his last penny, to let teenagers play so long as they lose, to borrow money in the securities markets that will never be repaid. They want a double standard in which expendables—dealers, cocktail waitresses, busted high rollers—face severe regulatory actions while owners and executives flout the law and risk nothing more serious than a fine. They want the *appearance* of regulation, and governments desperate for funds are giving it to them.

This growing alliance between the corporate gamblers and politicians is only the latest manifestation of a long history of mutually shared interests between those who understand games of chance and those who exercise political power. Twice before, corruption has brought an end to such alliances. But this third wave of gambling fever is rapidly gaining force, and no one knows when it will crest.

3

The Founding Fathers

Three Greek brothers gambled one day, testing their fates with the only higher authority they knew: chance. Their lots cast, Zeus won and became ruler of the universe. Poseidon did reasonably well, winning command of the seas. But the loser, Hades, descended into that awful hell known to every busted gambler.

From the earliest days of human society, casting lots—often by drawing straws or tossing dice made from the knuckle bones of sheep— was a way to ask the gods for answers to dilemmas. The high priest who wanted influence soon learned to become a "sharper," positioning the straws just right, shaving the dice, or even devising elaborate rules to ensure that more than random chance would determine the outcome. In many societies it was a serious crime for anyone but the high priest to touch the instruments used to divine the will of the gods. This imbued the dice with a sacred quality. It also made sure no one could tell if they were loaded.

The desire to risk is an essential part of human nature. Examples of gaming can be found around the world and throughout human civilization. As the Commission on the Review of the National Policy Toward Gambling observed in 1976, "Gambling is inevitable."

Gambling shaped the American character not just in the Wild West, but almost from the very start. Gambling subsidized one of the first English settlements in America and also bedeviled its residents.

The Jamestown colony in Virginia was settled, beginning in 1607, by poor people drawn from the streets of London with promises of opportunity to prosper in the New World. But these unwitting pioneers possessed few skills needed to settle a wilderness. To minimize idleness among the settlers, strict laws were passed to limit gambling. Their lack of work ethic, combined with harsh conditions, meant no profits for the Virginia Company of London. So in the company's third charter, in 1612, the crown granted the struggling company a license to run lotteries. In the following decade these lotteries became the major source of revenue sustaining the colony with fresh provisions and settlers, replacing those lost to disease, accidents and conflict with the Indians.

As other settlements developed gambling became an increasingly significant aspect of colonial life. George Washington, Thomas Jefferson and Benjamin Franklin sponsored private lotteries, making them the "numbers men" of their day. In 1774 Rhode Islanders spent the equivalent of three dollars per capita on the state lottery, economists Charles T. Clotfelter and Philip J. Cook calculated, an enormous sum considering the tiny cash incomes of the era. Harvard, Yale, Princeton and King's College (now called Columbia University) all relied on lotteries to pay for buildings. By the 1770s lotteries, both official and illegal, had proliferated so widely that King George III tried to eliminate those that did not directly benefit the crown or its colonial governments, or, worse, fueled opposition to British rule.

"The English colonies comprised the first in a series of American Wests where the affinity between gambling and the frontier stood out boldly," historian John Findlay wrote in his book *People of Chance*. "On the frontier as well as at gaming tables, Westerners found opportunities to get something for nothing . . . the adventurous outlook of westward migrants made the frontier an ideal breeding ground for distinctly American forms of gambling" like poker.

When the Continental Congress declared independence from England on July 4, 1776, it turned to gambling to finance the fight, sponsoring the United States Lottery to raise $1.5 million. This blending of patriotic impulses and gambling set a precedent that continues today in the symbol used to market Las Vegas—a red, white and blue banner with a star and stripes.

Other early American lotteries financed public works, their size growing along with the need for public improvements to develop the country. The great showman P. T. Barnum, said to have observed that "there's a sucker born every minute," got his start selling lottery tickets. In the early 1800s residents of Philadelphia, then the largest city in the New World, could visit three shops selling lottery tickets. Wagering grew so quickly that in 1831 Philadelphia was sustaining 177 lottery shops.

As lotteries expanded from predominantly small raffles among people who knew each other into large private enterprises, corruption followed. So did opposition from religious leaders. Public support dwindled as crooked operators became more numerous, some pocketing the money without awarding prizes and others arranging for confederates to win. State after state banned lotteries until, at the start of the Civil War, only three states—Delaware, Missouri and Kentucky—still allowed them.

Meanwhile, illegal casino games grew, especially among those on the long, boring journey to the outposts of civilization. Riverboat gamblers helped travelers pass the time, at great expense and often with the help of marked cards and accomplices. While fifties television series like *Yancy Derringer* and *Maverick* built their fanciful tales around riverboat gamblers driven to seek justice and possessed of hearts of gold, those who were taken by the sharpers felt quite differently. The real riverboat gamblers were called *blacklegs*, meaning cheaters and outlaws, and the bulk of the people hated them.

Blacklegs operated openly in the rough and dangerous port towns along the Mississippi River in the early 1800s, the major avenue of commerce in what was then called the American Southwest. In most towns they limited themselves to the water's edge and to the paddle wheelers that took days to work their way north from New Orleans to Memphis. In Vicksburg, Mississippi, ramshackle gambling dens were thrown up throughout the town. The gamblers' influence and economic devastation grew until vigilantes took to the streets in 1835, breaking down the doors of gambling halls and smashing faro and poker tables. When five sharpers barricaded themselves in one gambling joint on July 6, 1835, vigilantes tore the place apart, strung the five up, and left their bodies twisting in the wind until the next day. That same month, upriver in Memphis, citizens chased the local gamblers across the river into Arkansas.

I. Nelson Rose, a professor of criminal law who specializes in gambling issues, sees the end of the lotteries just before rebels fired on Fort Sumter as the end of what he calls the first wave of legal gambling in America. The second wave, he theorizes, began after the Civil War, as the defeated southern states, desperate for capital to rebuild public facilities, authorized a variety of lotteries. But the second wave came crashing to an end when the Louisiana Lottery Company, a private business that arranged its franchise by buying the votes of individual state lawmakers, tried to buy the Baton Rouge lawmakers wholesale. Congress passed laws barring use of the mails to sell lottery tickets, which devastated the Louisiana lottery, since about half of its tickets were sold that way. By 1894 state lotteries had all been voted out of existence.

The temperance movement and its offshoots—which led to the creation of such organizations as the Boy Scouts, Girl Scouts and Camp Fire Girls—also campaigned against gambling. Illegal casinos flourished, though, in back rooms in the big cities, while out west gambling remained as wide open as swinging saloon doors.

The temperance movement succeeded in having Nevada's gambling halls made illegal in 1909. But few closed. Instead the operators shared their winnings with sightless sheriffs, who sometimes opened their eyes just long enough to arrange a raid that maintained the appearance of vigilant law enforcement and reminded the operators of how wise it could be to make sure key public servants prospered. This corrupt system lasted until 1931, when the district attorney in Ely, a small but strategically located trading center in the high desert, shut down the gambling parlors for good. He said local officials were pocketing about five thousand dollars per month, an enormous sum in the depth of the Great Depression.

Soon Nevada newspapers were full of talk about a bill to make casinos legal and how lawmakers were saying—not for attribution, of course—that such a bill was sure to pass. Meanwhile, at public meetings, citizens debated the gambling issues. Many focused on how

26

illegal casinos financed corruption when legal ones could finance government.

On Feb. 12, 1931, the Reno *Gazette* printed the bill's text. The next day Republican lawmaker Phil Tobin introduced it. Soon opponents appeared. Some raised moral objections, not to gambling per se but to gambling that made corrupt officials rich and did nothing to hold down taxes in desperate times. A few analyzed the numbers and argued that the promised revenues would not amount to a government bonanza unless Nevada citizens gambled away every cent they earned. The casino operators came forth to criticize government regulation, too, denouncing the proposed licensing fees as confiscatory.

Then the Carson City lawmakers performed a sleight-of-issue trick that would set a pattern that decades later other states like New Jersey, Iowa, Colorado and others would follow. Nevada's solons wisely wrapped the talk of legalized gambling inside a less smelly issue, in this case salvaging Nevada's lucrative quickie divorce business from competition by other states.

In those days divorces were hard to come by in most states, with judges wanting to examine photos of a faithless spouse in flagrante delicto as evidence and the local newspapers often reporting such indelicacies. Those with the money to avoid scandal often came to Reno, staying at dude ranches in summer or skiing the High Sierra until their ninety days were up and they could get discreetly unhitched. But competition threatened this lucrative trade. Arkansas, a state much closer to the nation's major urban centers, was considering a quickie divorce law and it, of course, had its own flourishing illegal casinos. Idaho wanted to cash in on the easy divorce trade, too.

On March 6, the Nevada Assembly quickly and unanimously passed a new divorce law that cut the residency requirement to six weeks and kept the details secret. Three days later the Assembly voted 24 to 11 to make casinos legal. The Nevada Senate, without debate, passed both bills on March 18.

Across the Silver State gambling halls that had operated for years by paying off the county sheriff now operated openly after buying a license from the sheriff and paying taxes of $75 per month on each gaming table and $12.50 on each slot machine. Anyone could qualify for a license, even convicted felons, so long as they were not aliens. The law required

27

honest games. It contained one significant regulation, however: it was left to each county sheriff to determine whether a casino owner was fit for licensing, a vague power that assured the continued flow of money from casino owners to those sheriffs inclined to point out flaws in the casino owner's character or conduct.

In 1931, Reno was Nevada's only sizable city. Few foresaw American taxpayers pouring billions of dollars into Las Vegas, a town of barely six thousand desert rats. But Uncle Sam built Boulder Dam—a concrete colossus that brought cheap electricity to the desert Southwest in 1936—just as DuPont's creation of freon made air conditioning practical. To test the new warplanes being developed in anticipation of the looming global conflict, what is now called Nellis Air Force Base was built in the remote desert outside Las Vegas. And before long military planners anxious to expand the nation's industrial capacity began drawing lines on maps, lines that in the fifties and sixties would become interstate highways connecting the prospering millions in Southern California to Las Vegas.

4

"I'm Still Able to Do My Own Killings"

The growing prosperity in the bold days after fascism's defeat stirred entrepreneurs, including those in the business of risk, men like Benny Binion in Dallas, Moe Dalitz in Cleveland and Ross Miller in Chicago, all from the dark side of the American heartland. Binion, Dalitz, Miller and other gambling entrepreneurs saw opportunity in Las Vegas, for in Nevada their trade was not a crime. By pulling up stakes and going west they escaped the cost of corrupting the police, who provided imperfect protection because crusaders would come along demanding the vice laws be enforced, at least for a spell. They also escaped the risk of a real reform district attorney coming to power, one who could cost them time in jail just for being what they were—gamblers. Binion and the others foresaw the riches that would flow down the highways taxpayers were building to connect Las Vegas with booming Southern California and with the coming age of air travel for the masses.

Binion always said he grew up a West Texas cowboy. But by 1924, when he was nineteen years old, he was listed on police records as a tire thief. During the Depression and war years Binion ran a policy racket—a private lottery not unlike those the Founding Fathers sponsored—and illegal craps games in Dallas hotels. Among his players was a bettor who later would briefly become the most powerful force in Las Vegas,

29

the Texas oil man turned movie producer, airline owner, and major Pentagon contractor: Howard Hughes.

Binion, a heavyset man an inch under six feet with brown hair and penetrating blue eyes, enjoyed a cozy relationship with the city government and the county prosecutor in Dallas for two decades. The cops raided him frequently, but the misdemeanor charges were usually against those he employed. Binion once boasted that when Dallas fell on hard times in the thirties he agreed to a schedule of raids so his fines would keep the city government afloat.

Binion's sometimes cozy relationship with Dallas law enforcement came to an abrupt end as World War II concluded. A new police chief promised to root out corruption. He vowed to put Binion behind bars. As 1946 drew to a close, Binion, who was forty-two, shut down his casinos, loaded suitcases stuffed with cash into his Cadillac, and drove eleven hundred miles west to Las Vegas. Soon he filed his casino license application, which allowed him to open shop, and went to work.

Binion needed a permanent Nevada gaming license, though, and the Texas cowboy ran into opposition from Robbins Cahill, the executive officer of the part-time state Tax Commission. Cahill could justify licensing men like Dalitz and Miller, men he was certain had bribed cops and politicians, because the illegal nature of their business required payoffs. But Binion had been charged with murder twice, and after one murder conviction had been given a two-year prison term in 1932, although it was suspended. This was much too much for Cahill, who journeyed to Dallas, gathered up records, and came back determined to keep Binion out, to show that there were limits to how far Nevada would go to accommodate its growing new industry.

Binion tried every way he could to get Cahill fired or kicked upstairs, relying on the influence of new friends in Nevada on whom he showered cash, but to no avail. "The way I saw it, if we licensed Benny, it meant anyone could be licensed," Cahill recalled. When the day finally came for Binion to appear before the Tax Commission, Cahill figured he had a solid case that would revulse the prominent ranchers, mining executives, staid bankers and the governor who sat in judgment. But as the closed-door hearing progressed, Cahill could hardly believe what transpired.

Yes, it was true, pretty much like the newspapers said, Cahill heard the heavyset cowboy with the Stetson say about the killing of rival gambler Ben Freiden. Binion confirmed he had driven to meet Freiden, gotten out of his car, slapped Freiden around, pulled out his gun, and shot him three times in the heart. "He was a bad man, a very bad man," Binion explained.

"Binion had this very engaging style," Cahill recalled, "and he had the Tax Commission in stitches, just laughing at his killing a man. He said it was self-defense, that the man reached into the glove box, and he thought he had a gun. 'So I shot him,' Binion said. Then he was asked if it were true that he had killed another man and Binion said, 'Yeah, but he was just a nigger I caught stealing some whiskey.'"

When the laughter died, Cahill counted noses and realized that Binion was about to be licensed to run his little joint downtown on Fremont Street, a place where the craps tables were open to the street and the customers had leathery skin from working out of doors and wore faded jeans long before they became fashionable.

Binion was a crude fellow who friends said could neither read nor write. Standing on his casino floor in his customary cowboy outfit, sometimes he would spit on the carpet instead of into the spittoon and he liked to remind people about the time a gambler who did not pay his marker was stripped naked and set out on the sidewalk.

Cahill consoled himself with the certain knowledge that Binion ran an honest game at the Horseshoe. "I'd cheat people if it would make me one more dollar, but it won't," Binion told Cahill. "You always make more money with an honest game."

But it would not be the end of conflicts between Binion and the law, nor the end of people who had run-ins with Binion turning up dead.

After he was licensed in Nevada, Binion still ran his lotteries in Dallas. A 1949 raid turned up Binion's income tax return, which presented him to the government as more pauper than privileged. The local prosecutor gave it to the IRS and in 1953 Binion went to prison, serving concurrent terms for both federal and state income tax evasion. After that Binion sold the Horseshoe, though he continued to run it. First it went to a New Orleans gambler, but after Binion was released from prison his immediate family bought it back with almost half being owned by his oldest son, Jack. But the father was there every day and when anyone wanted credit he had to come to Old Benny.

For years Binion left the Horseshoe at five-thirty each afternoon to dine with his wife Teddy Jane and his children at home, until one day they fought. (Binion told associates that he could not stand her five-pack-a-day cigarette habit.) Teddy Jane got up, walked out the door and moved into a suite at the Horseshoe. Four decades later the modest stucco house looked untouched, thick with dust, clothes hanging in the closets, just as they were the day Teddy Jane stormed out.

In 1972 a bomb exploded in a downtown Las Vegas garage, killing William Coulthard, a former FBI agent whose family controlled the land under Binion's Horseshoe. Binion wanted a long lease at a low rental, while Coulthard had been holding out for a shorter lease and a lot more money. After the bombing Binion got a one-hundred-year lease on exceptionally favorable terms.

Binion's 1,298-page FBI file, heavily edited by the government before it was released, describes him as the prime suspect in the bombing. But try as they might FBI agents could not persuade Clark County sheriff Ralph Lamb to consider Binion as a suspect. Years later, when Lamb was tried for income tax evasion, documents showed that in 1970–72 Binion had loaned Lamb three hundred thousand dollars interest free and with no repayment requirement. (Binion boasted to FBI agents about his long, close associations with other influential people, too, notably fellow Texan Lyndon B. Johnson.)

Over the years the Horseshoe attracted plenty of unsavory folks, all of them welcomed. When Texas drug dealer Jimmy Chagra asked one of his confederates, Charles Harrelson, to rid him of a troublesome federal judge, the plotting took place at Binion's. Chagra paid Harrelson, father of *Cheers* actor Woody Harrelson, his $250,000 fee with cash that came from the Horseshoe. When Rex Cauble, famed for Cutter Bill's, his Dallas clothing outlet, was prosecuted as a major marijuana dealer, testimony showed that Cauble and his Cowboy Mafia laundered their drug money at the Horseshoe.

Violence flared again when an irate loser threw a chair through a Horseshoe window in 1979. He was chased out the door and down an alley by Binion's youngest son, Ted, and two casino security guards. When the cops arrived, they found the gambler dead, a 9 mm bullet in his head. Returning to the Horseshoe, police found Ted Binion and the security guards cowering in the casino cage. They had to tear down the cage door to arrest them.

Ted was charged with obstructing a police officer. A judge dismissed the charge. One of the guards pled guilty to manslaughter, saying his gun went off accidentally. He got probation. The FBI figured the guard was paid to take the blame for Ted. But while the government made the allegation in court papers, it never brought a corruption charge.

Investigations never seemed to bother Binion. He is described in his FBI file as both "ruthless" in his youth and as talkative and cooperative with FBI agents in his later years. But in his own mind Binion remained the vicious man depicted in his early FBI files. Shortly before he died on Christmas Day 1989, Binion bragged to a Texas newspaper reporter that "I'm still able to do my own killings."

Meanwhile, the Horseshoe developed a reputation as a place where card counters—blackjack players who use their memory to keep track of the cards and vary their bets accordingly—were at risk of being taken down to the basement and beaten within an inch of their lives. Blacks who ventured into the casino reputedly risked the same fate.

Through all of this Benny Binion became revered in Las Vegas as one of its most beloved characters. People anxious to raise a few bucks would bring him a belt buckle for his collection and haggle with him over whether it was worth eight dollars or three dollars, often taking two dollars. The Horseshoe grew famous for holding the World Series of Poker, for its Plexiglas horseshoe where tourists could get their pictures taken for free standing in front of $1 million cash. And everyone knew of the Horseshoe's policy of accepting whatever size bet a player was willing to make on the first play. Binion knew that was good business because the games he offered carried a built-in advantage, so if the gambler stayed long enough, the house had to win. "Just bring the money," was his motto. Once a customer asked to bet seven hundred thousand dollars on a roll of the dice. He won, doubling his money. Then, as Binion often told the story, the gambler let it all ride and lost. He walked outside and blew his brains out.

Whatever else they did the Binions knew how to make money. Internal financial records of the privately owned Horseshoe Club Operating

Company, never before disclosed, show that it is better than owning a gold mine.

As of June 30, 1988, the Horseshoe Club Operating Company had $84.9 million in retained earnings, after distributing $18.2 million to its shareholders in the preceding year, according to a confidential audit by the Grant Thornton accounting firm.

Each year the Horseshoe throws off incredible sums considering its small size and its location in downtown Las Vegas, away from the Strip. For the year ending June 30, 1987, the Horseshoe won $59,964,098. Add in profits from paying customers at its hotel, bars and restaurant and the net profit rose to $60.5 million. Of this, the Binions counted $19,271,822 as net earnings, nearly one of every three dollars they took in. Even these extraordinary net earnings understate how lucrative the Horse-shoe Club is because net earnings come after the salaries, fringe benefits and expenses that the family members paid themselves. That year the Binions raked in more than $20.5 million in dividends.

The following year, ending June 30, 1988, net earnings ballooned to $44.8 million, but most of the increase resulted from a land swap that allowed the Binions to unload a piece of land in the booming gambling town of Laughlin, on the Colorado River. The swap provided a signifi-cant benefit to the Binions, who in trade received the Del E. Webb Cor-poration's property next door, the Mint casino. Under Nevada law once a license is issued it lasts forever at that location. Building a Laughlin casino would have subjected the Binions to scrutiny by the regulators, but breaking through the wall into the Mint next door did not require a new license.

Nevada law prohibits the owners from being in the room when the day's winnings are counted. At the Horseshoe, former employees say, carts heavy with cash are wheeled into a room, one wall of which is covered by a curtain. When the drape is pulled back it reveals a glass wall, behind which matriarch Teddy Jane sits, smoking her cigarettes and watching the count.

The Binions own a huge Montana cattle ranch that, including land leased from the federal government, covers 250 square miles, an area larger than the city of Chicago. But mostly the Binions like cash. Their gaming lawyer, Frank Shreck, the state's former top casino regulator, says it's true that the Binions have collected masses of silver dollars that just sit, uncirculated, not even earning interest. "Their money management system is simple," Shreck said. "Just pile cash on the floor until the pile gets too big, then start another one."

Binion espoused another philosophy to one of his many admirers in the casino business, young Steve Wynn, who was just starting to build his own fortune as a casino owner by taking control of the Golden Nugget, located across Fremont Street from the Horseshoe. In contrast to the Wild West image of the Horseshoe, Wynn transformed the Golden Nugget into a Victorian lady with pristine white walls, gold filigree and lights that twinkle like diamonds. He expanded to more than nineteen hundred rooms. Once Wynn pressed the old man about why he did not expand his small casino and add to his eighty rooms.

"Better to have a little joint and a big bankroll than a big joint and a little bankroll," was Binion's sage advice to the ambitious young Wynn, who would later become the king of the world's gamblers. It was the kind of advice no one ever gave to Donald Trump or Merv Griffin.

While the Horseshoe prospered as a serious gambling joint, Las Vegas began to recognize that it had to offer more than poker, craps and slots to sustain itself. If Las Vegas was to lure affluent Southern Californians five hours across the desert, as well as attract conventioneers from Atlanta and Boston, it had to become an air-conditioned desert resort with swimming pools, horseback riding and, especially, that game favored by men with lots of money and time, golf. But amenities are expensive, and the traditional sources of capital, the big banks and Wall Street, wanted nothing to do with Las Vegas. They might arrange conventions there—and play—but the men who provided huge loans and sold stocks had no desire to do business with people known to enforce contracts at the point of a gun.

There were, of course, men with capital who wanted to invest: capital from loan-sharking, drugs and extortion. Legitimate business was willing to partake of Las Vegas as guests and its owners and executives were willing to lose vast sums at the tables. But the legitimate business world would not be involved as investors and financiers, so mob influence flourished. In response, as the fifties progressed, inquisitive U.S. senators Estes Kefauver and John McClellan and ambitious politicians without office, like Senate staff investigator Robert F. Kennedy, dug into the seamy world of Las Vegas.

When Democrat Grant Sawyer became governor of Nevada, he brought in men to run the Gaming Commission and the Gaming Control Board whom he felt would not bow to every element in the industry. He told them to keep out criminals, mobsters and their syndicates. "A gambling license is a privilege—it is not a right. If you err, err on the side of rigidity rather than laxity. Hang tough and you will be doing a great service to me, to the industry and to the state," Sawyer told journalist Wallace Turner.

Soon after that the state issued each casino a three-ring binder with eleven sheets of paper, each one containing the name, mug shot and the various police and FBI file numbers of men who were not to be permitted to gamble in the casinos. Among those named in what became known as the Black Book were Nick Civella, the Kansas City mob boss who would later turn up on FBI tapes as the secret beneficiary of a skimming operation at the Las Vegas Tropicana, and Marshall Caifano, a Chicago mobster better known as Johnny Marshall. Caifano was the first to test the Sawyer administration's Black Book, suing when the Desert Inn barred him because of pressure from gaming regulators. He lost in every court.

Another Black Book page profiled Sam Giancana, the Chicago mob boss with whom, it was revealed many years later, President John F. Kennedy shared the favors of Judith Exner. Giancana stirred a new crisis. In July 1963, he took up residence briefly in Chalet Number 50 at the Cal Neva Lodge on the tree-studded North Shore of Lake Tahoe. The room was registered to Phyllis McGuire, one of the singing sisters. Sawyer's regulators soon filed a complaint alleging that Giancana ordered food and drink, was chauffeured about by lodge employees, drove one of the casino's cars, and hung out with the Cal Neva's half owner, his friend Frank Sinatra.

When state agents told Sinatra to give his friend the boot, the crooner from Hoboken telephoned Nevada Gaming Board chairman Edward O. Olsen. This call prompted a new Gaming Board complaint written in the stiff but clear language of bureaucrats that made its point. Sinatra, the complaint alleged, "used vile, intemperate, obscene language in a tone which was menacing in the extreme" to Olsen.

The state also alleged that Paul "Skinny" D'Amato, whom Sinatra called his personal representative at the Cal Neva, had tried to force money onto two state auditors who were checking the win at its tables. D'Amato liked to call himself Mr. Atlantic City, after the town where in the twenties he started out running an illegal casino in the back of a cigar store. Later he owned the 500 Club, where Sinatra often sang and Dean Martin and Jerry Lewis got their start.

Sinatra's refusal to send Giancana away, plus the D'Amato bribe attempt, prompted the state to move against Sinatra's casino license. Sinatra told the state where it could stick its complaint, believing his license gave him the right to own not only half of the Cal Neva, but his 9 percent stake in the Sands on the Las Vegas Strip, too. The Black Book, Sinatra believed, would never stand up in court.

Sinatra's threat to fight created uncertainty about whether the state could retain the Black Book, whether it could bar someone it regarded as inimical to the interests of its major industry from playing in a casino merely on reputation. Then, on the night before a deadline to respond to Olsen's charges, Sinatra announced he had sold his stakes in both casinos. Sawyer's principle—that a casino license is a privilege and not a right—has since been tested by others and firmly supported by the courts.

Years later, Sinatra would continue to sing in casinos in both Nevada and Atlantic City, because he always packed the showrooms with free-spending gamblers, both ordinary fans and wise guys. He was reportedly paid $125,000 per performance to sing at the Sands in Atlantic City in 1991, when he was seventy-five years old, with the casino also paying for his band and entourage.

In the sixties jet travel made Las Vegas easily accessible from the Midwest and East Coast. The Strip flourished, with showrooms featuring Sinatra, Sammy Davis, Jr. and other entertainers who attracted the desired type of guests. Year by year the Strip grew, its bedazzling forest of neon drawing people from around the world to the first metropolis devoted to Mammon, to the love of easy money—making Las Vegas the world's first *Mammonopolis*.

Meanwhile, up north in Reno, another gambler had come seeking his fortune. William Fisk Harrah would soon be regarded as the best Nevada would ever get. He liked fine liquor, frisky women and fast cars. And he was a pioneer who would forever change gambling in America.

5

"Two and Two Is Nine"

Bill Harrah hated school. He ditched regularly to race about town with friends in the fancy car his dad had bought him. For a spell the teenager even had an apartment, until the high school principal found out. The money for his precocious Roaring Twenties adventures came from the gambling parlor his father ran on a pier in Venice, a little California beach town that is now a part of Los Angeles. Card games were illegal, so players bet on numbered balls at his father's place. But while Bill Harrah broke the rules all his life, he was not a man of violence like Benny Binion.

When his dad went bust in the Depression, Bill Harrah, barely a man, took over and decided the way to big profits was by catering to customers. Cushion chairs and curtains appeared. Soon folks who gambled in the ramshackle quarters next door became Harrah's regulars. Young Harrah made a lot of money, much of which he spent on the fastest motor cars available. But years later he recalled that he loathed operating "under subterfuge, and you have to look people in the eye and tell 'em, you know, two and two is nine. It's not fun."

Before long Harrah tired of trouble with the police. He climbed into one of his sleek motor cars and raced due north in 1937. He liked Reno right away because in Nevada the cops didn't put gamblers behind bars.

After faltering at first with a bingo parlor, Harrah opened his first casino. His please-the-customer style attracted business. He was the first in Nevada to carpet his casino floor and among the first to hire women dealers. Before long just about everyone in the state agreed that he knew how to run a casino better than anyone else, from treating customers royally to listening to advice from subordinates on how to improve his operations to watching the money. In 1955, he expanded, building a little casino on the remote south shore of Lake Tahoe, hard against the California state line, even though in winter Tahoe was often snowed in for weeks.

Harrah's players lost so much money that he was able to build the world's largest automobile collection: more than fourteen hundred Dusenbergs, Aston-Martins and other exotics. Among his favorites was the Jerrari, which mated the off-road Jeep with the awesome power of a Ferrari, as hot-rodding Reno teens learned when they pulled away from a green light expecting that the wiry old man in the boxy leather-covered contraption would eat their exhaust. Better yet, his lawyers persuaded the IRS that the car collection was part of his business, and that the giant warehouse Harrah called his car museum, a few miles east of Reno, helped draw gamblers to the tables. It worked. Generous Uncle Sam let Harrah write his hobby off as a business expense.

Harrah understood the benefits that can flow to a business owner from regulation, especially when it protects the owners from extortion. But Harrah detested the idea of soulless corporations owning casinos.

In the sixties Nevada law still required that casino owners be individuals, what the statutes called "natural persons," a distinction needed because of a nineteenth-century U.S. Supreme Court ruling that corporations were also persons under the law. Corporations could get part way around the natural-person requirement by becoming casino landlords who collected a portion of the casino win as rent. But because they could not run the games or count the money, corporate shareholders remained seriously limited by the law.

By the late sixties Robbins Cahill had retired from the state Tax Commission and gone to work as a lobbyist for the Las Vegas casinos, where one of his duties was to win passage of a corporate gambling act. Favoring the bill was Howard Hughes, the reclusive billionaire who had long employed the Del E. Webb Corporation, the firm that built Bugsy

Siegel's Flamingo, as his builder. Hughes bought six Las Vegas casinos and looked covetously at Harrah's profits. He turned for help to Governor Paul Laxalt, later to become a U.S. Senator and a close confidant of President Ronald Reagan. Harrah told journalist Wallace Turner that Laxalt sent a message one day that Hughes wanted to buy Harrah's, and that the governor thought that might be a good idea. Harrah was not interested. But recalling his prior tenuous existence in Venice, he realized his vulnerability to shifting political power.

Bill Harrah led the opposition to corporate-owned casinos. "Bill was very anti-, which was hard to figure because his operation had become too big for him to run and I figured that he, more than anyone else, stood to gain from" converting to corporate ownership, Cahill recalled. Harrah prevailed at first by getting a single word changed. The bill required corporate casino owners to meet one set of conditions *or* another. Harrah arranged to have the word "or" changed to "and," meaning that both sets of requirements had to be met, effectively rendering the bill useless when it became law. But when the part-time legislature convened again two years later, Harrah backed down, and Nevada's corporate gaming act passed.

One of the first to take advantage of the change was Bill Harrah. He said his lavish lifestyle and divorces had driven him to go public. "There was two reasons. One, primarily, I needed some money personally 'cause I could only pay myself so big a salary. And I could pay some dividends, but I needed more money than that because I'd had several divorces and divorces are very expensive. And I'd been living high so I just needed money badly."

There were also estate taxes to consider. He feared that the IRS might inflate the value of his business and take so much in taxes that the enterprise would be doomed. But he knew that with a publicly traded company the government could instantly calculate his worth to the penny based on its closing trade whatever day he died, taking only its share.

There was another consideration. As the majority shareholder Harrah retained absolute control, but in the event the political winds in Carson City turned against him, he had all those shareholders to join him in protecting their investment from the likes of Howard Hughes and other unwanted suitors who might come along.

40

When Mead Dixon, the lawyer who was Harrah's closest adviser, approached Dean Witter about underwriting a stock offering, the Wall Street firm turned him away. But one of Dean Witter's corporate finance executives called Jim Lewis, a friend in Los Angeles who worked for a small, local securities firm. "This is a company with a great record, great history, but its business is a might too gamy for us," Lewis was told.

Lewis put together a small stock offering, about $6 million, and with Harrah's attorneys went to the Securities and Exchange Commission for approval. The government lawyers knew nothing about gambling as a business. Caesars had already gone public, but through an existing publicly traded firm called Lum's. The Golden Nugget in downtown Las Vegas had stock, but it was state-regulated with trading officially limited to Nevada, even though shares sold all over Southern California. The SEC staff's main concern was skimming, and they spent weeks soaking up all they could about the controls Harrah had developed to make sure no one skimmed his win. With the regulators satisfied, Harrah's prospectus went out in October 1971, and although no Wall Street firm would touch the deal, it was promptly oversubscribed. The buyers came mostly from Northern California. Many investors were Harrah's players who hoped to get back a few of their losses and were attracted by the prospect of owning a piece of the best known gambling hall in Reno.

Knowing there would be a need for future stock and debt offerings to expand the company, Lewis took a keen interest in Harrah's annual meetings. For most companies the yearly ritual of accountability to shareholders costs money. Harrah's made money.

"There was nothing like them," Lewis recalled. "There was lots of food, lots of free drinks and people just had a good time." Shareholders would lob a few softball questions, sometimes about entertainers or a new twist to a game, and then everyone would retire to a cocktail party before heading for the casino.

"They all play the slot machines, so it works out pretty good!" Harrah once boasted.

When Harrah expanded his Lake Tahoe casino into a lavish high-rise hotel in 1973, against the advice of almost everyone, including Jim Lewis, his profits ballooned. Every room features a view of the emerald waters that Mark Twain called the Jewel of the Sierras. The rooms are as expansive as the views with beds big enough for a pasha and his harem, two bathrooms finished in marble, with a telephone next to each commode and a little television set on each sink counter.

Really big players got royal treatment from Harrah. He had two private planes to ferry customers. In the early seventies, his casino hosts spent more than one thousand dollars per week on call girls for his best players, charging their services to internal account 619 and sometimes writing on the voucher "customer satisfaction refund." When IRS auditors in 1976 found these expenses taken as business deductions they righteously objected. Harrah's agreed not to ask taxpayers to subsidize the sexual adventures of its high rollers and the IRS dropped the matter.

Some folks remarked how Harrah's Lake Tahoe reported more winnings than even bigger casinos in Las Vegas and wondered how Harrah could do it. Some speculated it was the size of his players' bankrolls. But what mattered was how he counted the money—no skimming allowed.

Harrah's prosperity attracted interest from a lot of places, including a motel chain out of Memphis that had been one of the hot success stories of the fifties and sixties but was now foraging for new profits.

6

On a Holiday

Interstate highways begat Holiday Inns.

Wide ribbons of concrete and asphalt began rolling across America after the Second World War, stretch marks on a victorious nation about to give birth to a prosperous new era. In each new cloverleaf, Kemmons Wilson saw opportunity. A family motor trip showed him that in 1951 even bad lodgings were hard to find. Wilson realized that the interstates would mean teamsters, sales people and vacationing families driving long distances, people who would steer toward a place with no surprises.

To make guests anticipate the pleasures of his lodgings after a monotonous day behind the wheel, Wilson chose the name Holiday Inn for his first motel in his hometown of Memphis in 1952. His signs resembled a movie marquee because the name came from the 1942 Bing Crosby–Fred Astaire musical. The concept was a phenomenal success. Imitators soon appeared, notably the Ramada Inn chain out of Phoenix.

By the early seventies Holiday's stock had soared to fifty-five dollars per share, making Wilson one of the richest men in America. But quality control problems bedeviled the firm as some inns deteriorated. Competitors like Ramada kept expanding, and when the Arabs turned off the oil briefly in 1973, Holiday stock plunged to four dollars. Wilson needed help and among those he turned to was Cincinnati developer Roy Wine-gardner, Holiday's biggest franchisee. Winegardner had become Holi-day's third largest individual shareholder when he swapped his inns for Holiday stock, which at the time was trading at forty-two dollars per share. On his increasingly frequent trips to Memphis to rehabilitate his investment, which had lost more than 90 percent of its value, Wine-gardner brought along his Harvard-educated lawyer, young Mike Rose, who would soon ascend from informal advisor to chief executive officer of Holiday.

In Holiday's files Rose found franchise agreements that Wilson had drafted on napkins, giving vast authority with few obligations, which explained why some Holiday Inn owners did not invest in refurbishing at the standard Holiday's customers expected. The company had made some bad investments, too, notably buying the second rate Trailways bus system in 1969. Rose's interest, though, was in what *could* be, and so he pushed Holiday toward strategic planning as a way to map a new future. As Rose's grip strengthened, he pushed Holiday to find new profits in businesses that complemented the Holiday Inns. Restaurants were a natural. So were casinos, and that was where Rose most wanted to go.

Unlike the Southern Baptists who filled Holiday's corporate bureau-cracy in Memphis, Rose had intimate acquaintance with gambling, a fact not widely known at Holiday's headquarters. His father had been a slots manager at the Desert Inn in the days before Howard Hughes, which meant when Moe Dalitz and his fellow mobsters ruled the place. One summer, when he was a University of Cincinnati student, Mike Rose worked as a front-desk clerk at the Castaways, across the Las Vegas Strip from the Flamingo. Another summer he interned at a Las Vegas accounting firm. These experiences prepared him to understand why Hilton Hotels Corporation bought its first casino, Kirk Kerkorian's Inter-national just off the Strip, in 1971. Kerkorian then opened the MGM Grand on the Las Vegas Strip and Rose watched as "that one casino made more than almost all of our hotels added together, which certainly got our attention."

Just as Holiday Inn was recovering, its stock coming back under aggressive new management, Nevada's monopoly on legal casino gam-bling in America was coming to an end. New Jersey voters decided in

1976 to legalize casinos in Atlantic City on the promise that gambling halls would be the catalyst to rebuild the resort and that an 8 percent tax on casino winnings would benefit senior citizens. The politicians also promised to keep the mob out, no small order since mob interests thoroughly infested the Garden State.

Casinos, New Jersey politicians repeated like a mantra, would be more highly regulated than nuclear power plants. The Benny Binions, Moe Dalitzes and Ross Millers would not be welcome, but owners untainted by payoffs to police or involvement with mobsters would be. It was a perfect opportunity for Mike Rose.

But how would the middle-class businessmen and families who stayed in Holiday Inns, a firm with Southern Baptist roots, react if the firm bought a casino? Even Rose was surprised when a 1978 survey found 94 percent of guests didn't care.

That year the first casino in Atlantic City, Resorts International, opened to a line stretching a mile down the Boardwalk. Once people finally got a seat at the blackjack and roulette tables more than a few literally wet their pants rather than let someone else replace them.

But while Resorts, and the companies that followed it in Atlantic City, nurture an image of gambling as simply another form of entertainment, they operate as ruthless slayers of big fortunes and little pocketbooks alike.

To restrict the rapacious nature of casino owners the state imposed limits such as the requirement that casinos close for six hours on weekdays and four on weekends. But the more relevant factor, credit, was generally extended less on the basis of one's income than on track record. Take out a marker, pay it off, get another one for as much or even more. After a while this system could reduce even a multimillionaire to the status of a coal miner who owes his soul to the company store.

That's how Michael Campanaro worked his way up to a sixty-thousand-dollar line of credit at Caesars. Campanara was just thirty-four but betting as much as ten thousand dollars on a roll of the dice got him treated like a big shot.

"I had never seen Frank Sinatra, Barry Manilow, Diana Ross," Campanaro later told journalist George Anastasia. "Now I'm sitting front row. Sinatra sweated on my table, that's how close. . . . I'd have a room. I could order lobster tail and champagne from room service. It wouldn't cost me five cents. I'd walk into the casino, they all knew me. 'Make room for Mr. C.,' they would say at the craps table. 'Would you like some cigarettes, Mr. C.? Would you like a drink? Do you want to go to dinner?' I felt like a king, like I didn't want to come home."

Home was a modest three-bedroom tract home in Union, New Jersey, the kind of place a county jail guard who made three hundred dollars a week in 1979 could afford. Mr. C's credit was cut off when he owed ninety thousand dollars and couldn't pay. The state indicted him, creating a powerful incentive for him to find a way to pony up to the "highly regulated" casino. A jury found Campanaro not guilty by reason of insanity.

David Zarin was a far more substantial player, a man used to the gamble of developing real estate. He quickly became Resorts' biggest customer.

One weekend Resorts gave Zarin eight hundred thousand dollars of credit, followed the next weekend by the same amount. His appetite for craps was enormous, and when it was momentarily sated, Resorts always had a suite ready upstairs so Zarin would not wander far from the Boardwalk jungle. When Caesars, the second Atlantic City casino, opened in 1979, a bidding war for Zarin's crap shooting erupted. Each gave Zarin even more credit and comps. In less than two years, Zarin wrote $15 million in checks to Resorts to cover his mounting losses.

When Zarin ran out of money and could not pay his markers, the state demonstrated where its interest lay—it indicted Zarin on ninety-three counts of theft by deception, charging that he signed markers knowing he didn't have money in the bank to cover them. Resorts sued Zarin for $4.1 million. He sued them back, contending that Resorts "induced" him to gamble beyond his means so it could expand its real estate empire by acquiring his interest in four hundred apartments he had built or was constructing in Atlantic City. Resorts denied it, but Resorts was the biggest landowner in Atlantic City, with vast tracts of derelict buildings and raw land totaling one third of all the developable acreage.

In the end the indictments were dropped, the suits settled privately, and the pattern set for how this supposedly "highly regulated" industry would be free to vacuum clean the bank accounts of rich fools.

46

Zarin was not unique in blowing a fortune on credit. Come along for one night of blackjack with another high roller, trucking magnate Leonard Tose, who owned the Philadelphia Eagles.

It was forty-four minutes into a new April morning in Atlantic City. The tall, dapper Tose sat down at a Resorts blackjack table. Blackjack, or BJ, is by far the most popular table game. It is also known as 21 because the object is to get more points than the dealer, but not more than 21. Face cards count 10, except aces, which can count 11 or 1, depending on which is more favorable. Winners are paid one-for-one, meaning a $10 bet wins $10. But if the player is dealt an ace and either a 10, jack, queen or king, then he or she has blackjack and is paid three-to-two, meaning a $10 wager wins $15.

Unlike baccarat, blackjack involves skill in deciding whether to ask the dealer to "hit me" with another card or to stand pat. The game often draws card counters, who try to keep track of how many 10-point cards have been dealt to help them decide when to ask for a hit and when to stand. To foil card counters many casinos put six or eight decks in the shoe from which cards are dealt and sometimes they reshuffle after each hand is dealt. Card counters have filed lawsuits accusing Binions' Horseshoe and other casinos of having them taken in back rooms and beaten (Las Vegas) or verbally harassed (Atlantic City).

Blackjack tables have seven spots for gamblers, and Tose liked to play all seven at once, placing bets as high as $10,000 on each spot or $70,000 per hand. It was the kind of action that drew gawkers. This night began when Tose signed a $25,000 marker.

In just nine minutes Tose was out of chips, so he signed another $25,000 marker. Seven minutes later he signed again, this time for $50,000. Busted again after three minutes, he drew another $50,000. For a spell his luck held because 27 minutes passed before he needed more credit. At 1:30 A.M. he signed for $15,000, then one minute later for $35,000, and four minutes after that for $50,000.

Tose rose and left the table. But shortly after three in the morning he was back, sitting at another Resorts blackjack table and signing a $50,000 marker. In the next 23 minutes he signed twice more for the same amount.

His total debt for less than three hours of entertainment? Four hundred thousand dollars. Credit gambling ate Leonard Tose's wallet, then dined on his bank account, and eventually starved him out of the Eagles nest. He sold the football team in 1985.

Money wasn't all he left behind at Resorts. Tose was married to a strikingly beautiful flight attendant named Caroline. After their divorce she married I. G. "Jack" Davis, the president of Resorts International.

Among the one in four Americans living within a six-hour drive or an hour or so helicopter ride from Atlantic City is a stadium full of rich men and women like Zarin and Tose. All the casinos had to do was make their acquaintance and get them to the tables. The hired hosts acted like their customers' best friends—willing to endure any unreasonable demand or abusive treatment or discreetly satisfy any whim—to get the customers' minds focused on whether the dice would come up seven.

Developer Lew Walter, a Holiday Inn owner in Southern California, wanted in on this action, but from the winners' side of the table. He shopped for a site, and for fifty thousand dollars optioned a plot of marsh owned by the head of the Atlantic County government, Chuck Worthington. Walters was rich, but not rich enough to build a $55 million hotel. He invited Kemmons Wilson and Mike Rose to hop Holiday's corporate jet to Atlantic City, a place Rose had never seen, for a tour of the newly opened Resorts and the marsh.

Rose flew in from Hilton Head, South Carolina, a booming and refined Eastern Seaboard resort that he liked as much as he disliked what he saw on the drive across run-down Atlantic City to broken-down Haddon Hall, a once elegant hostelry which had a slapdash paint job and a new marquee naming it the Resorts International Casino Hotel. "But when I walked into Resorts I realized there is this pent-up demand for casino gaming," Rose recalled, "and Atlantic City per se didn't really need to be an attractive place."

A few hours later, trudging through the marsh in muddy boots, the idea of investing in Atlantic City quickly grew on Rose. The marsh was "away from the least attractive part of Atlantic City; it was kind of sitting out there all alone. It didn't have all the negatives associated with the Boardwalk area," he said.

In September 1978, Holiday's board approved a joint venture with

Walters for a casino bearing the Holiday name. L. M. Clymer, Holiday's president, announced that same day that he was retiring at the end of the year because he could not reconcile his Presbyterian religious beliefs with gambling. Years later Rose would say that it was time for Clymer to go anyway. But Clymer did not go quietly, and two Holiday directors joined him in resigning on moral grounds.

That vote marked a significant turning point not just for Holiday, but for the country and the lines that distinguish legitimate business from that which is illegitimate. Throughout history gamblers could earn fortunes, but not much else. If they wanted the status of legitimacy, if they wanted respect, they had to take their money and get themselves or their children out of gambling and into businesses that were respectable because they added some value to society. The life of Robert Miller, the governor of Nevada, illuminates the usual path out of gambling and into respectability.

Governor Miller's grandfather was a coal miner. His father, Ross, operated in another underground: he ran an illegal casino and strip joint in Chicago. After the usual scrapes with the law, Ross Miller followed the trail already taken by Binion and Dalitz, to Las Vegas. In 1955, Ross Miller and a partner bought the Slots-of-Fun casino on the Strip.

Ross Miller, who was indicted but never prosecuted for skimming profits in Vegas, kept his boy away from his casino. He sent him off to Santa Clara University and then to Loyola Law School in Los Angeles so he would have a different life. His finances secured by a trust his father left, young Bob Miller became a lawyer in Las Vegas and the legal adviser to the police department. Later he rose to district attorney of surrounding Clark County and then lieutenant governor of Nevada. In 1989, he became governor of the Silver State. Given that he was just forty-three years old, Miller could look forward to a career in the U.S. Senate if he one day wanted it, and there were those in Nevada politics who thought the White House was not beyond imagining.

Mike Rose moved in the exact opposite direction. After graduating from Harvard Law School, he went to work in his home town, Cincinnati, where Roy Winegardner grew to like him and his work. Rose is blessed with an extraordinarily focused mind. His ability to identify problems, devise solutions and implement them, and his ties to Winegardner, made his influence at Holiday grow quickly. As his power expanded Rose took the firm not toward new heights in the boring but respectable lodging business, but instead steered the company into gambling.

The Atlantic City deal underway, Rose journeyed to Nevada. Behind the River Boat Casino on the Strip, right across from the Castaways where Rose had checked guests in and out one summer long ago, Holiday already owned a hotel and convention center. In August 1979, Holiday bought a 40 percent interest in the River Boat casino, acquiring the rest of it in 1983.

Rose also jetted to Reno. He had learned from Wilson's mistakes— making deals on napkins and buying a second-rate company like Trailways—that operating on the cheap could become very expensive. Rose wanted the best. He wanted Harrah's. But Bill Harrah refused to see Rose. Mary Ellen Glass, who recorded Harrah's oral history, recalled that Harrah took enormous pride in the classy image the Lake Tahoe property created for his name. "Bill Harrah said *Holiday Inn* with kind of a sneer in his voice," Glass said.

But Rose made nice with Mead Dixon, Harrah's trusted attorney and a company director, and then took the plane back to Memphis. Bill Harrah died a few months later and his estate needed cash to pay death taxes. Dixon, who had become both the casino company's chief executive officer and the executor of Bill Harrah's estate, started negotiating with Rose, though both denied it at first. The deal was closed in February 1980. Holiday paid $300 million, a figure that shocked Wall Street as extravagant, even foolhardy. But Holiday got the premier casino operator in Nevada for its money, a firm with the best managers and the most effective cash controls. These controls protected all the money that flowed across Harrah's gaming tables from the moment it left a gambler's sweaty palm until it had completed a perilous journey through the counting room and on to the owner's bank account.

Years later the price would be shown to have been a bargain for another reason. The excesses of the eighties pumped up the value of Bill Harrah's car collection faster than Donald Trump's fame. Rose was smart enough to cash in by selling most of the cars for $100 million and giving the rest to a nonprofit Reno museum, which soon discovered that admission fees were not enough to support itself and became an albatross to the city government.

Rose quickly decided to slap the Harrah's name on his Atlantic City casino. It opened in November 1980, and five months later Michael D. Rose was elected chief executive officer of Holiday.

7

"The Better People Place"

At night, a halo often seems to hover over Atlantic City as moist sea air gathers into low clouds that reflect the floodlights and the brightly lit signs of high-rise casino hotels. From a distance this halo looks appealing, and as one motors along the Atlantic City Expressway's last four miles, through the flat marshlands, the sudden appearance of an urban skyline with bright lights heralding Caesars, TropWorld and, again and again, Trump, is strangely engaging. But the halo effect is deceiving. Atlantic City is no heaven on earth, but an urban hell that brings together the filthy poor and the filthy rich.

The expressway does not lead to a charming gateway, the kind Disney World or even some national parks erect to attract and enchant visitors. Instead it dumps onto an urban street. To the left is the backside of the busy bus depot, the air around it thick with foul diesel smoke around the clock. To the right stand angled rows of brick apartments, the bleak public housing project known as Pitney Village, where a popular sport among agile teens is racing down the street, bounding in three leaps from car hood to roof to trunk and then on to crinkle the sheet metal on the next vehicle.

To reach the Boardwalk casino zone players must pass through blocks of urban ruin. Yet the lure of gambling is so powerful that the only place on the East Coast with legal casinos until 1991 could boast that it had become the nation's Number 1 tourist destination. Each year more than thirty million people came, more than visit Disney World, although the average stay in Atlantic City is for just six to eight hours and, other than a stroll on the Boardwalk, few of these tourists venture outside the self-contained cities that are the casino hotels.

Casinos were supposed to be the catalyst to rebuild Atlantic City. Instead they have transformed it into the place where the South Bronx meets Las Vegas–by–the–Sea, where heroin and hookers are readily available and armed robbery is a constant danger, especially for old folks.

Publicists like to put on airs about a grand and glorious old Atlantic City. In truth the town was conceived as an excuse to sell train tickets. Civil engineer Richard Osborne, who witnessed but did not share in the profits created when a little lake port became mighty Chicago, shepherded thirty-four rich Philadelphians onto barren, windswept Absecon Island in 1852 and asked them to envision a workingman's resort that would make them richer still. The well-to-do already had their beach resort at Cape May Point thirty miles south at the Garden State's southern tip. Osborne picked this shifting sand not because of any natural beauty, but simply because it was the closest straight line between the sea and the crowded workshops of what had been, until a few years before, the dominant city of the Western Hemisphere. This was the easiest way for Osborne and his partner, Shore physician John Pitney, to profit from train fares and real estate.

The first train filled with beach goers arrived in Atlantic City on July 1, 1854. The first Boardwalk went up in 1870, a cultural oddity eight feet wide and made in sections so it could be hauled back for storage in winter. The Boardwalk was an industrial-era sensation, for it allowed visitors to experience nature vicariously, looking out at the beach, the crowds and waves while escaping the messy reality of wet sand. The world's playground was born. Soon bigger, permanent planking was in place and grand hotels like Haddon Hall, the Marlborough-Blenheim and the Traymore rose beside the boards.

Despite these few elegant hostelries Atlantic City was always honky-tonk, with saloons during Prohibition, back-room gambling run by the likes of Skinny D'Amato, and lots of hype. Mob guys played there, too,

53

because it was an open city where nobody was supposed to get rubbed out. The Miss America Pageant began there as a publicity stunt in 1921, held after Labor Day to coax from tourists one more weekend of hotel revenues.

But Atlantic City did not share in the prosperity of the Pax Americana that followed World War II. No interstate highway was built to Atlantic City. Instead, the new superhighways, along with jet travel, opened up new vacation possibilities for Atlantic City's traditional market as people from Philadelphia, New York and Baltimore hit the road, filling Kemmons Wilson's Holiday Inns. Television hurt Atlantic City, too. The giant Boardwalk showrooms—where tourists could type a letter on a two-ton typewriter, sample Heinz's 57 varieties, and watch the famous diving horse in between—closed down as network television offered a cheaper way to hawk wares to the masses.

New Jersey was a Northern state in the Civil War, but Atlantic City lies south of the Mason-Dixon Line both geographically and in spirit. When changing vacation patterns meant that the big Boardwalk hotels could not sustain themselves, the absentee owners took their profits elsewhere and let upkeep slide, a process known as disinvesting. Whites who could find better jobs moved out either to the surrounding suburbs or far away. But the blacks who made the beds, entertained in the black nightclubs in the summer, and got by on relief in the winter were not welcome in the suburbs and lacked the resources to move anyway, so they stayed on. By 1976, when city fathers, merchants and the local newspaper were organizing the second statewide vote for casinos, the most popular bumper sticker in town said, WILL THE LAST PERSON TO LEAVE ATLANTIC CITY PLEASE TURN OFF THE LIGHTS.

The New Hampshire lottery began making state-sponsored gambling acceptable in the sixties and the New Jersey lottery had proven immensely successful, especially after it produced the first million dollar annuity winner. But the 1974 vote showed New Jerseyans did not want casinos in their own backyards. The 1976 measure limited casinos just to Atlantic City, promising that they would be a "unique tool of urban redevelopment." The people believed the promise and passed the initiative, which exempted licensed operators from the statutes that made gambling a crime.

Chief among those promoting gambling was Steven P. Perskie, an assemblyman from Atlantic County. His family had long been influential in South Jersey politics. Years later it would be Perskie, more than anyone else, who would show that the assurances of strict casino regulation were nothing but politicians' promises.

Authorizing casinos did not change the old ways of Atlantic City. By 1991 the casinos employed nearly fifty thousand people, yet unemployment in Atlantic City remained higher than in the rest of New Jersey as well as the nation because the casinos prefer to hire their workers from the suburbs, which are overwhelmingly white. The state government encourages this policy in myriad ways, including studied indifference to the casinos' flouting of the fair employment laws and by subsidizing bus fares from white communities an hour away, while only rudimentary and costly transit is available in Atlantic City's poorest areas.

While Atlantic City nurtures its romantic image as the Queen of Resorts, the harsh truth years after legal casinos started is that a greater portion of its people live in public housing than in any other city in America.

But not all of Atlantic City's dozen temples of chance stand by the city's slums. Harrah's Casino Hotel is on the northwestern edge of Atlantic City just off another road across the marsh to Absecon Island, the White Horse Pike. Just before reaching the public housing projects that stretch for block after block, players can turn north and head through the stands of phragmites and sedges to Harrah's or its sole marina neighbor, Trump Castle Hotel & Casino Resort by-the-Bay.

In its advertising Harrah's appeals to those who do not want to be reminded of the underclass by so little as a passing glance at a poor person through a car window. Harrah's calls itself "The Other Atlantic City." This slogan worked so well that Harrah's added a second: "The Better People Place." Its billboards, newspaper ads and posters feature smiling middle-aged and elderly white couples, often in expensive attire, endorsing Harrah's as a fun place for people like themselves. When leading Atlantic City blacks like Pierre Hollingsworth, the retired deputy fire chief and former city commissioner, complained that the slogans exuded a subtle racism, Harrah's responded by adding a very few black faces to its posters, particularly the faces of blacks who serve casino patrons.

The hotel at Harrah's Marina is a fancy Holiday Inn with nearly five hundred plain vanilla rooms and a few suites. Later a tower with 264 suites was added, using cookie-cutter architectural plans from a new lodging chain that Mike Rose developed, Embassy Suites. To this, the company added a slew of restaurants, some boutiques and sixty thousand square feet of blackjack, craps, baccarat, Big Six and roulette tables surrounded by enough one-armed bandits to fill a prison. As casinos go, Harrah's defines prosaic. It has plenty of marble and more than a few mirrors, but the colors are muted and outside the only neon sign is a graceful outline of a sailboat against the hotel's blue-glass walls. The areas beyond the darkened casino are bright and airy, with walls of glass that give visitors sweeping views of a little marina filled with sailboats and, in the distance, the Atlantic Ocean. Overall Harrah's looks and feels more like a prosperous suburban mall than a gambling joint.

The affluent suburbanites Harrah's targets are often as boring as their beige Buicks and maroon Mercurys. But typically they own their cars outright, unlike the leased Mercedes and BMWs of many Trump Castle players. Mostly Harrah's gamblers are fifty or older, with grown children and houses bought and paid for long before escalating real estate prices prompted the phrase "affordable housing." They had picked the right time to be born, and as their hair thinned their wallets thickened so much that they could afford literally to play with their money.

Harrah's management, like the other Atlantic City casinos, railed about excessive regulation, but it was government regulation that sometimes inadvertently helped the place prosper. To save money, management wanted to pave enough wetlands to park seven hundred cars, with plans to spread more asphalt if business warranted. But the New Jersey Department of Environmental Protection said no. Wetlands serve the sea as a filter and a nursery. To conserve as much of this life-giving resource as possible, the bureaucrats insisted on high-rise parking. Harrah's built a garage for twenty-one hundred cars, adding thoughtful amenities. The garage featured a carpeted lobby, heated in winter and cooled in summer, with banks of telephones and spotlessly clean rest rooms. When the other casinos sold parking spaces to players for as much as twelve dollars on a Saturday night, Harrah's gamblers parked free. A glass-walled skywalk let gamblers stroll in comfort from their cars to the gambling area. That customers appreciated these touches could be seen on the garage's top deck. Blotches of dripped oil mottled the cement floor, while the top deck of the neighboring Trump Castle garage was nearly spotless years after it was finished.

Soon after Harrah's opened in November 1980, its slots became the most popular in town. They were priced from a nickel to one hundred dollars per pull, with quarter and dollar machines predominating. Harrah's offered players every slot available: fruit reels, video poker, even rare Silver Ghost Nudge machines, which give players a second chance when they narrowly miss a winning lineup, allowing them to push a button and nudge a reel up or down one stop.

Many slots featured 3 spinning reels with 22 symbols per reel. Some players calculated that the potential number of combinations was 22 times 22 times 22, or 10,648. They were wrong. Originally, slot machines were mechanical, with metal gears that allowed 22 or so stops on each reel and that paid a small jackpot, a big jackpot or kept your money. But these new machines were governed by a computer chip. The handle players pulled simply triggered the computer to start an electric motor that spun the reels. The outcome was already determined, not by the coin the player just inserted, but by the previous play, because the computer always worked one game ahead. These calculating devices could electronically generate millions of combinations from the 22 symbols on each reel. Jess Marcum and other mathematicians referred to these electromechanical devices as "virtual reel" machines because the computer could create a virtually infinite number of combinations, making possible a vast array of payouts, from two coins to a million dollars or more.

The variety of payouts attracted players who made Harrah's slots phenomenally lucrative. A video-poker machine cost about five thousand dollars in 1991. That year Harrah's Marina won more than $103,000 from each of its 1,739 slot machines. Compared to the motel business, it was a stunning margin. It would take years for a typical Holiday Inn room, which cost far more than a slot machine, to generate that much in nightly rentals.

Harrah's was among the first casinos to invest in computers to track its regular players and provide personalized service that made steady customers feel special even when several thousand people jammed its casino floor. Customers at several were offered plastic cards, embossed with their name. Harrah's was called the Gold Card. At other casinos

57

players could get a Trump Card, become an Island Ambassador at the Sands, or join the Officer's Club at the Showboat.

These frequent-gambler cards carried a magnetic strip on the back, like those used to withdraw cash from bank teller machines. Inserted into a device on a slot machine, the card tracked play. It also triggered an electronic greeting welcoming the player by name. Often this would be followed by congratulations on a wedding anniversary or the arrival of a grandchild or recommending a new kind of slot machine that had been installed since the player last visited.

Simultaneously, a screen would light up just off the casino floor, announcing to the crew of casino hosts, as floor sales agents are called, the player's name, nickname, tidbits like a recent birthday or wedding anniversary, and the player's favorite beverage. A cocktail waitress could be sent to the player's machine with a drink even before the player asked. A casino host could also stroll by and strike up a conversation using her personal knowledge of the player or the information gleaned from the computer. New tidbits collected from these chats would then be added to the computer database so the casino would have fresh material to strengthen its bond with the player on future visits.

Frequent-gambler cards allowed Harrah's to keep a perfect record of how much each player bet, on what kinds of machines, how fast he or she played, the total amount wagered and how much the player had won or lost. In this way Harrah's could grade its players into profitability categories without the uncertainty and errors formerly made when casino hosts rated players by recording their guesstimates on slips of paper. These precise records allowed Harrah's to calculate exactly how much to reward each player with comps, which is gamblerese for complimentary meals, drinks and rooms and, for really big players, gifts of jewelry, cars, even trips around the world.

Comping was a huge factor in the Atlantic City casino business, unlike Las Vegas, where only the biggest players received comps. In 1991, Atlantic City gamblers collected $488.6 million in comps. The casinos gave away another $247.7 million in coins and coupons to bus riders, in all enough to pave the entire New Jersey Turnpike, Garden State Parkway and Atlantic City Expressway with quarters.

The law barred casinos from comping players based on their losses, but this was of no consequence because comps could be dispensed based on the amount of play. Since the slot machines all paid back less than people put in them, and the amount was predictable to within a fraction of a percentage point because of the computer chips that determined payouts, all the casino had to do was calculate its theoretical win to set the level of comps. One player might win or lose much more than the arithmetic suggested, but the universe of players would be efficiently categorized and comped according to their worth.

The wealth of information these frequent-gambler cards generated also enabled Harrah's to target its marketing through such techniques as identifying comp-hungry players who came on busy weekends and offering a free room or even a suite if they switched to gambling on Tuesday mornings when business was slow.

The marina location, the better people slogan and steady management worked so well that year after year Harrah's was the most consistently profitable casino in Atlantic City. Since the day it opened this prosaic building in the marsh, far from the blight and Boardwalk, had paid for itself three or four times. It earned phenomenal net profits that became the talk of the gambling and hotel industries. During more than eleven years of operation net profits averaged more than $1 million per week. In the time it would take the Holiday corporation to net that much from the franchise fees paid by a typical Holiday Inn, a couple could marry, have a child and see their offspring off to college.

Mike Rose liked those profits so much that he started working on how to dump the Holiday Inns so he could build a new future, one with the potential to make enormous profits by operating gambling halls across America and around the world.

The prospect of making millions and millions fast and easy drew lots of potential investors into the casino business once Atlantic City opened up the market and, with the state lotteries, whetted the natural appetite for gambling. Steve Wynn came to Atlantic City early on and in 1982 Merv Griffin came for the first time. Before long Jack Bona and Donald Trump would seek fortunes there. Meanwhile, Holiday's chief hotel competitor, Ramada, was going into the gaming business in both Las Vegas and Atlantic City. And an eccentric rich Californian named Mitzi Briggs was getting out.

S

Stripped Naked

Bare breasts brought Mitzi Briggs to Las Vegas. One of her grown sons wanted to invest in the *Folies Bergère* at the Tropicana, one of the many topless shows the Vegas casinos use to lure patrons and fire them up for the tables, and she wanted to check out this potential investment. Briggs was rich, thin and four times married, a genteel woman with the pursed lips of a church secretary. She doted on her six children, lavishing money on them, supporting their auto racing and travel. Friends said she gave her children so much that they loved her purse more than her, though Briggs could never see that.

Her fortune began in San Francisco with her maternal grandfather, who founded the Stauffer Chemical Company in 1881. Much of the fortune went to her mother, Marie Stauffer Sigall, who leaped to her death from the fourth floor of a San Francisco hospital in 1951, according to the newspapers. Mitzi always insisted her mother had fallen. Mitzi, then twenty-two, an only child earning As studying philosophy at Stanford University, inherited the $2.8 million estate. Before she graduated she married marine biology student Jack Briggs, then divorced him and married his brother, R. Carlyle Briggs, whom she divorced in 1958. She married and divorced twice more.

While her love life was mercurial, she had a way with money, especially in real estate. By the late 1960s, court records show, her fortune had grown to $44 million. Mitzi Briggs also had become a deeply troubled soul.

She converted to Roman Catholicism in 1967 and came to believe that she had become, in succession, Christ's sister, wife and mother. She later told the story of her religious experiences, including the rapture of sex with God, in a rambling vanity book titled *Naked Before Thee: A Religious Autobiography*, which she wrote under the name Maria Josefa. Copies were available in the Tropicana bookshop during Briggs' years there.

Shortly before Christmas in 1970, one of her daughters committed her to a mental hospital in Belmont, California, prompting a hearing a month later on whether she was sane enough to manage her money. The hearing revealed that some of the money she had made in shrewd deals had quickly disappeared in generous gifts. She had donated $5.5 million to the Catholic Church. She had given 184 acres of land in San Jose, California, worth six hundred thousand dollars, to people she believed were militant Native Americans involved in occupying Alcatraz Island. She testified that this gift averted a "Red Power" uprising in which the Indians planned to "blow the faces off Mount Rushmore." John E. Thorne, a Bay Area attorney who represented Briggs during the hearing and who had represented many sixties radicals, would describe her years later as "the kindest, gentlest, sweetest and most generous person you could ever meet." And among the most gullible. Said Thorne of the land she gave away: "The people she was involved with turned out not to be Native Americans at all."

After the hearing a judge freed her from the Belmont hospital and briefly placed her in a conservatorship under her son John David Briggs, then twenty, and the San Mateo County public guardian. The judge put her money under the control of a bank, but not for long.

In 1975, when she came to check out her son's interest in the *Folies*, the Tropicana was a struggling gambling hall at the far south end of the Strip, a casino built by mob guys who, unlike Briggs, never learned the three rules of real estate: location, location and location. Besides being far from the Strip's center, the Tropicana had too few hotel rooms to keep its Polynesian-theme casino hopping. It was better known for big-name entertainers such as Sammy Davis, Jr. But what fills a casino is hotel rooms, not showrooms. As Briggs saw it, with some fixing up, and some more rooms, the Trop could be a gold mine. She bought in for $6.4 million.

Still, the Tropicana kept losing money, so she poured in an additional $8.6 million. She took little or nothing out. Casino executives routinely charge first-class airfare to their expense accounts, but Briggs always flew coach and often paid her own way.

Briggs never understood how to mingle with the customers, how to appeal to their desire to feel lucky and, when they lost, to soothe their egos with gifts and kind words. For a casino owner she held some bizarre views. One evening, soon after she arrived, Briggs hosted a dinner at the Trop for her executives and commission sales people, known as junket reps. Among her guests was another part owner, Deil O. Gustafson, who had bought into the Trop in 1972 and promised to turn it into "the Tiffany of the Strip." Seated near her was the charming Joseph "Caesar" Agosto, the *Folies* producer, who played a much bigger role in running the Trop than Briggs realized. And among the many wrinkled faces at dinner that night was a lone college student named Rob Goldstein, who was filling in for his father, an old-time gambler who had fallen ill just as a planeload of his players descended on the Trop. The father ordered his son to fly west even though exams started the next week. The room was elegantly prepared, with the best china and stemware and a card, made by a calligrapher, telling each guest where to sit. After the meal the hostess rose to make a speech about her philosophy as a casino owner.

"Mitzi told us about how she didn't understand gambling and how it was evil," Goldstein recalled. "I thought she was nuts." Like the others, though, Goldstein kept his thoughts to himself.

The money Briggs poured into an expanding enterprise she regarded as evil was enough to finance a new tower of desperately needed rooms. When it opened in 1978 the Trop's casinos filled with gamblers. But the turnaround came to an abrupt halt in 1979, when the FBI revealed that the Kansas City mob was skimming millions of Tropicana dollars. There was no question about the skim; the feds had wiretapped Nick Civella, the Kansas City mob boss, and *Folies* producer Agosto was all over the tapes.

Briggs had no idea the mob was robbing her blind or that Agosto was an intimate of Civella. Despite the wiretaps Briggs could not believe that the gracious Agosto had cheated her. She flew to his prison to ask whether it was true.

"Mitzi, I couldn't help it, they had a gun to my head," Agosto told her. She believed.

Later a jury in St. Paul, Minnesota, convicted Gustafson, a Minnesota banker and self-made multimillionaire, of bank and wire fraud, conspiracy and other charges connected with a check kiting scheme that he and Agosto ran to keep the Tropicana afloat. Gustafson was sentenced to ten years in prison.

Briggs was never charged with anything. Even years later law enforcement officials spoke of her sympathetically, as that eccentric woman who was robbed blind by the mob. It was not the last time she would be robbed.

The wiretap evidence was too much even for the laid-back Nevada gaming regulators, who were used to working with people often accused, but seldom convicted, of crimes. The regulators told Briggs and Gustafson to turn in their licenses. But instead of tossing them out, the regulators told them they could sell if they found a buyer fast.

Gustafson worked out a deal to sell the Trop to Ramada, which operated the world's third-largest lodging chain from its headquarters in Phoenix. Ramada was so anxious to get into a business in which it had no expertise, but was certain would produce phenomenal profits, that it agreed to terms that years later would cost it $35 million and would play a major role in making Briggs a pauper. Time would show that the soulless corporations Bill Harrah so disliked could be just as high-handed and heartless as the mobsters who stole the winnings from the Trop.

Since its founding in 1954, Ramada had played the motel industry's Burger King to Holiday Inn's McDonald's. Like Holiday, Ramada built predictable roadside inns. Its reputation was for doing business on the cheap. And while Ramada became a brand name, it was Holiday's that became the icon. As gasoline taxes financed ribbons of concrete, moderately priced lodging chains that built along the interstate highways boomed. Ramada became a Wall Street darling after it went public in 1962. More than a decade later the first Arab oil embargo created lines at gasoline stations and the major interstates were completed. As the eighties loomed Ramada, like Holiday, knew it had to find new lines of business to keep growing. Casinos seemed an obvious extension for a hospitality firm. Unlike Holiday, which in Harrah's bought the premier operator in Nevada, Ramada tried to move into gaming on the cheap. Holiday's shareholders got a bargain; Ramada's saw their money wither.

The kind of people who built the Tropicana and who ran Las Vegas in those days were not strangers to Ramada's founder, Marion W. Isbell, Sr. The company's publicists like to tell how Isbell was a restaurant man from Chicago who had sort of retired to Arizona and how, just to keep himself busy, he had built a motel in Flagstaff in 1954 with some friends, including entertainer George Gobel. Isbell noticed how much money Kemmons Wilson was making with his Holiday Inns, copied the idea of efficient, standardized motels and quickly made *Ramada*, a Spanish word meaning shady resting place, a household name. Left unsaid was the story of Isbell's ties to Chicago gangsters.

During World War II, Isbell was president of the Chicago Restaurant Association and later continued as a director. The association employed Abraham Teitelbaum who, according to the New Jersey Division of Gaming Enforcement, counted among his clients Al Capone. Like Capone, Teitelbaum served time in federal prison for income tax evasion.

In 1959, when Senator John McClellan was busy investigating labor racketeering, he focused for a spell on the Chicago Restaurant Association. His Senate Select Committee on Improper Activities in the Labor or Management Field issued a report showing that among Windy City eateries that did not belong to the Chicago Restaurant Association an amazing number of them, 124 in all, were bombed or burned. McClellan's committee reported that gangsters handled labor relations for the association.

In 1969, after Ramada paid Teitelbaum seventy-five hundred dollars for settling in two days a months-long strike against its hostelry there, Isbell wrote a letter of recommendation for Teitelbaum, commending his "great ability and integrity." That was just one of several ties the New Jersey regulators found between Isbell or Ramada and the mob, ties that Isbell insisted until his death in 1988, at age eighty-three, were illusory. The New Jersey Casino Control Commission heard all this and more but bought enough of Isbell's claim that it licensed Ramada.

Despite his familiarity with Teitelbaum and others close to Capone and the gangsters who succeeded him in Chicago, Isbell kept Ramada away from the gambling business. Isbell refused requests by casino owners for Ramada franchises because he thought gambling would tarnish the chain's image. But when Isbell's son, Bill, became chief executive officer in 1976, that policy changed.

Four years later Bill Isbell had Ramada acquire a 7 percent stake in the Del E. Webb Corporation for $10 million from nine dissident shareholders, including Frank Sinatra. Webb was the contractor who as World War II ended built the Flamingo, the first real gambling palace, for Bugsy Siegel. Later Webb became half owner of the New York Yankees and his company became a major player in gambling with the Sahara casinos in Las Vegas and Reno, the Mint in downtown Las Vegas, Del Webb's High Sierra at Lake Tahoe and later, after Webb died, the Claridge in Atlantic City. For a year Isbell tried to merge Ramada and Webb. Finally he gave up and sold the stake, earning a $3 million profit for Ramada.

Bill Isbell kept looking for a way into gaming until his eye settled on not just one place, but two. Ramada leaped into the casino business in both Las Vegas and Atlantic City. It was one of many disastrous decisions in Ramada's history, one that nearly sank the company as spending escalated into world-class cost overruns. The son not only picked bad locations in both cities, he installed abysmal management.

In Atlantic City everything about Ramada's operations ran backwards, starting with the legal name of its subsidiary there: Adamar.

To buy land on the Boardwalk, Ramada hooked up with James G. Ryan, a convicted felon free on bail pending an appeal and awaiting trial on counterfeiting charges. Ryan arranged for Ramada to buy two old hotels near the south end of the Boardwalk. As part of the deal, Ramada assumed a mortgage whose beneficiaries included members of the Genovese crime family. One of them, convicted loan shark John "Johnnie Gray" Wademan, stood to earn five hundred dollars a week for years to come in return for putting up five thousand dollars, a return of 10 percent per week.

It was just the kind of deal that should have set off alarm bells among regulators who claim to be the world's toughest and whose mission was, as Governor Brendan Byrne put it, to make sure the mob kept its "filthy hands" off Atlantic City's casinos. But the Division of Gaming Enforcement sought only headlines when it disclosed the arrangement. It did not focus on just how Wademan came to enjoy these extraordinarily profitable benefits, only on how to get rid of him.

These were the early days in Atlantic City casinos, when what mattered most was getting more casinos open, creating more jobs and bringing in more casino taxes to fund programs for the old folks who always voted. In cases like Ramada's the regulators acted as if their duty was only to make embarrassing disclosures, not to deny the privilege of a casino license to people who had rubbed shoulders with mobsters and done business with them or their fronts. A decade later they often would not even bother with the disclosures, except when they involved small fry.

In 1981, in hearings that by law were to determine whether Ramada possessed the "honesty, integrity and business ability" to hold a New Jersey casino license, the enforcement division concluded that Ramada had not known that mobsters stood to benefit from the deal and therefore it rationalized clearing Ramada of any regulatory taint. The enforcement division also did nothing more than put in the record the curious method by which Ryan was paid a quarter-million-dollar finder's fee for arranging purchase of the site. Instead of handing Ryan a check directly, Ramada agreed to increase the price it paid by one quarter million dollars and let the sellers pay the fee, thus insulating itself from Ryan, if only slightly.

Ramada's first Atlantic City plan was to build the Phoenix Hotel, named in honor of its hometown, at a cost of $50 million with the promise to spend $20 million more to expand the casino, add a theater, meeting rooms and other amenities. Instead of tearing down the old Ambassador Hotel, Ramada tried to scrimp by saving the steel girders and rebuilding.

In April 1979, the Casino Control Commission temporarily shot down the proposal to cheapskate, because it would mean fewer jobs for the powerful ironworkers union and other craft unions whose work rules made construction in Atlantic City far more costly than in New York or Philadelphia. Plus, there were demands for payoffs to keep the jobs going. Thomas Kepner, the corrupt local ironworkers boss, eventually went to prison for extracting payoffs from contractors, such as a free condo for trysts with his mistress, and stealing members' benefit money.

Governor Byrne backed his casino commissioners, declaring that the run-down Ambassador epitomized Atlantic City's decay. "We are going to have new first-class hotels," Byrne announced. "We will have Boardwalk hotels and attractions that are supportable in themselves" so if other states made casinos legal Atlantic City would continue to prosper as a destination resort offering more than just games of chance.

A few days later Steve Perskie, who had moved up to the New Jersey Senate from the state Assembly, boarded a jet to Phoenix, where he spent six hours reassuring Ramada executives that he wanted them. "I went specifically to answer some of their questions about bureaucratic problems and regulations," he said. "This is a first-rate hotel chain with an impeccable reputation," a character judgment that would later prove dead wrong.

When plans were approved, Ramada budgeted the Atlantic City Tropicana at $130 million, by far the most expensive facility Ramada had ever built. Even so, the company opted to use the so-called fast-track construction method in which the architects raced to keep ahead of the construction crews. Fast tracking saved neither time nor money.

Costs skyrocketed so fast that Ramada was forced to sell ninety of its hotels and motels to raise cash. Still, it nearly went broke.

Continued cost overruns in Atlantic City had become so significant that no one thought in terms of a budget anymore, only of finishing the project. The lack of controls so infuriated Continental Illinois, the lead bank on the project, that it began demanding changes. The giant Chicago bank wanted either an end to cost overruns, which was unrealistic, or Bill Isbell's head.

The bank took its gripes to Ramada's two outside directors, Edward M. Carson, president of First Interstate Bank in Arizona, and newly appointed director Richard Snell, the Phoenix lawyer whose father was regarded by many as the most powerful man in the Grand Canyon State.

Carson and Snell were mulling what to do when in August the *Wall Street Journal* published a hard-hitting story alleging that mob influence continued at the Las Vegas Tropicana under Ramada's ownership. Ramada bitterly denounced the story and initiated a libel suit. But two days after its publication Ramada's directors met in Phoenix to consider the multiple crises threatening the firm's existence, especially Continental Illinois Bank's very pointed demands that Isbell be fired.

As Snell recalled the directors' meeting, Isbell resisted. Finally, Isbell left the room and Carson turned to Snell. "There are only two people in this room who can run this company and I like my job and I'm not leaving it," Carson said, according to Snell. Minutes later Isbell was asked for his resignation. He agreed to a buy-out of his contract and Snell became chief executive officer on the spot.

Snell's law firm had worked for Ramada on and off for years, but he knew little about its inner workings. In the twenty-seven years since he had graduated from Stanford Law School he had never run a company, much less one as troubled as Ramada. Soon Snell was so busy trying to keep the Atlantic City fiasco from sinking the whole company that he hardly had time to cope with the Las Vegas Trop. When he did, Snell would act swiftly and arrogantly.

By the time the Atlantic City Trop was finished in 1981 Ramada had built the most expensive hotel in the history of the world. It cost more than $400 million, including work that it deferred temporarily. But this was no Ritz. The exterior consisted of giant beige walls, many with no windows, and the lobby was cramped. Had the facility been magically transported to the Las Vegas Strip, it would have been regarded as the most boring place in town.

The Atlantic City Tropicana cost an astounding eight hundred thousand dollars per room—more than twenty times what an average Ramada Inn room cost and more than triple the cost per room at Harrah's Marina. And the Trop rooms were about as prosaic as those Ramada Inns just off the turnpikes.

Al Glasgow, the contractor turned casino newsletter publisher and later Donald Trump consultant, stood on the Boardwalk one day looking at the rambling, unthemed Trop and grinned at his own thought. "In trying to save a few bucks by using the old steel," Glasgow opined, "they got a building that looked like it was designed by the U.S. government and cost like it was financed by the mob."

The Atlantic City Trop was not the only fiasco at Ramada. Out in Las Vegas, Ramada's desperate financial condition would strip Mitzi Briggs of her fortune, though a day would come when she would win vindication, though not restitution.

9

The Junk Man Cometh

From the day it opened in the spring of 1981, the Playboy Hotel and Casino offered Atlantic City gamblers irresistible, well-stacked views. It was not the voluptuous young bunnies serving free drinks that made the Playboy stand out; it was three stories of floor-to-ceiling windows that formed the casino's east wall and let gamblers break their concentration by gazing out at the Boardwalk, the beach and the sky beyond.

Casinos are built without windows or clocks because the owners want nothing to remind players of the passage of time. In Atlantic City the odds at all games favor the house, so while some individuals will win because they leave when they are ahead, overall the longer gamblers stay at the tables and slots the more money the house wins from its crowd. Thus anything that reminds players about time is the casino owner's enemy. Playboy's windows violated that unwritten rule. But building a casino with windows was only the first of many rules the Playboy's owners flouted.

Constructing an Atlantic City casino cost so much that even Hugh Hefner, renowned for his mansions and his private DC-9 with its revolving, round bed, needed a partner. He chose even richer Chicagoans, the Pritzker family, whose $5 billion fortune grew in large part from the Hyatt hotel chain, which they had nurtured into a lucrative future as a publicly traded company and then decided to make their private property. Along the way the Pritzkers had continual access to cash from the Teamsters Central States Pension Fund, a cookie jar for many Las Vegas casino owners.

Hyatt shareholders were bought out in 1979 with some cash and ownership of Hyatt's gambling arm, the Elsinore Corporation. Elsinore owned the Four Queens, a low-roller joint in downtown Las Vegas, and the Hyatt Lake Tahoe, a lonely outpost on the North Shore, far from Harrah's, Caesars and the other gambling halls at the south end of the lake a half hour or longer drive away. The High Sierra location would later prove very useful to the Pritzkers. The partnership with Hefner meant a third casino for Elsinore, whose largest shareholders were the Pritzkers.

No one but the Pritzkers knows just how many millions they made from Hyatt after they took it private in 1972. That they made a fortune is certain, though, for the Hyatt chain grew in size to become in the minds of many the nation's premier lodging chain.

But the company the Pritzkers gave shareholders in partial payment, Elsinore, was a disaster, largely because it lost a total of $228 million in Atlantic City over the next decade.

In late 1978 and early 1979, Playboy and the Pritzkers arranged to buy a 1.8-acre site on the Atlantic City Boardwalk. Given that the gambling floor alone covered 1.5 acres at a typical Atlantic City casino, it was a tiny piece of land. This parcel was so small that instead of a single sprawling casino floor, the Playboy had to be built with three long, narrow floors connected by escalators that carried players past those picture windows. Even so it ended up with just 50,516 square feet of casino, the third smallest in town.

The site's main feature was five hundred feet of Boardwalk frontage next door to Convention Hall, the aging cavern where Miss America is crowned each September and where Lyndon B. Johnson was nominated for president in 1964. It was still considered a lousy location because the Playboy's entrance stood at the end of a man-made canyon with an incongruous name that suggested flat land—Florida Avenue. One side of the long street was a blank concrete wall towering skyward. The other side was a beige brick wall that formed part of the Convention Hall annex. From miles away, where the Atlantic City Expressway crosses the marsh into town, gamblers could see the twenty-two-story glass tower with the Playboy name prominently in the skyline. But by the time customers drove within a block of the Playboy the tall walls of the Florida Avenue buildings made it hard to spot. Even when a sharp-eyed driver did see it, he beheld the glamour and sex appeal associated with the Playboy name surrounded by massive images of industrial gloom.

Three months after the $159 million Playboy casino opened in April 1981, management was sacked. The effete London-style gaming the Playboy offered simply turned off the street-wise crowds that frequented Atlantic City.

The new marketing types brought in plenty of action and plenty of unsavory characters as they dispensed credit freely. A Main Line Philadelphia dentist known as Dr. Snow because he made a fortune selling cocaine—before heading off for a forty-two year prison term—favored the Playboy's tables. At suites provided free by management he hosted days-long parties where booze and drugs flowed freely and he served himself up as the filling between a pair or more of coke whores in what he liked to call a human sandwich. So long as the drugs stayed in the hotel part of the building, or at least weren't openly snorted at the gaming tables, the agents from the self-proclaimed toughest regulatory agency in history didn't get a whiff of the real action.

Meanwhile, Hefner could not secure a permanent license. Investigations raised questions about the huge loans the Pritzkers obtained from the notorious Teamsters Central States Pension Fund, but those questions could not compete for the attention of regulators, or the press, with the problems of Hefner, who showed up at one hearing with Playmate of the Year Shannon Tweed, later a star of HBO's *First and Ten* series.

The Division of Gaming Enforcement sleuths focused their attention on bribes paid for the Manhattan Playboy Club's liquor license in the sixties. That payments for liquor licenses were routinely extracted by corrupt state officials, or that Playboy was later commended by prosecutors for helping them, was of little interest to the enforcement division's highly selective vision. Here was a man whose very business reeked of immorality, at least in the eyes of the division. Besides, there was a scandal at Playboy's London casinos, where Arab sheiks were allowed to circumvent credit rules because it was good business. Similar rules violations would occur frequently in Atlantic City in the years that followed, punished with fines that represented a tiny fraction of the increased sums the casinos won by breaking the rules. Hefner had never been charged with any crime, but the New Jersey Casino Control Commission decided Hefner was unfit anyway and ordered him out.

Playboy was entitled to a buy-out from Elsinore at the amount invested or an appraiser's valuation, whichever was lower. Given the Playboy casino's track record—it lost $10.8 million in 1982, its first full year of operation—Hefner faced a huge loss on his $51 million investment. So the casino commissioners let Hefner sell his stock to Elsinore for what he had put up, receiving a $45.4 million note at 10 percent interest, due in installments over six years, plus $5.6 million in management fees. This was in April 1984, when interest rates were still in the teens.

The interest on the existing Playboy casino debt was at floating rates that had risen to the point where the casino's balance sheet began to tip, the interest costs pouring onto its books like seawater weighing down a stricken ocean liner. The new obligation to Hefner only weighted the casino down with more interest burdens. But it set a pattern for financial manipulations that would long plague Atlantic City and that would extract a heavy price from investors whose money went into future deals by Donald Trump and Merv Griffin.

In June the Playboy was rechristened the Atlantis Casino Hotel. "Atlantis suggests mythological associations with the legendary kingdom of fabulous riches," Elsinore president Robert R. Maxey said, revealing a superficial, or at least highly selective, reading of history that ignored the awful thought of an entire continent and all its inhabitants disappearing from the face of the planet. Players, perhaps fearful their money would disappear in this monument to unparalleled disaster, began avoiding the Atlantis.

That fall Elsinore refinanced the Atlantis courtesy of Drexel Burnham Lambert, which operated as a securities brokerage but was in fact a vast criminal enterprise with sixty thousand employees but only one power center. The power sat behind an X-shaped desk not on Wall Street but in Beverly Hills. His name was Michael R. Milken, a brilliant man facile with numbers, whose greed exceeded that of even casino owners.

Milken was a hero to owners and executives of the casino industry for he provided them with access to the capital needed to build ever more costly glittering temples of chance, buildings so lavish that in time $100 million would only be enough for a refurbishment.

Milken's product was junk, not the kind the heroin addicts shot up in the burned out buildings a block from the Boardwalk casinos, but the kind that made casino executives rich by injecting millions of dollars onto their books. The deals Milken designed were structured so that he and the executives who brought him their business would make fortunes in fees, stock options, warrants to buy stock and other devices.

Milken's first major junk bond deal was a casino. He raised the money for Steve Wynn's Golden Nugget (of downtown Las Vegas) to build an elegant fantasy vision of Victoriana on the Atlantic City Boardwalk. Golden Nugget borrowed thirty times its net worth for that deal, akin to a renter with a few thousand dollars in the bank getting a mortgage for a gated mansion in Beverly Hills. It was a gamble, but a good one. Wynn knew how to attract serious gamblers; on a Saturday night, if he steadily raised the minimum bets from $10 to $15 to $25 to $50 the tables remained full and the Golden Nugget's bank accounts fattened. Wynn's Atlantic City casino won more money per square foot than any other gambling hall in New Jersey or Nevada, taking in nearly twenty dollars per square foot each day in July 1986, more than double what Donald Trump's Taj Mahal would report four years later.

But while the Atlantic City Golden Nugget bonds proved to be as valuable as the casino's name implied, before long Milken was doing casino deals that made Drexel and him rich from fees but were disasters for the bond buyers.

The deal Milken worked up for the foundering Atlantis was one of his worst. He arranged for Elsinore to pay off its bank debt with $115 million of Drexel bonds. Technically they were not junk bonds because the term implies unsecured obligations, the corporate equivalent of credit card debt, while $90 million of the Elsinore bonds were secured by a first mortgage on the money-losing Atlantis, which an appraisal claimed was worth $190 million. Securing the balance of the bonds was a $25 million lien on the Hyatt Lake Tahoe.

Milken's customers knew the bonds were junk because they insisted on a whopping 15.5 percent interest before forking over their money, one point higher than the Atlantis had been paying the banks. The bonds were still warm from the printers when interest rates began sliding to single digits. But this decline provided no relief to the Atlantis, which would have seen its interest rate fall to 9.5 percent had it stuck with the bank debt.

On another front, the Pritzkers did get some dandy relief from high interest rates.

While Elsinore held title to the Lake Tahoe property, it was a thoroughly Hyatt operation, which meant the Pritzkers ran the show, typically collecting $1.2 million in management fees annually. Elsinore paid Hyatt another $704,000 for insurance plus legal fees and a host of other costs. On top of that, Hyatt charged Elsinore one hundred dollars per hour for any work Hyatt headquarters executives did related to the Lake Tahoe property. When the Internal Revenue Service challenged the Lake Tahoe tax deductions, however, it was Elsinore, not Hyatt, that agreed to pay the final tax bill. But for the Pritzkers the sweetest part of the deal was a loan from the Hyatt Lake Tahoe for $20 million. Elsinore borrowed through Drexel at 15.5 percent and then loaned money to Hyatt at 8.5 percent.

The Pritzkers could arrange such sweetheart deals because they controlled Elsinore. Even after Jay Pritzker quit Elsinore's board the family maintained a firm grip by placing one of its most trusted attorneys, Charles Evans Gerber of Chicago, on the Elsinore board. The Pritzkers had started out with almost 22 percent of the company, but issuing more shares in lieu of cash interest on the Drexel bonds reduced their stake to 6 percent, still the largest single block. Meanwhile, other Elsinore shareholders, who did not get such fabulous deals as the Hyatt Lake Tahoe loan for themselves, watched the value of their stock sink from a high of seventeen dollars until in 1991 each share was worth less than the cost of one pull at a dollar slot machine.

In April 1985, one year after the regulators let Hefner swap his stock for a note, the Atlantis financing subsidiary, Elsub, failed to make a four-hundred-thousand-dollar payment to Playboy. It was the first sign that cataclysmic money woes would engulf the casino named for the lost continent.

A few days later Marvin B. Roffman, the flint-eyed casino securities analyst at the Janney Montgomery Scott brokerage in Philadelphia, issued a report comparing the efficiency of Atlantic City's casinos. Roffman gave the Atlantis poor marks and he showed that excessive interest costs were not the only problem. "The casinos with the highest profit margins—Bally's, Harrah's and Resorts—are also the most niggardly with their giveaways," Roffman said. The Atlantis was among those which liberally dispensed free booze, bread and beds and whose bottom line suffered. Another way to examine efficiency was to treat a casino like a retail store and examine its sales per square foot, Roffman noted. By this measure the Atlantis came in dead last. It won $3,291 per square foot of gaming area the year before, nearly 30 percent less than the $4,594 average among all Atlantic City casinos.

And the Atlantis was beginning to lose market share, with disastrous consequences for the bottom line. The old Playboy had eked out a profit only once, earning almost a half million dollars in 1983, when players lost $168.2 million. The next year net losses were $9 million because costs rose while the amount players lost was virtually unchanged. The loss, and word around town that the Atlantis was slowly sinking, prompted Elsinore to assure its shareholders in June that it could pay its bills. Just three months later, though, Elsinore said that it would miss its next payment on the $45.4 million note due Playboy.

Then, in November, the Atlantis failed to pay the nearly $9 million interest due on the Drexel bonds Milken and his minions had sold. The hapless junk addicts who bought the bonds had received a single payment, for six months interest, before their investment soured.

Two weeks later Playboy sued Elsinore in U.S. District Court in New Jersey alleging wrongful conduct by a "complex web of affiliates and subsidiaries" that controlled the Atlantis. The suit made detailed allegations of conduct that, if true, would disqualify Elsinore and the Pritzkers. The suit charged that

> Elsinore caused entities it controls to fraudulently convey millions of dollars to it for Elsinore's own benefit, thereby preventing [Playboy] from receiving the payments promised for the sale of its interest and depriving the Atlantis Casino of sufficient funds to pay its creditors . . . Elsinore caused its controlled entities to place a $90 million mortgage on the Atlantis Casino and then diverted substantial proceeds of this mortgage away from the Atlantis Casino to pay obligations of either Elsinore subsidiaries (unrelated to the Atlantis

Casino) to the Teamsters Pension Fund or for other improper purposes.

Elsinore, according to the suit, caused two subsidiaries, Elsub and Elsinore Shore Associates, "to make a secret conveyance" of land that harmed the Atlantis and benefited Elsinore. Playboy also complained that Elsinore refused to provide financial information required by the Playboy note. And Playboy also attacked Elsinore's announcement to shareholders the previous June that it could pay its bills, saying the statement "intentionally misrepresented" the facts. Hefner's firm then forced the Atlantis into bankruptcy.

The New Jersey Division of Gaming Enforcement and the casino commissioners could have treated the Playboy suit as an outline for a case to revoke the Atlantis gaming license or even as a tip sheet for an investigation. They could have tested the allegations Playboy made, especially the allegations of fraud. They could have read into the claims questions about whether Elsinore met the integrity and business ability requirements in the Casino Control Act.

Instead the regulators focused on how to keep the Atlantis open, which would protect the Pritzkers' investment, the sixteen hundred Atlantis jobs and the state's flow of tax monies.

New Jersey's Casino Control Act requires that a casino prove "by clear and convincing evidence" that it is financially stable to qualify for a casino license. The law placing this burden on the casino does not define financial stability, so the commission relied on projections of expected revenues and expenses prepared by the casino and analyzed by its staff and the enforcement division to test fiscal fitness. The commission also began using an old Bankruptcy Code definition of stability: the ability to pay bills as they come due. That definition proved a boon to Elsinore in its fight to keep the Atlantis open.

It may seem axiomatic that a casino seeking refuge from its creditors in federal Bankruptcy Court is not financially stable. But the commission found that reorganizing debts under Chapter 11 of the Bankruptcy Code could actually create and even enhance financial stability. How did the commissioners reach this conclusion? When a business is reorganizing in Bankruptcy Court it pays only those bills it can afford to pay. Under bankruptcy law any bills that cannot be paid simply do not come due.

Gamblers did not take such a sophisticated and charitable view of the Chapter 11 filing. The amount the casino won from its players dropped quickly and continued to slide, even though the casino commissioners did insist that enough money be set aside to ensure that all winning bets would be paid.

The crowds with designer suits and silk blouses moved on to Wynn's Golden Nugget and the newer places like Trump Plaza next door. Replacing them were the down-at-the-heels gamblers who didn't play enough to make them worth a free Coca-Cola. But even when the crowds shrank the place appeared to be busy. The casino had been designed so that the first floor offered slots, the second table games with a few slots, and the third was a lavish salon for high-rollers. Except for busy weekend nights in the summer the salon stayed closed. Because the building's layout made the salon level accessible by escalator and elevator, the Atlantis had to post guards around the clock to turn away the few people who wandered onto the third floor. It also meant that instead of having fifty thousand square feet of gaming area the Atlantis effectively had only thirty-four thousand square feet, barely half the size of most Atlantic City casinos. On all but the slowest winter days it appeared that the Atlantis was packed.

When Jeanne Hood became Elsinore's president in the fall of 1985 she drove many of the Atlantis' high rollers away with a new marketing plan. Gone were lavish parties, big-name entertainers and liberal comps. In their place she offered blackjack tables with $2 minimum bets, down from $5, and $1 minimum craps bets. "There wasn't much choice, we did what we had to do," she said. Hood said she wanted to draw middle-level players, but what the Atlantis attracted were people with even less in their pockets than the denizens who frequented Glitter Gulch in Las Vegas and preferred the seedy places down the street to Elsinore's Four Queens, which Hood also ran.

For three years lawyers and advisers for the Atlantis and its creditors argued over how much it could afford to pay on its mortgage and to its suppliers. Both sides charged their fees to the casino. By the time a plan of reorganization was finally approved in September 1988, the Atlantis had shelled out more than $15 million in fees and costs, far more than the shortfall it faced when its troubles began.

Atlantis employees, meanwhile, went without a pay raise. Local 54 of the Hotel and Restaurant Employees International Union had a uniform contract with all Atlantic City casinos to represent bartenders, cocktail waitresses and many other workers, but not dealers. A scheduled wage hike in September 1987 was refused by the Atlantis. The union struck, its lines of pickets and some scattered violence driving away even more business.

Hood, who had taken over as Elsinore's president just before the bankruptcy filing, said the Atlantis could not pay higher wages while it was in bankruptcy proceedings. The union pointed to examples of corporations that had paid wage hikes while reorganizing their debts and demanded that Hood ask Bankruptcy Judge Rosemary Gambardella for permission to pay the wage hike, which totaled about a quarter million dollars for the coming year. Hood refused.

Then she enraged the Atlantis workers by arranging a huge pay hike for herself. The way striking workers figured, the sixty-year-old widow personally got their money.

Hood earned $120,000 in 1984 at the Four Queens. The next year she took over the Atlantis as well. Its losses ballooned from $9 million to nearly $34 million, while Hood's pay rose to $189,000. Then the bankruptcy proceedings began and the Atlantis refused to pay any wage hikes. But Hood saw her pay more than double in 1986 to $457,000, including both a bonus and a supplemental bonus. Hood earned even more in 1987. Her salary was increased to $250,000, she received a $110,000 bonus, and she persuaded Elsinore's board to pay her an extra $140,000 bonus. Hood's argument that the money came from Elsinore, the corporate parent, and not the Atlantis did nothing to soothe the anger among Atlantis workers, nothing to inspire them to provide the best possible service to customers who came to the casino hoping to win money but who usually went home losers.

Hood also arranged a golden parachute worth more than $1.3 million if new investors acquired just 20 percent of Elsinore's stock.

Despite the continuing strike, in March 1988 the Atlantis gave the casino commission projections showing it would bring in more gamblers who would lose more money, and that the casino would turn a profit.

To provide expert support for its case to win a new license, Elsinore hired Stephen Cooper, a specialist at helping firms work out their problems with creditors. Cooper testified that the bankruptcy proceedings were coming to an end, which they did six months later. And he spoke glowingly about how the commission could take comfort in the projections because they established that the Atlantis was regaining financial strength. The union wanted to take on Cooper's testimony, but the commission refused to let it intervene in the hearings. Based on the projections, and particularly on Cooper's expert testimony, the commission granted a one-year renewal.

But the Atlantis was not getting stronger. The amount it won from players had fallen to $6.5 million per month, less than half what it took in at its peak in 1983. Rooms were let for as little as $29.95 a night, less than half the average at the other Atlantic City casinos.

Elsinore was so cash poor that in September 1988 it paid its bondholders not cash, but more than nine million shares of stock. Its stock traded at two dollars per share just before this payment-in-kind to bondholders. Within a few months it would trade at thirty-seven and a half cents and Hood would seek approval to issue one hundred million more shares of stock to meet future bond payments.

Worse, while every successful business is organized to bring in more cash than it spends, dollars began flowing out of this enterprise at an increasing rate. No matter. Before long the Atlantis would become the property of another junk bond addict: Donald Trump.

10

The Art of Deception

Although he polished his image as a self-made billionaire, Donald Trump grew up riding through New York's outer boroughs in his mother's Rolls-Royce. His father, Fred Trump, was reportedly Chase Manhattan's biggest depositor in Queens. Fred built working-class apartment complexes, huge brick fortresses often financed with government subsidies that he arranged in part through his close ties to politicians, notably New York mayor Abe Beame and Meade Esposito, who for decades ran the Brooklyn Democratic party organization.

Donald Trump wanted more than his father's obscure wealth. He lusted for the glamour of Manhattan. He wanted to build with marble, not brick. He wanted to house the glitterati, not their servants.

With his father's financial backing and political connections, young Donald made some amazing deals. He started by turning the broken down Commodore hotel next to Grand Central Station into the Grand Hyatt. The amazing part was not the Hyatt's ostentatious design, with a glass-walled lounge slung out over the sidewalk, or the favorable financing or the partnership with the Pritzker family that owned the Hyatt name, but the way City Hall poured taxpayer money into Trump's pockets. The Beame administration made the Grand Hyatt the first hotel in New York City exempted from paying property taxes. The exemption covers forty-two years, a gift easily worth $400 million by the time it expires in 2020.

Like Holiday Inn's Mike Rose, Trump realized in the mid-seventies that the profits in hotels and even development deals pale beside the potential return from a casino. He boasted in 1978 that the Grand Hyatt was designed so that when it opened it could accommodate a casino. But when efforts to legalize casinos in New York faltered, and Resorts proved a phenomenal success after it opened in 1978, Trump started scouting Atlantic City and became an ardent foe of casinos in New York.

In January 1980, his top aide, attorney Harvey I. Freeman, wrote to Kenny Shapiro about leasing one of the choicest sites on the Boardwalk, straight ahead of the Atlantic City Expressway and next door to the Convention Hall where Miss America is crowned each September. Several years later Shapiro would be identified by federal prosecutors and by the New Jersey's State Commission on Investigation as the Atlantic City investment banker for Nicky Scarfo, the vicious killer who ruled the Philadelphia Mafia, the most murderous mob family in America.

Dealing with unsavory characters was not new to Trump. He bragged that his projects always came in on time and under budget (Trump's public budget pronouncements were inflated so it was easy to meet them), and it was remarkable how Trump always had labor peace, especially with the mob-controlled cement workers union, which took charge at most of his projects, including the concrete colossus known as Trump Tower. What Trump did not boast about or even publicly mention was that he hired mob-owned firms like S & A Concrete, whose secret owners were the two top Mafia figures in New York: Anthony "Fat Tony" Salerno, head of the Genovese crime family, and Paul Castellano, head of the Gambinos. Trump also made extensive use of attorney Roy Cohn, the notorious fixer, whose clients included Salerno.

Trump boasted in his first autobiography that when he sought a casino license he persuaded John Degnan, the New Jersey attorney general, to limit his probe to six months. Trump became the first applicant that the attorney general's Division of Gaming Enforcement recommended for licensing. The division had either opposed or taken no position on the others.

That Trump was not fully investigated by the enforcement division was obvious to anyone who read its 1982 licensing report. But it was almost a decade later that investigative reporter Wayne Barrett's biography of Trump revealed that the developer also had been the target of a 1979 federal bribery investigation. No charges resulted from the probe, which had been inspired by one of Barrett's disclosures in the *Village Voice* newspaper. But Trump had not listed the probe in his license application, and the Casino Control Act mandates license denial for anyone who omits a relevant fact. The key court case upholding the disclosure provision involves a woman denied a license as a blackjack dealer —a much lower level of license than casino owner—because she did not report that she had been forced to resign from a retail clerk job for selling friends a few items below their ticketed prices, a matter handled in court as misdemeanor shoplifting.

The licensing report did reveal that Trump had failed to list on his application an investigation of alleged racial discrimination against tenants. Still, the enforcement division recommended Trump for approval because he disclosed this matter just before he was to be questioned under oath about the omission.

The licensing report's most interesting portions examined Trump's finances, disclosing a pattern that would continue into the future: modest executive salary ($100,000), minimal savings ($6,000), fat fees from his deals ($1 million commission on the Grand Hyatt), and enormous debts ($35 million unsecured credit line at Chase Manhattan Bank).

The report also gave a glimpse into his efforts to avoid income taxes by owning his properties through partnerships. At first Trump cut his siblings Maryanne and Robert in on some deals, but in his casinos and many other of his celebrated deals Trump was almost always both the sole general partner and the sole limited partner, a strategy designed to reduce income taxes. It worked fabulously to lighten the burden of supporting the United States government. By 1978 Trump had yet to build Trump Tower or any of his casinos, which together created opportunities for multimillion dollar deductions each year, by vastly enlarging his opportunities to report a negative income to the government while at the same time living the vaunted Trump lifestyle on cash flow.

THE RESULT:

	Income	Federal Income Tax Paid
1975	$ 76,210	$ 18,714
1976	24,594	10,832
1977	118,530	42,386
1978	(406,379)	0
1979	(3,443,560)	0

Although his tax returns have not been publicly disclosed since 1979, Donald Trump has had such enormous write-offs available to him that he probably did not pay a penny in federal income taxes through at least 1986, when an overhaul of the Internal Revenue Code made it modestly more difficult to avoid paying income taxes.

The Casino Control Commission licensed Trump in March 1982, after a perfunctory public hearing. The terms of his license were both extraordinary and prophetic, finding on the basis of the incomplete investigation only that he had established, by clear and convincing evidence, his good character and integrity, while his business ability and financial stability were found in need of further proofs.

No matter, Trump now had the extraordinary privilege of a New Jersey casino license in hand, and he got busy developing his narrow Boardwalk site. Since his Grand Hyatt and Trump Tower were not yet finished, he needed a partner. He turned to Mike Rose. The Holiday corporation enjoyed such phenomenal success with Harrah's Marina that coordinating operations with a Boardwalk casino seemed like a good marketing strategy.

Immediately Trump set out on a course that, by his own account, raised questions about the one favorable finding in his casino license. He set out to deceive his prospective partners: In his first autobiography Trump wrote that Holiday's board wanted to "assess our progress in construction," which worried him "since we had yet to do much work on the site."

To create the illusion of progress Trump jammed the site with bulldozers and dump trucks, not caring if they accomplished any work so long as they looked busy. Trump's construction chief told him it was the strangest request he had ever received. One Holiday director asked Trump why a hole was dug and then filled. "This was difficult for me to answer," Trump wrote, "but fortunately this board member was more curious than he was skeptical." The deception worked.

Although Trump claimed that Holiday came to him seeking a partner, Holiday put up the financing and was to run the place. All Trump brought to the table was his lease and his extraordinary ability to escape the usual union work stoppages. This was enough, though, to provide Trump with an incredible deal. All he had to do was build the 614-room casino hotel and then sit back and collect half the profits. He was even guaranteed against any losses in the first five years.

It would soon turn out to be a joint venture from hell. It would also set a pattern that relied on deception, especially feigned raids on his competitors to weaken their ability to compete against his casinos. His crucial allies in these moves to damage competitors would be the New Jersey Division of Gaming Enforcement, which repeatedly failed to seek sanctions for his conduct while demanding strict obedience to the law by others, and the Casino Control Commission, whose duty was to foster the industry while also making sure that casinos remained "highly regulated." The division and the commission sometimes behaved like watchdogs with other casinos, but they made themselves into Trump's trusted lapdogs.

The Boardwalk lots Trump leased were so narrow that the only way to make a hotel and casino attractive was to build not only skyward, but to create a wider space out of thin air. Here his Atlantic City real estate lawyer, Patrick McGahn, proved invaluable.

Paddy McGahn's ability to win favors from City Hall had been profitably demonstrated a decade earlier when Jim Crosby's Resorts hired him before it opened the first casino in Atlantic City. McGahn liked to tell how he took his pay in Resorts stock for winning City Hall rulings that gave Resorts control over a crucial strip of land, variances and other arcane matters. When the crowds packing Resorts caused its stock to skyrocket to more than two hundred dollars per share, McGahn sold, making him worth somewhere between $12 million and $18 million.

His dark, paneled office a block from Resorts included a shrine of his

Marine Corps days in Korea, where as a young officer he led troops up bullet-raked hills and claims to have personally strangled communist soldiers, a tale that has earned him the moniker "piano-wire Paddy." Other walls held photographs of McGahn with Donald Trump, President John F. Kennedy and the Pope. Friends said McGahn's connections went all the way to God; enemies regarded him as the devil incarnate.

McGahn's influence grew from his flattery of petty officials at City Hall and the many independent authorities that ran parts of Atlantic City. He knew intimate details about their lives, inquiring how surgery had gone for a sick aunt in North Carolina or how the new grandson was doing, thus making the unpaid members of the zoning and planning boards and the obscure bureaucrats at City Hall feel important.

McGahn realized that the solution to Trump's narrow lot problem was to build out over Mississippi Avenue, which separated the site from the Atlantic City Convention Hall. Trump had no right to build beyond the curb, however. McGahn solved this by persuading Convention Hall officials to lease a one-foot strip of its property for ninety-nine years in return for a one-hundred-dollar fee. At City Hall McGahn argued that control of both sides of the street gave Trump air rights, and the people he had cultivated went along. Above this thin air Trump built the high-roller area where Akio Kashiwagi, Bob Libutti and others would later blow millions of dollars.

The enforcement division, which originally agreed to Trump's plan that Shapiro and Sullivan be his landlords without getting licensed, suddenly changed its stance in 1983 and demanded they apply for licenses as financial sources. This shift occurred after prosecutors had publicly detailed the depth of Shapiro's ties to mob boss Scarfo. But Sullivan noted that it was also after he notified Trump that he was in default on his lease, jeopardizing Trump's lucrative deal with Holiday. Knowing they would never be licensed, Sullivan, Shapiro and their partners sold the land to Trump. Later, Sullivan sued the enforcement division, alleging that it had improperly helped Trump gain an advantage in a business dispute. He lost on a technicality before a trial could be held on the merits of his claim.

When Harrah's at Trump Plaza opened in May 1984, it was as prosaic as Harrah's Marina. To support its thirty-nine floors the lobby sprouted a forest of tall columns covered with red cloth and mirrors.

86

The tallest building in town also suffered from a costly omission. While Harrah's Marina prospered in good measure because of its luxurious garage, Harrah's at Trump Plaza opened with only a surface lot across Pacific Avenue. Donald Trump had bought up most of that block, with half the money coming from Harrah's. But he balked at building a garage, threatening at one point to sell the land while insisting that the casino be renamed only Trump Plaza in his honor. The difference parking made showed up on the bottom line. Each week Harrah's Marina earned a bigger net profit than Harrah's at Trump Plaza earned in all of 1985.

Trump had a good reason not to want a garage. He wanted to buy out Holiday's half, which would cost a lot more with a garage helping to pump up profits. He did persuade his partners to rename the hotel, removing the Harrah's name and calling it Trump Plaza Casino Hotel. Mike Rose was unhappy at Trump's actions, but he would not sell, confident that eventually Trump would have to fulfill his obligation by building the garage.

But a series of events no one could have seen coming—involving the Casino Control Commission, the prime minister of the Bahamas, junk bond king Milken, and the late Conrad Hilton's eloquent will—changed Rose's mind. These events nourished the myth of Trump as an artist whose medium is deals.

These events began with the 1985 license renewal for Resorts International and a political scandal in the Bahamas. The opposition party in the Bahamas showed that $431,000 had flowed from Resorts into the pockets of Prime Minister Lynden O. Pindling.

Division of Gaming Enforcement director Thomas O'Brien said the $431,000 looked like a bribe to enable Resorts to keep its Nassau casino. New Jersey attorney general Irwin I. Kimmelman backed O'Brien, saying Resorts was unfit to operate in Atlantic City. After hearing the evidence, Commission chairman Walter N. Read concurred, finding that Resorts had failed to prove its honesty and integrity by clear and convincing evidence, as the Casino Control Act required. But the other commissioners did not share Read's view, and on Feb. 26, 1985, the commission voted 3 to 1 to renew Resorts' license.

The vote touched off a fire storm of criticism that the commission was letting economic interests shape policy and was not upholding the integrity and character standards that voters were promised would be paramount in casino regulation. That fire storm was still exploding two days later when the license application of Hilton Hotels came up for a vote. The commission shocked the investment world by denying Hilton Hotels a gaming license on a 2 to 2 vote.

Hilton had almost finished work on a sixty-thousand-square-foot casino with a grand skylit lobby in the marina, across a road from Harrah's Marina. It had built 614 rooms, with the main building designed so that additional hotel towers with several thousand more rooms, and some suites, could be easily added if the volume of business warranted. A Hilton casino held out the promises of solid management and more convention business from Hilton's sales force.

The commission found that Hilton's major sin was hiring Chicago attorney Sidney Korshak, whom law enforcement agencies said was a key tie between the legitimate business world and the underworld. Korshak's power lay in his supposed ability to insure labor peace for Hilton Hotels. The focus on Korshak, who was paid fifty thousand dollars a year and worked far from Hilton's headquarters in Beverly Hills, California, was a sharp departure from the policy followed with Trump, who worked closely with attorney Roy Cohn. The fact that Cohn, who had been indicted four times, was acceptable while Korshak, who had never even been indicted (much less convicted, or disbarred, as Cohn later was), would not be acceptable showed the capriciousness of the casino regulators and added to the growing evidence of official favoritism toward Trump.

Hilton's greater sin, one not found on the official record, was its haughtiness. Barron Hilton would not bow and scrape before the casino commissioners, as Jim Crosby did at Resorts' hearings. Hilton neither confessed errors nor thanked the commissioners for showing his firm the light, promising never to repeat any mistakes, as Crosby had done, nor did he meekly listen to criticism, as Trump soon would. Hilton failed to grasp that humility fostered the appearance of regulation.

Years later commissioner Carl Zeitz would look back on that week with regret. Zeitz had voted for Resorts and against Hilton, but he came to believe he should have voted the other way, against Resorts, which would have thrown it out, and for Hilton.

Having $320 million sunk into a single-purpose building without a license to open forced Hilton into a fire sale. Worse, its Beverly Hills neighbor, Drexel junk bond–meister Mike Milken, who was near the height of his powers and hungry for the fees hostile takeovers brought him, immediately saw Hilton Hotels as another company from which he could reap huge fees.

Like most hotel chains, which had lots of real estate that had risen in value faster than their stock price, Hilton Hotels was vulnerable to a takeover. But the firm was vulnerable for another reason: the greed of chairman Barron Hilton.

Barron Hilton was deep into a court fight with some nuns and the state of California over his father Conrad's estate and how a single phrase had come to afflict an otherwise flawless will. A mystery writer might have called it The Case of the $641 Million Clause. Instead of a "whodunit," this intrigue was a "who gets it."

Conrad Hilton frequently revised his will, giving less and less of his hundreds of millions to his children until his thirty-fourth version left Barron a Palm Springs manse and three quarters of a million dollars. Conrad left 99 percent of his estate to a foundation bearing his name, instructing the trustees to foster world peace and "shelter little children with the umbrella of your charity."

After his father was in the grave Barron went to court seeking to snatch as much as $641 million from the mouths of these children and put it into his already deep pockets.

Under federal law a foundation and members of the donor's family together cannot own more than 20 percent of a publicly traded corporation. Conrad Hilton had owned 27.4 percent of his hotel chain and Barron owned 4 percent. Conrad's thirty-fourth will solved this problem neatly, though, by requiring that any excess be given to the Jesuits, who are a public charity unaffected by this limit. Had this will been in effect at his death, the foundation would have received about 16 percent, Barron would have kept his 4 percent, and the Jesuits would have received the rest of Conrad's stock.

Before Conrad Hilton died in 1979, at age ninety-one, however, his will was revised one more time. The changes came on the advice of Donald Hubbs, a veteran tax attorney whose clients included Barron Hilton. Hubbs recommended that his client's father change his will to give any stock above the IRS limits to Barron instead of the Jesuits.

89

After Conrad died Barron put forth a novel interpretation of his father's will. Since he and the estate together owned nearly one third of the company, and he could not be forced to sell his stake, Barron argued that the 20 percent rule meant that his father's entire estate was in excess. The only solution to this dilemma, Barron argued, was for the estate to sell him all of Conrad's stock and then give the cash to the Hilton Foundation.

He also argued that this stock, which would insure his control of Hilton Hotels, was worth less than market price on the day his father died—an argument that was not merely self-serving but ludicrously so in an era of hostile takeovers in which Drexel clients routinely paid huge premiums above market price for the controlling shares of a company.

The California attorney general, as guardian of charitable assets, challenged Barron in court. Years later a negotiated settlement gave Barron much of what he wanted, but in March and April of 1985 the outcome of the estate fight was in doubt and, therefore, so was Barron's continued control of Hilton Hotels. Combined with the New Jersey casino license rejection, the battle over how much Barron would take from the starving made Hilton Hotels vulnerable to Milken's takeover machine. Milken ally Steve Wynn immediately dove into these uncertain waters.

Wynn had been touting plans to build a second casino on a marshy marina site, which would have mimicked Mike Rose's strategy of combining a Boardwalk property with one in the marina. One week after the Hilton license denial Wynn announced that Golden Nugget was abandoning plans for a $350-million marina casino. Savvy observers realized at once that Wynn was not withdrawing at all, but signaling that he wanted to buy the Atlantic City Hilton or perhaps the entire Hilton Hotel Corporation. Even though Hilton Hotel was vastly larger than Golden Nugget, Wynn had credibility as a seasoned passenger on Milken's junk-bond juggernaut.

Four weeks later Golden Nugget offered seventy-two dollars per share for the stock in Conrad Hilton's estate and promised a similar price for the rest of the company. For the world's suffering children it was a much better deal than Barron proposed. Wynn was offering $488.3 million for the estate's stock, more than two and a half times what Barron had offered. Implicitly, Wynn was pricing the entire Hilton com-

90

pany at $2 billion and that day Hilton's stock jumped $8.50 per share to just above the price Wynn offered. But Barron Hilton had the advantage of being the foundation's chairman and attorney Hubbs had become the foundation president. The estate rejected the bid on April 12.

Milken and Wynn failed, although they inadvertently helped impoverished children by raising the price Barron ultimately would have to pay for his father's stock. Meanwhile, Donald Trump was busy working on a deal that would leave Barron Hilton employed at Hilton Hotel while extricating the company from Atlantic City, and without destroying Barron's efforts to buy his father's estate at a discount.

Barron Hilton took the Trump deal. Afterward, Trump publicly savaged Hilton, as he would others who did deals with him. In *The Art of the Deal* Trump dismissed Barron Hilton as a member of the "lucky sperm club" who owed his lofty position to his father. Trump wrote that after the license denial Hilton "ended up selling to me at the last minute, under a lot of pressure, and without a lot of other options."

Hilton got the better part of the bargain, though, for what the dealmeister did not mention was that at this fire sale he paid one hundred cents on the dollar.

Trump borrowed every penny for the deal and then some. Manufacturers Hanover loaned him his $70 million capital contribution. Bear Stearns, a New York securities firm anxious to get in on the casino junk business Milken had developed at Drexel, peddled $353 million worth of mortgage bonds. The deal was so fat that Trump even sliced off a $5 million fee for himself.

The Casino Control Commission certified the deal, which required finding that Trump had demonstrated his financial stability and his business ability. The latter finding came even though Trump had no experience running a casino, only building one and sharing in the profits. The commission also found that the casino would be financially stable, meaning it could pay its bills as they came due, an important consideration for prospective bond buyers who want to get their principal back.

To run his first casino Trump picked someone who knew even less than he did about the casino business—his wife. Trump boasted that Ivana was "a natural manager" and the commissioners went along even though there was no way Ivana could prove by clear and convincing

91

evidence that she had the experience and business ability to run a casino hotel.

Immediately, the Trumps began remaking his marina property in his image, starting with a new name: Trump's Castle. When it opened six weeks later, on June 17, 1985, the previous owner's giant "H" was still visible everywhere and the "Beef Barron" restaurant featured a $7.50 "Barron's Burger." Soon those symbols would be gone, along with Hilton's well-conceived marketing plans.

Mike Rose was not happy to see Donald Trump with his own casino, especially since it was across the road from Harrah's Marina. Earlier Rose had reluctantly agreed to remove the Harrah's name on the Boardwalk. Now Rose calculated that Holiday spent $8 million promoting Trump's name while his erstwhile partner was competing head-on for players with Holiday's most valuable asset, Harrah's Marina.

The day Trump's Castle opened Mike Rose took Donald Trump to court. Holiday's lawsuit sought to block Trump from using his name in the marina, saying it would confuse patrons, and to bar Trump from using its confidential list of players. The suit charged that Trump's delays in repairing the Boardwalk casino's many construction defects, his threat to sell the parking site, and his failure to build the garage were predatory and "unmistakably" part of a plan to drive down the value of the Boardwalk partnership to force Harrah's to sell its stake cheap.

Trump countersued, alleging Harrah's management was so sloppy that it had "badly bloodied" the Trump name.

U.S. District Judge Stanley Brotman brought Trump and Rose to his court in Camden, New Jersey, in an attempt to forge a settlement. Brotman noted that nothing in their contract barred Trump from opening his own casino.

Nine months later, in March 1986, Rose threw in the towel and sold Holiday's half of the Boardwalk casino. Trump paid $223 million, two thirds of what he paid for the Hilton, but then he already owned half of the Boardwalk casino. Again, Trump borrowed every penny and then some. The day the deal closed Trump announced the property would now be known as Trump Plaza Hotel and Casino.

Trump also announced that work would begin right away on a badly needed garage.

11

The Art
of Management

From low-rent Arctic and Baltic to costly Boardwalk and Park Place, the streets of Atlantic City have been familiar to millions since the board game Monopoly was invented by a pair of down-and-out locals during the Great Depression.

Donald Trump looked on Atlantic City as a real-life monopoly game where he wanted all the choice pieces. In Monopoly imprudence can lead to bankruptcy. Luck and other players' mistakes can also be more important than skill.

Once Trump got full ownership of Trump Plaza on the Boardwalk in May 1986, he cast aside Mike Rose's concept of coordinating marketing between a marina operation primarily outfitted with slots and a Boardwalk house geared to table players, a strategy intended to give a pair of jointly owned casinos an advantage against everyone else. Instead Trump started his two casinos competing against each other. They not only vied for the same players, they competed for entertainment talent, executives and sales staff to entice players. The economies possible by jointly purchasing supplies and advertising were ignored in favor of duplicate, competing operations.

This wasteful and ruinous policy went unnoticed in many of the breathless newspaper and magazine stories touting Trump's supposedly smooth-running Team Trump and his claimed ability to promote people like Ivana into positions far above their experience and make them winners. So did the cold reality that the Trump Organization operated in constant chaos, his empire run on office intrigues. Long-range planning consisted not of how to build for next year and the year after that, but of how best to vanquish the executive in the next office.

Al Glasgow, Trump's loyal casino consultant, shook his head in disbelief at the costly warfare, which he called "disorganized crime," among the Trump executives. "Instead of bringing in the business and making money they're all stabbing each other in the back, all busy trying to figure out how to fuck the other guy and get on Donald's good side," said Glasgow, himself a skilled veteran of the in-fighting whose sensitive antennae detected early on which executives were rising and which were heading for the door.

In such a battle a novice like Ivana, working with the Castle, ordinarily would be no match for the competition at Trump Plaza, which was run by the experienced and steady hand of Steve Hyde. But ordinary was poison in the Trump Organization, where ability or even success at bringing money to the bottom line was sometimes less important than one's relationship with Donald. Minor talents sometimes rose to great heights, briefly, before Donald abandoned them. When it came to intimacy with Donald, Hyde was no match for Ivana, at least not at first.

Trump planted stories that Ivana had been on Czechoslovakia's Olympic ski team. She had not, nor had she ever made such a claim. He called her a top Canadian fashion model. She had been an anonymous runway model. He did not mention that Ivana Zelnickova Winklmayr Trump had married before.

After Norman Vincent Peale married them in 1977, Ivana used Donald's growing income and desire for media attention to make them both Manhattan society charity-ball regulars. Now, in the summer of 1985, she reigned over Trump's Castle and the depth of her management talent quickly became apparent.

Hilton had designed for the mass market, but Trump did not want his name associated with the common men and women whose steady play earned a million dollars a week in profits for neighboring Harrah's Marina.

Christian Mari, who had run the hotel side of the Atlantic City

Golden Nugget before coming to work as Ivana's senior hotel executive, urged adherence to Hilton's marketing plan. "We should be a slot house," he told the Trumps. "That is what Hilton designed, that is what the marina market is." The memos, the charts and the logic got him nowhere. "You just couldn't talk to Donald. He would not listen to advice from his executives."

Egged on by Donald, Ivana wanted to fill the Castle with high-stakes gamblers, even though the Castle lacked the kind of excessively opulent suites that whales and other preferred players could command elsewhere.

To the eternal high-roller question, "Whaddya gonna gimme?" Trump Castle needed an answer. The really suite deals were at Atlantic City's two high-roller houses, Caesars and Steve Wynn's Golden Nugget. Caesars marketing offices in Medellín, Hong Kong and other cities where great fortunes were being accumulated provided a steady flow of people who demanded the most luxurious and flamboyant lodging.

Wynn was a polished showman who understood that it was good for business to give people bragging rights, to be able to say not that the Golden Nugget had given them a suite, but that their friend Steve Wynn had reached into his pocket and given them the key to one of his suites. Golden Nugget's entertaining television commercials, in which Wynn acted out vignettes with Frank Sinatra and Dolly Parton, enhanced those bragging rights and brought in more people willing to gamble heavily to get his suite keys.

Even the tiny Sands, wedged onto a small lot a block from the Boardwalk, offered nine opulent suites, including the four-thousand-square-foot Versailles, which sprawled over two floors.

The Castle had only one fancy suite and Ivana took it for herself.

Her competitor, Steve Hyde, was a Mormon with seven kids, an accountant who had learned the business at the Caesars and Sands casinos in both Atlantic City and Las Vegas and at Atlantic City Golden Nugget. He had made one major career mistake, one that taught him an important lesson about how credit gambling can hurt the casino as well as bankrupt players. Hyde had agreed in 1981 to run the Las Vegas Sands for Pratt Hotel Corporation while his rival, Bill Weidner, would run the Atlantic City Sands. "After I got to Las Vegas I realized that the place had depended on one player—Adnan Khashoggi," Hyde explained. The arms merchant "owed millions, but he didn't pay his markers and the place went bust." Weidner, not Hyde, went on to become president of Pratt Hotel.

Hyde returned to Atlantic City and joined the Golden Nugget, where Wynn regarded the big bear as a solid executive, but not a star. Wynn did admire Hyde's ability to smooth stormy waters, to not confuse personal tiffs with getting the job done. This ability, this willingness to absorb verbal assaults and go on about the job, became crucial once Hyde moved to Trump Plaza.

During this time Trump suddenly faced his first major problem with casino regulators. One of them accused him of lying under oath.

The issue grew out of Hilton's promise to help finance part of a $40 million project to improve the only road into Brigantine, the island town immediately across an inlet from the marina. Trump lawyer Nick Ribis promised the casino commissioners that Trump would stand in Hilton's shoes, but once the casino changed hands Trump renounced the commitment and filed a lawsuit.

Valerie Armstrong, an ambitious young Republican lawyer who had lived in Brigantine and who was recently appointed to the Casino Control Commission, pressed the matter. Attorney David Sciarra of New Jersey's Public Advocate office said seven days of testimony made it clear that Trump never intended to build the roadway, a charge which, if true, could cost Trump his license because it would show he lacked integrity.

"There is a cloud over this license which must be dispelled," Armstrong said, noting that "every week this commission denies licenses to people . . . because they refused to treat the commission with honesty and openness, even in cases where the matter withheld itself might not have constituted cause for denial" of a license. Incensed, Armstrong complained of "numerous direct and sharp conflicts" in the testimony, concluding that Trump's version of events lacked "candor and honesty."

But while Armstrong believed Trump had failed the Casino Control Act's integrity and character tests, she had only one vote. By June 1986, Trump had already become a powerhouse, owning two of Atlantic City's eleven casinos. His license was renewed on a 4 to 1 vote.

That vote, and Armstrong's remarks about how others were kept from casino jobs if their candor was in doubt on even minor matters, illustrated the stark truth of casino regulation—that it was based on two standards of justice, separate and unequal. One standard held those seeking licenses for jobs as cocktail waitresses or blackjack dealers or supervisors to the absolute letter of the law, and those suspected of violating it were sometimes rousted from their beds at night, prosecuted and, if that failed, forced into licensing hearings that would drain their life's savings. The other standard assured casino owners of a convenient time for an appointment before any questioning and, often enough, the government agents would travel to the owners office to save him the trouble of travel. In arranging such appointments the enforcement division attorneys could choose to give no hint of their purpose or they could explain just what they were after, affording the owners an opportunity to prepare answers to the questions they knew would be asked.

Once the testimony was in, whether it be about bribing a foreign head of state or a commitment to build a road, casino owners also received the benefit of the doubt. The worst they risked was that Armstrong or one other commissioner would vote against them and the others would speak a few critical words.

Armstrong asked for a thorough investigation of the road issue. But nothing ever came of her request and six years later the road improvements remained only a promise.

With his license renewed the deal artist made his first major foray onto Wall Street. In his first autobiography Trump told how Daniel Lee, the casino analyst at Drexel Burnham Lambert, and some colleagues came to his Trump Tower office at 4 o'clock on a summer afternoon "to discuss being my investment bankers on a deal to purchase a hotel company."

Drexel never became Trump's investment banker, but Trump's actions made Drexel more than $100 million in fees.

The unnamed hotel company Lee and Trump discussed was the Holiday Corporation. Trump bought 1.1 million shares of his former partner in the summer of 1986, borrowing every cent from his bank credit lines and his broker, Bear Stearns.

Trump had plenty of motivation both to weaken Holiday financially and to divert management's attention from its smoothly running Harrah's Marina next to his Castle. Far more than Hilton, Holiday's real

97

estate assets had risen in value faster than its stock price. What put a scare into Holiday was Trump's announcement that he intended to file for a casino license in Nevada, a necessary step before he could take over Holiday, because it operated casinos there.

Mike Rose was already working on strategies to restructure Holiday, including having management acquire the firm from shareholders in a leveraged buy-out, when Trump came hunting.

Rose recalled later that

> I really didn't believe Donald Trump was a serious corporate raider. This was before he had established his reputation as a greenmailer. I just couldn't quite picture him as running a big company. But he had put us in play clearly, and our stock was moving, and arbitrageurs were taking big positions, and something had to happen, so we got hard to work with Goldman Sachs [Holiday's investment banker], and we started talking about alternatives. And frankly I wasn't satisfied with whether we were exploring all the alternatives; it seemed we got sort of a canned response from them.

For advice Rose turned to James Wolfensohn, another investment banker, who later became a Holiday director.

"The best in this sort of situation is Drexel," Wolfensohn said, adding this caution: "Now they've got this reputation."

"Yeah," Rose remembered replying, "what scares me about Drexel is, [after] we go in and talk to them, we don't know if one of their clients ends up doing something to us."

Wolfensohn arranged a meeting in Beverly Hills with Drexel chief executive Fred Josephson, deal-maker Peter Ackerman, and Milken, who was listed on company records as a mere bond trader.

"They convinced me of two things," Rose said. "One, they were reputable people, they weren't going to take any information we gave to them and do anything untoward and, secondly, before we had ever met them, just from public information, they knew more in a constructive sense about our company and our industry and how to think about our business than Goldman did in all of the years we had worked with Goldman. . . . I got a real appreciation for these guys, who really did their homework and who think like businessmen as well as bankers."

98

The meeting convinced Rose that he wanted Drexel working for Holiday, never against it. Of course, Drexel had already been working against Holiday, with Lee recommending that Trump buy the stock and bringing Drexel's mergers and acquisitions experts in to advise Trump on Holiday's prospects as a takeover candidate.

To thwart Trump, Drexel recommended that Holiday take on $2.4 billion of junk bond and bank debt. Most of the money went to pay a special dividend of sixty-five dollars per share.

Overnight Holiday's balance sheet changed from understated black to bright red. Now Holiday was weighed down with nearly a billion dollars more in liabilities than assets, making it ugly to Wall Street raiders. To shed this debt and get its balance sheet back into the black Holiday would have to sell hotels fast and at premium prices.

Not only was management's attention diverted, but the company had little money to reinvest in Harrah's Marina, a prospect that thrilled Trump.

David Hanlon, who ran Harrah's, had scale models built for a convention center, added hotel rooms and other improvements that could have pushed profits even higher. Rose rejected this sensible plan to reinvest in Holiday's most profitable property. Rose did not trust regulation in New Jersey either to let him run his business as he saw fit or to control Trump's predatory behavior.

Trump, meanwhile, sold his Holiday stock in November for a gross profit of $18.8 million, made entirely with borrowed money.

Drexel fared much better, earning $95 million in fees and expenses from Holiday.

The Casino Control Commission could have stopped Trump's Holiday raid. The Casino Control Act states that "the economic stability of casino operations" is in the public interest and that competition is "desirable and necessary" to insure varied attractions to draw tourists. The act also directed the commission to prevent economic concentration and "encourage and preserve competition."

But the commission ignored these duties. Trump got the implicit message. Within days of cashing in his Holiday position Trump started buying stock in another competitor, Bally Manufacturing.

Drexel could not have asked for more in a rainmaker, because this time Trump's putative raid brought it a series of lucrative junk bond deals, and Drexel didn't even have to pay Trump a finder's fee.

Bally had begun as a pinball and slot machine maker. It equipped state lotteries, owned the popular Pac-Man video game, ran health clubs featuring sultry Sheena Easton in its television spots, and owned three casinos, two in Nevada and one in New Jersey. It also had a history of mob ties and before the New Jersey Casino Control Commission would license it in 1979, Chairman William O'Donnell denied any impropriety but was forced to resign and sell his stake.

Trump liked Bally's Park Place. Its magenta-and-green casino produced the largest cash flow in Atlantic City and Bally's Park Place also profited from a classy-sounding address, Boardwalk and Park Place, the most expensive squares on the Monopoly board. Like Harrah's, Bally's also had steady management under former stockbroker Richard Gillman and his crew. But its corporate parent did not do nearly so well—except when it came to extraordinary pay and perks for executives and directors. The price of Bally Manufacturing stock was low relative to the company's value, making it attractive to raiders.

Trump, again using borrowed money, bought nearly 10 percent of Bally Manufacturing in the last two months of 1986. Drexel's Dan Lee advised Trump as he made these stock purchases.

Within days Bally sued Trump, accusing him of antitrust and securities law violations, and Trump countersued. Bally also hired Drexel.

In February 1987, Bally settled the litigation with Trump by buying back his stock at an inflated price and paying him a $6.2 million fee to go away for ten years. Trump's gross profit, including the fee, was $21 million. Drexel made much more and this time Trump not only saddled a strong competitor with debt, he got a bonus when an even tougher competitor, Steve Wynn, quit Atlantic City altogether.

Because Trump owned two casinos, Bally could block a takeover by buying a second gambling hall. That's because New Jersey law limited him to three. Bally bought the Atlantic City Golden Nugget, paying a wildly inflated price of $440 million. Wynn's company had only $255 million invested in the baroque palace at the south end of the Boardwalk, whose early profits had not been sustained. Over the previous three years combined it had lost more than $6 million.

Bally's spendthrift reaction to Trump's raid left Bally drowning in red ink, unable to compete effectively in Atlantic City (or Nevada) and the raid prompted Wynn, one of the two high roller specialists, to leave town. For Trump it was a straight win-win. He had eliminated one tough competitor, Wynn, and he had saddled two more casinos with the oppressive debt loads that held back Harrah's from expansion.

Right after Wynn left town the badly needed garage was finished at Trump Plaza. On the side facing the casino were a few potted plants and two black hansom cabs, each drawn by a life-size bronze horse. Displaying the kind of chutzpah that Trump relished, Hyde claimed that the garage was a work of art and that its entire $30 million cost should be credited against Trump obligations under a city ordinance requiring investments in public art. (The ploy became moot when the ordinance was gutted.)

Despite the hansom cab many thought the garage an architectural and urban planning atrocity, for it confronted motorists coming off the Atlantic City Expressway with a gigantic blank wall, to which were added huge red lights declaring the name Trump Plaza. More than any other structure in town the Trump Plaza garage demonstrated that the casinos were in Atlantic City, but not of it, that the casinos wanted to be walled off from the rest of the city.

Whatever its aesthetic values the garage gave Hyde the tool he needed to outshine Ivana's Castle. In 1986, Trump Plaza's net profit was four times Trump Castle's. In 1987, with the garage open only seven months, Trump Plaza's net ballooned to more than ten times the Castle's.

Still, during the last week of July 1987, Ivana nearly won her fight with Hyde. Ivana hired Christian Mari from the old Golden Nugget. But he wasn't coming to work at the Castle. Mari's contract read "senior vice president, hotel operations, Trump Plaza." Mari was to be Ivana's Trojan horse.

Hyde got wind that Ivana's hire would show up in a week and warned his top aides that it was time to look for new work. In cold fury he told associates: "Ivana can have the Castle and she can have the Plaza and she can run them both into the ground." Hyde turned to the only two men in New York who could sway Donald's mind, brother

Robert and lawyer Harvey Freeman. The next day Ivana called Mari to her office and told him her plan had failed, but his contract would be honored at the Castle.

Having won this battle Hyde renewed his efforts to make Trump Plaza the successor to the Golden Nugget as high-roller heaven. Among those Golden Nugget players he lured up the Boardwalk was Robert Libutti, a compulsive gambler with a hair-trigger temper and a habit of using vulgar street language when addressing women and minorities, habits that the Mormon Hyde ignored so long as Libutti was willing to while away hours risking up to twenty thousand dollars on each roll of the dice.

What Hyde discouraged was the lusty interest Trump took in Libutti's only daughter, a stylish divorcée named Edie.

"Don't ever let him go out with her, Bob, don't ever," Libutti said Hyde warned him. "I'll lose a customer and I'm going to lose a boss."

"Why?" Libutti asked.

"You'll wind up killing him and you'll never come back here again."

Libutti said he was furious that a married man would want to bed his daughter and he finally confronted Trump, ordering him to stop asking her out.

"Donald, I'll fucking pull your balls from your legs," Libutti said he threatened. "Remember, I know what you are. I will literally amputate your nuts from your body."

Hyde had another reason to want to keep Trump away from Libutti's daughter and it had nothing to do with his religion's rigid morality.

Hyde had gained in the competition with Ivana by helping Donald hide his mistress, Marla Ann Maples. The bosomy Georgia blonde stayed at Trump Plaza, signing for anything she desired in its restaurants and shops. So long as Donald stayed focused on Marla, Trump kept his wife away from Trump Plaza, which meant Hyde and his team remained secure in their cushy jobs.

Although Trump always surrounded himself with bodyguards, sometimes he abandoned them and drove himself to Trump Plaza to reduce the number of mouths that might spread stories about his secret liaisons. This precaution was not perfect, though, for a few insiders could not keep the secret.

To really win Donald's heart Hyde and his team needed to establish Trump Plaza as the premier high-roller joint. Like Harrah's Marina, Trump Plaza was built as a prosaic place. Hyde remade it, covering the floors, walls and the columns with Italian marble and arranging Mike Tyson's fights next door at the Convention Hall, as well as other glamour events.

Meanwhile, Donald had his own plan to attract high rollers to Trump Castle. (The 's had been dropped from the name, a grammatical refinement that Trump claimed cost a half million dollars.) Trump wanted suites. Ivana could spend lavishly on dinners, fine wines and gifts, but high rollers still wanted their egos fed by spending their hours away from the table in fantasy lodgings with marble and tapestries or brass and gauche colors, depending on their taste.

Christian Mari thought the plan to build the Crystal Tower was nuts, the $75 million cost pure waste. "I was absolutely against it," Mari said. "We should have continued the phased plan Hilton had contemplated, we should have competed with Harrah's."

Ivana, anxious to please Donald's fantasy of offering only the best to the richest, ordered more marble, more chandeliers, more art. While Donald continued selling himself to the world as a master developer who always came in on budget, the Crystal Tower cost overruns ran wild. The final price was more than $110 million or, by one official estimate, $115 million. All this bought what looked, from the street, like a hospital wing.

This monument finished, Trump did something that was absolutely amazing given his practice of claiming wildly inflated values for his properties. At the start of 1988, Trump had paid Appraisal Group International to value the Castle. It settled on $636 million. Nearly two years later, just as the Crystal Tower was about to open, Trump's confidential net worth statement valued the Castle at $635 million.

Perhaps Trump never compared the two statements, but nonetheless by his own account he had written off the entire $110 million expansion as less than worthless—it sliced a million bucks off the Castle's value.

In reality the Castle was worth nowhere near either of these figures, which were more than twenty-seven times the cash flow the casino hotel produced in 1987. Except for extraordinary circumstances, such as

103

Bally's desperate purchase of the Golden Nugget, getting six times cash flow for a casino would be a good price. At the start of 1988 that made the Castle worth $234 million, about one third the figure set by Appraisal Group International.

Trump's willingness to ignore tried and tested relationships in real estate and business between cash flow and purchase price was not limited to producing inflated appraisals for properties he owned. He bought the Plaza Hotel on Central Park South in March 1988, for more than $400 million, again borrowing every penny and then some. The price was in line with his valuations of the Castle, since he paid about twenty-five times cash flow. It also meant the deal was written in red ink that the bankers, anxious to collect financing fees, somehow failed to notice.

Shortly after he closed the deal Trump flew in his black Super Puma helicopter from Manhattan to the Castle helipad to close the book on the competition between Ivana and Hyde. He gathered a dozen Castle executives around the mahogany-and-granite conference table in the windowless executive boardroom and called Manhattan on the speakerphone.

"Ivana, I'm here with some of your friends in the room," Trump announced, according to two of those present. Then Trump told Ivana that she was no longer their boss.

Executives seated around the table, even those who detested Ivana, were aghast that Trump would publicly demean his wife instead of talking to her in private. The cruelty of it was mitigated when Donald continued, saying that he was promoting her to a new position in the Trump Hotel Corporation and putting her in charge of his newest property, the Plaza Hotel on Central Park in Manhattan. Over the speakerphone Ivana's whimper could be heard. One witness to this exchange recalled thinking: This man has freon in his veins.

Hyde had won and with him came the hope of reliable, competent management. With Ivana confined to New York the little resort that called itself the World's Playground was safe for Donald to play with Marla.

Trump, who often said money was the measure of success in business, had told the world how much he valued Hyde and Ivana. He paid

Hyde seven figures to run his casinos. After her promotion Donald paid Ivana "one dollar a year and all the dresses she can buy."

But instead of focusing on his two casinos, on building the business, the easily distracted Trump would soon cast his eye on another casino—one that would soon entomb his presumed fortune.

12

A Shell on the Beach

On April 10, 1986, Jim Crosby's oxygen bottles stopped helping him. Nicotine had killed him. He had been an international playboy whose will doled out money to seven women, a man famed for chartering helicopters to go to dinner, a man who put the brother of mobster Meyer Lansky's closest confidant in charge of his company's Bahamas casino. Crosby had also been the force behind Atlantic City's casinos, the man who saw the opportunity to get rich by ending Nevada's monopoly in the United States and who persuaded the citizens of New Jersey to see gambling as a benefit for themselves, an idea that would revive Atlantic City and help old folks pay their medical bills. Crosby did it by transforming the Mary Carter Paint Company into Resorts International, a casino company in which he and his family became controlling shareholders.

In Atlantic City he started out on the cheap, slapping fresh paint on the broken-down Haddon Hall before it opened on May 26, 1978. But he wanted a monument, too. On the sandy soil next to Haddon Hall, Crosby started work on the world's largest casino, the Taj Mahal. But while players like developer David Zarin and Philadelphia Eagles owner Leonard Tose lost millions at Resorts' tables, Crosby was blowing even bigger fortunes with bizarre investment schemes. Resorts bought gold futures as the price was dropping, losing nearly $22 million. It blew $23.7 million trying to take over troubled Trans World Airlines. At Crosby's death Resorts owned 11 percent of another losing airline, Pan Am. In 1984, Resorts had earned a $21.7 million profit, but the figure sunk to $3.2 million in 1985 as the crazy investments and the Taj ate cash and the wheezing Crosby slowly drifted away.

Resorts International had an unusual capital structure. It had no mortgages, but it borrowed $605 million through junk bonds, the corporate equivalent of credit card debt. It also had two classes of stock that traded roughly in tandem, even though the Class B shares carried one hundred votes each and the Class A just one vote. The B shares traded at forty-seven dollars just before Crosby died. But they rose sharply the next day because it was obvious Resorts was ripe for a takeover, ripe for a new buyer who would apply sound management to exploit the torrent of cash still flowing from its casinos in Atlantic City and the Bahamas. I. G. "Jack" Davis, Crosby's right-hand man, insisted the company was not for sale, but no one believed him.

Five months passed before the first buyer appeared. Pratt Hotel Corporation, a Dallas firm which owned the Sands in Atlantic City, bid $100 that September for the controlling B shares, a deal that would have cost about $73 million. On the stock market the B shares quickly soared to $150 amid speculation they would rise to $180 each before Pratt would close the deal.

Pratt was in the same business as Resorts, but it was worlds apart in its history. It hardly made any profits, though it paid its executives very handsomely while its shareholders saw the value of their stock steadily decline, from $5.62 a share in the early eighties to less than twenty-five cents a share in early 1992. And its founders came from a very different background than Crosby.

At age seven Jack Pratt hawked newspapers on the streets of Joplin, Missouri, to help his father, a shipping clerk, get the family through the Depression. At sixteen Pratt and his brother Ed, nineteen, bought a run-down diner on Route 66 and turned it into a round-the-clock truck stop where they flipped hamburgers and pumped fuel until Jack finished high school. They claimed that they sold out for a quarter million dollars in 1950 when the Korean War draft tapped Jack.

Over the years Jack, Ed and younger brother Bill parlayed theater

107

snack bars and Dairy Queens into a chain of Holiday Inns and other motels they called Inns of America and, eventually, into ownership of the Sands in Atlantic City and Las Vegas. But even in these cash-rich businesses they operated on a shoestring. A doorman at the Sands in Atlantic City could open his coat, showing its lining worn through, but on the first of each month a check went to Dallas to cover the management fee Pratt Hotel charged its casino no matter what.

"Jack's a determined salesman," observed Ed Tracy, a onetime Pratt executive who later ran Trump's casinos. "He's the master of the Texas walking paper. If he needs to borrow fifty million dollars and no bank will loan him more than one million dollars, Jack will walk into banks all over Texas until he finds fifty that will each loan him a piece of what he needs."

Jack Pratt was the last owner Jack Davis wanted for Resorts. At sixty-one, Davis's tanned face had crinkled into a ghoulish grin that made him look like he was already long in the grave, while the rest of his body was as taut as a teen athlete's, kept in shape by rigorous exercise and lots of skiing. Davis graduated in the top third from the Harvard Business School, a member of the famous class of 1949, which produced an inordinate number of great executives. While no elitist, Davis did not need a boss with barely a high school education. Besides, Pratt already had the services of William Weidner, a smooth executive who knew marketing, and thus would have no need to keep Davis on the payroll. Davis had labored for years under Crosby, addressing his quixotic demands while building the business. Now it was his turn to be the boss. All Davis needed was an angel to buy the B shares, someone with deep pockets who could finish the Taj, but who also needed his management experience.

To Jack Davis, Donald Trump looked like a better bet than Jack Pratt. Trump was near the peak of media adoration. He had gone to Wharton, his lifestyle indicated deep pockets, and his ego would drive him to finish the Taj, Davis figured. Davis lined up the Crosby family for Trump and in March 1987, Donald Trump arranged to buy the B shares held by the Crosby estate, Crosby's relatives and some others. For $96 million they would give him stock controlling 88 percent of the votes. Trump, of course, borrowed all the money.

Trump rewarded Davis with a lucrative new employment contract that quickly quadrupled his pay to $1 million per year and that could mean nearly $20 million in pension payments to Davis and the lithe young Caroline, the former Mrs. Tose.

All Trump needed to close the deal was the Casino Control Commission's approval. The Casino Control Act limits an owner to three casinos. Since Trump already had the Plaza and the Castle, this posed a problem since Resorts already ran one casino and the commissioners also wanted the Taj finished. The logical choice was to close the casino in the existing Resorts while keeping open its restaurants and hotel rooms. Trump would then own three of the city's dozen casinos, but because the Taj casino was the size of the Plaza and Castle combined he would have as much floor space as four casinos. Would this much power in the hands of one owner diminish competition? Would it mean the kind of economic concentration the law prohibited? And was anyone willing to see a casino close?

To make his case that buying Resorts would not result in undue economic concentration Trump relied on Marvin Roffman, the casino analyst at the Janney Montgomery Scott brokerage who reflected the views of Main Line investors by emphasizing capital conservation, not daring investments. Roffman testified that letting Trump buy Resorts would not cause undue economic concentration because there were so many other sites available for others to open casinos. Two days after Roffman testified the commission advised Trump he could finish his deal and could close Resorts when the Taj was completed. Almost immediately events began unfolding that made Roffman regret his testimony.

Once in control Trump signed a "comprehensive services agreement" with Resorts that paid him a percentage of gross revenues in return for his management expertise. But Trump had no such expertise. The stock market saw immediately what the agreement meant that Trump would drain off money as an expense, insuring that he got his— even if nothing but red ink flowed to the bottom line.

Trump asserted that he was only charging a fair price for his expertise. But the three independent directors of Resorts—whom the casino commissioners insisted upon to maintain a semblance of checks on Trump—were wary. They hired David Schulte, a savvy Chicago investment banker, to review its terms. Schulte quickly showed just what a steep price Trump wanted for his comprehensive services. Over the agreement's thirty-year term, Trump stood to collect about $1 billion, Schulte figured.

The comprehensive services agreement required Casino Control Commission approval. Trump testified that the comprehensive services agreement was not his idea, but Jack Davis's. Some commission staffers argued internally that the agreement provided no benefit to the casino company and would weaken it, that it ran contrary to the commission's duties.

That Trump knew next to nothing about how to actually run a casino, that Resorts already had or could buy on the open market far more qualified managers for much less money, and that the contract posed a direct conflict between Trump's pecuniary interests and his fiduciary duties to other shareholders was of no heed to Chairman Read, who stuck to his decidedly narrow view that it was not the commission's job to protect shareholders. So long as the agreement did not interfere with the integrity of casino gaming and did not threaten the financial stability of the casino, Read would go along.

Emboldened by the laissez-faire approach that Read articulated on making money in what the law promised would be a "highly regulated" industry, Trump pressed on. Just five days after the commissioners rubber-stamped the services agreement Trump offered the rest of Resorts' owners fifteen dollars per share, or $85.6 million, to get out. It was the clearest possible evidence that Trump had not acted in the best interest of shareholders, whose stock was worth more than three times that just before Crosby died and more than five times as much the day after he died. Trump's fifteen-dollar price was for all shareholders, both the lowly A shares and the rest of the B shares, whose one hundred votes per share no longer carried any weight because Trump already had a majority of the voting power. Trump announced that unless he owned Resorts outright he would not risk his own money to finish the Taj, although anyone who had been following Trump's business style knew he would never risk his own money even if he won complete ownership of Resorts. (Trump later risked only the money of bank depositors and bond buyers on the Taj.)

Trump had another tactic to get the other shareholders to sell out

110

cheap. He threatened to shutter the Resorts casino in Atlantic City, to throw it into bankruptcy, saying the company was a mess, which it was. He even took stock analysts on a tour to see the horrors of what happens when a hotel built at the start of the century is not maintained for decades. Rooms priced at $150 a night featured peeling wallpaper, rotted window frames and stained carpets. The better rooms had wheezing air conditioners. But many rooms were like the hallways, steaming in summer and chilly in the winter.

The fifteen-dollars-per-share price appalled Schulte, whose opinion Resorts' independent directors had sought to insulate themselves in the shareholder litigation. He called it "grossly inadequate." Schulte pronounced $22 per share fair, an opinion worth almost $40 million more to the other shareholders and worth a $1.8 million fee to his firm, Chilmark Partners. Presented with Schulte's appraisal on January 12, Trump did the expected. He said he wouldn't buy at any price.

A few days later a new character walked onto this stage, blowing his nose.

Fidelle V. "Dale" Scutti said his sinuses bothered him. His cure was a trip to Atlantic City, a curious vacation spot in January for a multimillionaire auto dealer from suburban Rochester, New York, given that he also had a home in sunny Ft. Lauderdale. Scutti checked into the Showboat casino and strolled the boards in an overcoat, filling his nostrils with cold salt air. He didn't gamble. But he did spend a lot of time looking over the Taj Mahal with its forty-two stories of smokey-blue windows that shimmered even in the winter.

From outside the Taj looked nearly complete. Inside it was a mess, with openings that let in rain and the corrosive sea breezes. More than five years and $512 million after Resorts International broke ground on what was to be the world's largest casino, the Taj was just another pretty shell on the beach.

Scutti said he read in the newspapers that Trump would invest the $525 million needed to finish the Taj only if he could make Resorts his private property. How, Scutti asked himself, could it cost a half billion dollars to finish that building? Scutti was not in Trump's class financially, but he had built auto malls, strip shopping centers, and restaurants and had an idea of what construction cost.

111

Scutti figured that Trump's game was to scare Resorts shareholders into selling out cheap so he wouldn't have to share the spoils.

"Trump helped to make the stock price drop with threats of bankruptcy, with threats that no one could complete the Taj Mahal except him, and with threats that he was the only one who could finance the Taj Mahal," Scutti said. Shareholder suits making similar claims were already being heard in Delaware Chancery Court, where Resorts was officially organized. Trump denied the allegations.

Dale Scutti said he left Atlantic City convinced that Donald Trump had stumbled onto a great real estate play. Scutti wanted in on it. On January 19, Scutti bought one hundred thousand Resorts Class A shares at $13.50. Soon he would invest more than $5 million until he owned nearly 6 percent of the one-share, one-vote Class A stock. But he needed someone to force up the stock price to make any real money.

Meanwhile, Trump's withdrawn fifteen-dollar bid disturbed others and not all of them were shareholders dismayed at getting fifty dollars less per share than they could have had before Trump took charge. Casino Control commissioner Valerie Armstrong, who just months earlier had voted against renewing Trump's casino license because she believed he had lied, said Trump's conduct could be interpreted as intending to drive down the price of Resorts stock, which would be a violation of his fiduciary obligation to all shareholders.

Trump's withdrawal of the fifteen dollars per share bid was a bit much even for the other four casino commissioners. When the commission announced that it would hold hearings in two weeks to reconsider the approval of the comprehensive services agreement, Trump realized that Armstrong might have allies willing to kill the lucrative services agreement.

Trump got the unstated message, that an independent party had set a fair price for Resorts stock and Trump had better meet it or he could see his billion-dollar comprehensive services agreement voided. Two days later Trump said he would pay twenty-two dollars for the rest of the Resorts stock, which ended the commission's interest in any hearings.

Shareholders, though, seemed not to think much of Schulte's opinion or Trump's sudden willingness to pay twenty-two dollars per share. By March just 3 percent of the Class A shares had been tendered. On March

18, the Delaware Chancery Court was scheduled to rule on what price would be fair for Resorts and it might take a more generous view than Schulte.

Back in Rochester, Dale Scutti kept buying Resorts stock. He also retained Morris Orens, a New York lawyer who worked the securities bar, to help find a buyer for the company, an angel, a raider or anyone who would drive up the price of Resorts stock.

Orens took this request to a client of his named Ernie.

13

"I'm with You"

The tiny brokerage just off Wall Street bore the pretentious name of Equities International. John Connolly, a former New York police detective who held the equally pretentious title of national sales manager, was instructing some of his novice stockbrokers in the art of generating commissions when the telephone interrupted.

"We have to talk right now!" Peter Aiello screamed out of the earpiece.

"I'm busy. I'll call you back," Connolly yelled back.

"I'm at Ernie's!" Aiello hollered before Connolly put his receiver down.

A minute later Connolly phoned Ernie's. His conversations with Peter Aiello would play a crucial role in the most celebrated business deal of 1988—Merv Griffin's hostile takeover of Resorts International from Donald Trump. The battle of the moguls was a story dear to the hearts of the glitzmongers who pose as journalists at many of the nation's leading news organs. Before the deal was finished, exactly eight months later, network television would chronicle the fight, major newspapers would carry the exchanges of witty barbs on their front pages, and breathless magazine covers would herald how Merv had taught the deal artist a lesson. Virtually all of these accounts would be based on how the highly

114

paid publicists for both men described the deal, not on its written terms, although they were open to public inspection. Hardly any of these accounts examined who profited, and why, from a casino deal that would soon cost banks and junk bond investors nearly a billion dollars. None of these accounts would mention the conversations that day between Peter Aiello and John Connolly, conversations that showed how close mob associates and stock swindlers were to Merv Griffin, the richest entertainer in history.

Connolly was a muscled Irish cop who was about to receive a gold detective's shield when he abruptly quit New York's finest in 1976. "Overeducated and underpaid," was how he explained giving up a career that began auspiciously in 1965 when he graduated at the top of his police academy class and quickly grew into plum detective work digging into the Gallo and Gambino crime families.

A dozen years later Connolly wore expensive suits, had his once red hair sculpted, and was riding the Wall Street boom. He also had more than a few clients looking to lynch him, mostly single and divorced women who said the slick stockbroker had wooed them into becoming clients and then executed trades without permission, steadily reducing the number of zeros in their net worth until some neared their last digit.

He was about to get out, to become, he said, a screenwriter, when Aiello showed up with his pal Ernie. Although Ernest G. Barbella paid two hundred thousand dollars for 48 percent of the firm just before 1987 ended, Aiello was as much in the deal as Ernie, he just could not be listed anywhere officially. Aiello had what *Forbes* called "a list of securities violations a mile long" for things like taking money from firms where he worked to repay his personal debts. At the time Aiello was barred from being a principal of any securities firm, so he used a title indicating he worked in marketing and recruitment—and used Ernie as a front.

At that first encounter with Aiello and Barbella, Connolly opened his ruddy ears wide as they explained how their connections would make them all rich. On his way home Connolly dropped a quarter into a phone and called a lawyer friend who worked for the Securities and Exchange Commission. "Some wise guys are taking over this place," Connolly reported.

On the afternoon of March 16, 1988, when Connolly called back, Aiello was so excited he could barely get his story out.

"Have everybody start buying Resorts International," Aiello ordered.

"Why?" Connolly asked, fishing.

"Just buy it," Aiello said.

"Why?" Connolly insisted.

"Merv Griffin is going to make a bid for the stock and my people are connected with his people. He'll go as high as forty-five dollars a share," Aiello explained.

"Right away," Connolly promised. But first Connolly walked outside to a phone booth and called his SEC contact. Insider trading done with the SEC's knowledge is not a crime and once Connolly's pal told him to proceed he knew he and his clients could keep their ill-got profits.

That afternoon Equities International clients bought eleven thousand shares of Resorts International for about twenty-two dollars per share. The next morning thousands more Resorts shares were purchased and not just by Equities International clients. Aiello, for one, bought twenty-five hundred shares in his own account at another securities firm. He also bought five thousand shares in his father's name.

When Aiello called Connolly with orders to buy Resorts stock he was in an excellent position to know Griffin's plans. He was calling from Ernie Barbella's office, which also just happened to be the headquarters of The Griffin Company.

The sign on the door, on the eighteenth floor of the European American Bank Building at 900 Third Avenue, read "Morgan Capital Corporation," a venerable Wall Street name that Barbella had picked up after its former owners shut down in 1983. Behind the sign, in an office ten feet by twenty, Barbella sat at a desk back-to-back with Michael Nigris, his roommate years ago at Baruch College. Barbella and Nigris were partners in Morgan Capital and many other ventures.

Nigris also wore another, much bigger, hat as he worked in this office. He was also president of The Griffin Company, Merv's holding company and the firm that on the following day launched a hostile bid for Resorts.

When the Dow Jones News Service reported Merv Griffin's offer the

116

next day Donald Trump immediately faxed a copy to Nick Ribis, his casino lawyer.

"I looked at it and figured it was a mistake," Ribis said. "The Dow said the offer was thirty-five dollars per share. I figured it was a typo. They meant twenty-five dollars. It had to be a mistake. Donald was offering twenty-two dollars per share so there was no reason anyone would pay thirty-five dollars."

A more jaundiced view came from Richard D. Greenfield of Greenfield & Chimicles, a law firm that has grown rich pursuing shareholder suits against corporate managements. Greenfield said Griffin's offer seemed "more designed to cause mischief and to affect the market in Resorts stock than to legitimately consummate a transaction with the company."

Trump had no interest in Merv's deal. Having paid $135 per share for his Resorts stock, it would be a disaster for him to sell. The market, however, pushed the price of Resorts shares from twenty-two dollars to near the thirty-five dollars Griffin was offering. To some it looked like a chance to recoup from some of the damage Trump had done. Connolly said he quickly got his clients out of their Resorts position and filled in his SEC pal.

Over the following weeks Trump and Griffin fed the glitzmongers with cute one-liners, but no progress was made toward a deal. Griffin made a second offer, doomed from the start. Then the two moguls met at Trump Tower and afterward Griffin's aides designed an offer that showed he had come to appreciate a fundamental requirement of any deal with Trump: Donald's cash machine had to be fed.

This third proposal bought Trump out of his management contract for $63 million cash, sold Trump the unfinished Taj at a fire-sale price of fifty cents on each dollar Resorts had invested in it, and paid Trump back every penny he spent to buy the controlling stock held by the Crosby estate, Crosby family and Jim Crosby's lady friends. The other Resorts stockholders saw their deal sweetened by a buck to thirty-six dollars per share.

The deal depended on saddling Resorts with $325 million of new debt that would be sold by Mike Milken. This new debt would be in the form of mortgages on Resorts casinos in Atlantic City and the Bahamas. Because this debt was secured by mortgages it meant that if the company could not afford to pay all its obligations the mortgages would be paid first, ahead of the $605 million of existing junk debt that, like credit card balances, was secured only by the company's promise to pay.

That summer Griffin flew around the country in his Canadair jet, meeting with the agents from mutual and pension funds who bought Drexel junk. The roadshows came to an abrupt halt in late August 1988.

Griffin and three dozen of his lawyers, accountants and underwriters tasted canapés around the dining table in his suite at the Helmsley Palace Hotel in Manhattan when he saw a man he did not recognize. Ever the affable host he appeared to be on his talk show, Griffin strolled over and put his hand out.

"Who are you with?" he asked.

"I'm with you," replied Ernest G. Barbella.

"I apologize," Griffin said. "There's so many people around now. What do you do?"

As Barbella explained that he was an unpaid consultant helping Nigris, Griffin noticed jaws dropping among those listening in.

Drexel's Laurie Martin spoke to Griffin after the Barbella encounter, accompanied by Tom Gallagher of Gibson Dunn & Crutcher, Griffin's senior lawyer.

"You don't know who Ernest Barbella is?" Martin asked.

"I never heard of him," Griffin replied.

It was an amazing statement, not only because Barbella worked out of The Griffin Company headquarters, but because Barbella had been in on the Resorts takeover from the start. Barbella had helped arrange for the video shown to prospective investors at the roadshows as well as the lighting for that day's roadshow in New York.

Further, Barbella had signed the contract that made Mike Nigris chief executive of The Griffin Company. Nigris had a personal services contract, but in 1986 it was redrawn so that Griffin actually retained a firm controlled by Nigris and Barbella, which in turn supplied Nigris.

Earlier, on July 12, Barbella, Nigris, their friend Martin Kern and their wives flew to the Bahamas, at Griffin's expense, to check out the Resorts casino there. Kern was Griffin's monitor at Resorts, where since May he had worked out of Jim Crosby's old office in the Atlantic City casino. The Bahamas trip came just after Nigris had vacationed in Sicily, a place even Griffin thought odd given the pending casino license application in New Jersey and the Casino Control Commission's sensitivity to Mafia matters. Griffin flew directly from his European vacation to Nassau in his personal jet. Together, Griffin and Nigris went to see Prime Minister Lynden O. Pindling. Griffin and Barbella were at Resorts' Bahamas hotel at the same time, but Griffin said they never met.

Griffin said he was unaware of the back-to-back desk arrangement at The Griffin Company headquarters because he had never been to the headquarters office of his own company. Griffin said he worked by phone, from hotel suites, and that when he was at his Holmby Hills mansion he did business poolside under the Southern California sun.

Alarmed at Griffin's ignorance of Barbella, Drexel hired Kroll Associates, a global detective agency, to investigate. What Drexel managing director Ken Moelis quickly got back was a verbal report not only on Barbella, but on Nigris as well. A second report, prepared later by Terry Lenzner, the former Watergate prosecutor, who runs Investigative Group Inc., was chilling: "Barbella is a member of the Gambino organized crime family, according to one highly placed confidential law enforcement source."

Barbella has flatly denied being a member of the Gambino family. But there is no question he is a stock swindler with a long history of involvement with other convicted white-collar thieves.

Of Nigris, Lenzner wrote:

> According to a highly reliable but unconfirmed source with knowledge and proven credibility, in several instances Nigris has been known by law enforcement to be associated with members of organized crime. Our investigation has focused on a number of close business associates of Nigris who are purported organized crime figures, convicted fraud artists and securities swindlers.

The report then went on for six pages detailing how a variety of stock swindles and some dubious stock deals were all run out of the eighteenth floor of 900 Third Avenue. The report showed that Nigris and Barbella were principals in a variety of companies whose other principals included Kern, Aiello and disbarred lawyer Herbert S. Cannon, a convicted bank and securities swindler. It noted that Barbella had paid an eighty-five-thousand-dollar fine to settle a federal administra-

119

tive complaint against a meat brokerage he owned that allegedly bribed a supermarket executive. Barbella and Nigris had also been principals of Musikahn, a firm that was heavily in debt when it raised $2.3 million through a stock offering in 1984 and then went broke, its pool of cash drained. Barbella later pleaded guilty to fraud charges in the Musikahn swindle; Nigris was never charged.

The report also mentioned National Car Care Inc., a quick oil-change firm that was trying to raise money from investors and was headquartered in the same offices as The Griffin Company. SEC records showed that the firm's chairman was Kern and its attorney was Morris Orens, the lawyer who brought Dale Scutti's Resorts proposition to Ernie Barbella.

With the initial detective report in, Drexel's Moelis called Griffin at his home in California's Carmel Valley. Moelis said he had information so sensitive it should be discussed in person. They haggled about who would fly up or down the California coast. Finally Griffin could not stand the suspense. "Ken, I'm in a sweat. What is it you found?" Griffin pleaded. Moelis gave him a summary, including Drexel's concerns about underwriting the deal.

Griffin and Moelis flew east together to plot strategy with Howard Goldberg, Griffin's Atlantic City casino lawyer. Then they went to Trenton, where in an unusual Sunday meeting at the Division of Gaming Enforcement headquarters they told Director Anthony J. Parrillo and his top aides what they had found. Parrillo would later say the division was already onto the same story but had not completed its investigation when Griffin volunteered his version.

Griffin fired Kern, a former vice president of the A & P supermarket chain whose name had turned up on secretly made FBI tapes of Anthony "Fat Tony" Salerno. Kern was spoken about as the kind of guy in a corporate setting with whom the mob could do business.

Curiously, Griffin did not fire Nigris. He merely suspended Nigris from Resorts matters, while keeping him on as president of The Griffin Company. Griffin's casino lawyer, Howard Goldberg, gave reporters a very polite version of what had happened that made no mention of Barbella, the stock swindles or Lenzner's report that put a supposed mob associate right in The Griffin Company headquarters. Goldberg said only that Nigris and Kern "voluntarily stepped aside. They withdrew their applications because their background investigations might be too time-consuming."

With Nigris out Drexel told Griffin he had to hire a credible casino executive if the $325 million of junk were to be sold. Goldberg introduced Griffin to David Hanlon, the polo-playing manager of Harrah's Marina. Hanlon was known more for traveling and playing than hard work, but the casino he oversaw made phenomenal profits, and while he had a reputation for imperiousness, his reputation for honesty was spotless. Griffin dangled before Hanlon the prospect of a global chain of first-class Merv Resorts, a once-in-a-lifetime opportunity to run a really big show.

Hanlon had his own reasons for wanting a new job, even if leaving meant giving up Holiday stock worth $6 million. When Trump forced Holiday into restructuring Mike Rose arranged for the senior executives to receive 10 percent of Holiday's stock over eight years as an incentive to keep the team there and working hard. But the only executive showered with enough stock and other benefits to make leaving out of the question was Mike Rose. In one of the many accounts from which executives got special payments Rose one year received thirty-four times as much as Hanlon, who ran the property that generated 28 percent of Holiday's profits.

Hanlon wanted big money; Griffin gave it to him. He was to be paid more than $2 million in his first year, nearly five times the $415,900 he collected the year before at Harrah's. And Hanlon also stood to get 5 percent of Resorts stock once Merv took over.

Ten months later, right after Griffin finally fired Nigris, the enforcement division asked Griffin under oath just why he had delayed that action. Griffin said the initial detective reports seemed to be only hearsay.

Deputy Attorney General Mary Jo Flaherty then asked Griffin why his casino license materials included an extensive report from the DeMatteis Organization, a New York firm that Nigris retained to perform what Griffin had told the commission would be massive development in Atlantic City. Griffin said he knew Fred Dematteis was a world-class developer.

121

Then Flaherty asked Griffin if he knew "that Mr. DeMatteis was named in a federal criminal proceeding against the Salerno crime family with the concrete scandal."

"Good lord, no," Griffin replied. "From the tone of today's interview, it sounds like I know of nothing but the Mafia or criminals."

14

The Dancing Duck

The New Jersey Casino Control Commission, still smarting from the Hilton debacle three years earlier, was determined to license Merv Griffin. The commissioners did not want Trump to close the original casino in town and they wanted the Taj finished. They also wanted a new player in town to counter Trump's influence and the risk of what might happen to Atlantic City if Trump ever got into trouble. Griffin, with his Hollywood connections, held out the prospect of restoring to the Boardwalk some of the glamour that left when his buddy Steve Wynn returned to Las Vegas.

Getting Griffin through the licensing process required deft work, though, to make sure no facts came into the public record that would interfere with the commission's desire. And the commission had to act fast because the junk bond market was collapsing and federal prosecutors were moving toward indicting Drexel, which would make it ineligible to sell New Jersey casino securities.

For their part, Howard Goldberg and Tom Gallagher, Griffin's top lawyers, needed to focus attention on Griffin's promises and away from the financial realities of his deal with Donald Trump. They had to come up with a way to make the deal appear financially stable even though the added Drexel debt would push interest costs to $300,000 per day while Resorts cash flow was at best running $192,000 per day. And those were the optimistic numbers before the deal closed.

The Division of Gaming Enforcement's role in expediting commission approval required that it accept claims that Griffin would cover this $108,000-per-day shortfall by cutting costs while bringing more players to his casinos. The enforcement division also had to ignore the fact that the Resorts deal was born of a stock manipulation run right out of The Griffin Company headquarters where Ernie Barbella worked for years. It was not a situation that the prosecutors could dismiss lightly as an aberration. In fact, it bore a striking resemblance to what had happened six years before, the first time Griffin had tried to get into the casino business.

At a January 1982 news conference Griffin had stood beside a detailed architectural model of the proposed Camelot, a one-thousand-room gambling palace with a medieval motif that was to rise next to Harrah's in the marina. A gleaming sword, the proposed casino's symbol, lay across two chairs. "We hope to have a shovel in the ground by next spring," Griffin declared.

A shovel never appeared, but the men who joined Griffin that day did a good job of digging into the $20 million they raised from ten thousand investors, the "little guys" they said they wanted to help own part of a casino.

The Camelot was to be built by American Leisure Corporation. Griffin was a director and an employee with the title of vice president and director of special events. American Leisure's president was Nate Jacobsen, who had been the visionary Jay Sarno's partner in building what, in 1966, was by far the grandest and gaudiest betting parlor in history, Caesars Palace in Las Vegas. Caesars Palace was built with money from Jimmy Hoffa's Teamsters and its silent partners included a dozen mobsters, among them bosses "Fat Tony" Salerno and Sam Giancana. Sometimes Caesars hosted Griffin's TV show, although Griffin said he had never met Jacobsen during those years.

Jacobsen sold Caesars Palace to the Perlman brothers from Florida, Clifford and Stu, who would later be barred from Atlantic City because of organized crime ties. The federal government claimed Jacobsen and other officers skimmed $1.1 million from Caesars, money they denied taking. They did, however, return that sum back to the casino after they had left, ending the inquiry. Federal raids also showed Caesars was used for illegal bookmaking during the Jacobsen days.

After Caesars, Jacobsen moved across the Strip to the Bonanza, where he hired as manager a bright mathematician named Jess Marcum who had once been with the RAND Corporation. The place soon went bust and was later torn down to build Kirk Kerkorian's MGM Grand. Jacobsen moved on to King's Castle, another beneficiary of the Teamsters's pension fund. It also went bust while he was there. King's Castle later became the Hyatt Lake Tahoe.

Jacobsen was arrested in 1971 for kidnapping and extortion. After he was acquitted he freely told the story of how he and a security guard had kidnapped the victim, whom he suspected of cheating the casino out of one hundred fifty thousand dollars in a keno scam.

American Leisure was born out of another firm, one that had been created by one of Jacobsen's buddies, Irwin Lampert, who earned his fifteen minutes of fame by trying to sell the semen of a crossbreed of beef and bison called the beefalo. Jacobsen and Lampert came up with a plan that they said would let the little guy investors share in the lucrative benefits of casino ownership. In December 1979, operating as American Leisure, they offered the public 10 million shares at $2.50 each, saying the $25 million would help finance the Camelot. The company said the Camelot would cost $42 million, a figure that even then was ridiculously low given the initial cost estimates of other casinos.

The SEC alleged in a 1980 lawsuit that American Leisure's securities offering was fraudulent. The sale was underwritten by only one brokerage, Blinder, Robinson & Company, a Denver penny-stock firm that *Forbes* magazine would later refer to as "blind 'em and rob 'em." Blinder, Robinson later went bust and in 1990 its principal, Meyer Blinder, was indicted on racketeering and securities fraud charges in Las Vegas connected with a swindle. A key attraction to "little guys" was a written promise that if the entire $25 million worth was not sold in ninety days American Leisure would give back the money it did raise. The sale fell $5 million short.

The creative men who ran American Leisure devised a solution, though, to avoid returning all that dough. They used some of their investors' money as collateral for a loan so a friend in Florida could buy more stock. When the SEC uncovered this scheme it wanted to force return of the money, but a judge said the company could compensate investors with IOUs or more stock.

Shortly after this Irwin Lampert brought Griffin into American Leisure, giving the company's badly tarnished image a glamorous connection and focusing attention away from its past problems.

Griffin came to his first board meeting accompanied by a young accountant named Michael Nigris. During the meeting Griffin heard that Jacobsen was a kidnapper. Years later Griffin recalled, wrongly, that the matter involved locking up a union official to force negotiations on a contract. Griffin said he dismissed the information as inconsequential. After all, New York mayor Fiorella LaGuardia had done the same thing in the thirties, hadn't he? Griffin said.

Other directors, Griffin recalled years later, leaned across the table and whispered more about Jacobsen.

"You know that he can never be licensed in Atlantic City," one director said.

"What the hell are we all doing here?" Griffin asked.

Griffin later tried to buy the company and take it private. So did others. The Camelot casino was never built, but the little-guy investors lost their money just as surely as they hoped players would.

A thorough inquiry in 1988 into this past attempt at casino ownership, especially given the Nigris-Barbella role in the Resorts deal, could have sunk Griffin's takeover of Resorts. To avoid this disaster Griffin's lawyers and the enforcement division set out on a course that would later become routine. Instead of tying all the relevant facts into one presentation, they agreed to break issues into pieces and then gently float them past the Casino Control Commission, bobbing lightly above the hard truths whose jagged edges lurked just beneath the surface.

The actual terms of the Trump-Griffin deal were largely ignored in favor of obtuse testimony about side issues and inflated claims about cost savings. The dangerous Nigris and American Leisure matters were put off until the following year, when Griffin would have to undergo full personal license hearings. For the deal to close, both sides agreed, all he needed was a temporary license, which could be issued based on an incomplete investigation of Griffin's fitness since it appeared, or at least what was in the public record made it appear, that nothing was amiss.

Griffin's advisors also began a whispering campaign to make him appear to be dumb, a guy who relied on experts for everything and who really did not understand his own deal with Trump. Hanlon's ability and integrity is what should be of greatest concern, the Griffin team said. Griffin contributed to this by claiming ignorance of some parts of the deal and by telling self-deprecating stories, like the one about the Vegas duck.

As Griffin told it, he was doing his talk show from Caesars Palace when he dropped by Circus Circus, the kind of low-rent joint where his viewers were more likely to gamble. There he saw a live duck in a glass case with a sign saying it would dance for a quarter. Merv dropped in his two bits. The machine played "Tea for Two" and the duck danced. Merv stood amazed because ducks can't be trained. Then he dumped in another quarter and another and then another. The duck always danced. Griffin could hardly contain himself. This would be fantastic for his show. People would be fascinated, ask their friends if they had seen the dancing duck on *The Merv Griffin Show*.

Stirred to excitement by the boss, his staff hunted down the duck's owner and arranged an appearance. Just before airtime the duck's owner had a question.

"Do you have an extension cord?" the duck owner asked.

"For what?" Griffin said.

"For the shock plate."

Aghast, Griffin canceled the act and contacted the humane society.

The implicit message was that Griffin could see the potential in the duck act, be taken in by the illusion, without recognizing the reality just beneath the surface, just as he could be taken in by people like Nigris and Jacobsen.

This supposed lack of perception contradicted the image Griffin had sought to project in the past, that of an astute businessman with such canny insights that his career had grown from singing a novelty tune about "A Lovely Bunch of Coconuts" after World War II to a place on the Forbes 400, the richest entertainer in the history of the world. How could a man who grasped early on that it was owning television shows, not just performing in them, that made for real wealth, and who devised game shows so lucrative he sold them to Coca-Cola for a quarter billion dollars plus eight-figure annual fees for the rest of his life, fail to notice what the people around him were up to? The New Jersey casino regulators avoided this issue simply by not asking questions that might produce answers they did not want to hear.

These items from the past and present were not the only matters that could sink the takeover. There was also the nasty little problem of the future financial stability of Resorts once Griffin weighted it down with more debt. The problem was not just the debt, it was that the solution Griffin's lawyers and Drexel were advancing had been publicly repudiated one June day in 1988 by Merv Griffin himself.

Although the deal was far from done, Griffin flew to Atlantic City. The afternoon began with a clever remark by Griffin, a preemptive strike against Trump, whose style was to finish a deal and then denounce whoever sat on the other side of the table as a chump. Griffin, followed by his official companion, Eva Gabor, and by Brent Plott, who would later sue him for palimony, stood before a battery of television cameras in a Resorts ballroom that had been freshly painted and carpeted, unlike much of the rest of the deteriorating old hotel.

Asked if he intended to put his name on Resorts hotels in Atlantic City and the Bahamas and on his recently acquired Beverly Hilton in California, Griffin replied with a reference to the huge red letters on another Boardwalk casino: "No, not unless I can get Merv to be as big as Trump—or get the T off Trump." Griffin's clever way of calling Trump an ass revealed the emnity between the two moguls that again and again threatened to blow up their deal over the following four months, a prospect the casino commissioners wanted to avoid.

It was Griffin's other remarks that day that should have alarmed the casino regulators and those who financed the deal, for if Griffin meant what he said, then Resorts was guaranteed to end up in bankruptcy soon.

Griffin planned to put up $100 million cash, while Mike Milken's Drexel would peddle $325 million of junk. On the surface it seemed like a good deal. A family buying a house, for example, usually can borrow four dollars for each dollar they put down, though buyers with strong credit histories can sometimes borrow as much as nineteen dollars for each dollar they put down. Griffin's deal appeared to involve borrowing $3.25 for each dollar he put up. Add in the existing credit card–style junk debt that the company was already carrying, however, and Griffin's Resorts would be borrowing more than nine dollars for each dollar he put up. Still, that was a reasonable ratio in the eighties junk bond takeover era.

But half of Griffin's money would be in Resorts for just one day. Six weeks later Griffin planned to withdraw another $25 million, and he planned to continue withdrawing money until he had less than $8 million tied up in Resorts, giving him $121 of borrowed money for each dollar of his own.

Even Milken's most addicted junk buyers were savvy enough to realize this was bad stuff, so bad that before the deal closed they demanded that Griffin leave $50 million in Resorts and put up an extra $10 million in the form of a letter of credit that they could call on if Resorts failed to make an interest payment on the Drexel debt. The existing junk bond owners got no such deal.

To make the interest payments on all $930 million of debt just through 1990, Resorts had to sell enough assets within two years to raise $85 million. After that, according to financial projections that the Casino Control Commission accepted, Resorts would be winning so much money from players that it could easily meet its interest obligations. The projections of huge growth disregarded evidence that the casino market in Atlantic City had stopped growing after a decade, ignored the potential impact of Trump's plans to open the Taj next door to Resorts, and failed to consider the run-down condition of Resorts.

To raise the $85 million Resorts would have to sell land. Resorts was the largest private landowner in Atlantic City, controlling one third of the developable acreage. Griffin and his publicity machine set to work in June to create the impression that this could be done with ease. The *Los Angeles Times Magazine* even swooned about how in teaching Trump some new deal artistry, homeboy Griffin had won "150 acres of prime real estate in the heart of Atlantic City."

But Griffin had no intention of selling the real estate needed to make the Resorts deal work, even if buyers existed. He said so himself that warm June afternoon in Atlantic City. Griffin claimed that proposals had already started coming in from developers who wanted to buy or develop Resorts land in Atlantic City, land that was mostly surrounded by the bleak signs of decay, weed-filled lots in a ghetto. These purported proposals, Griffin said, were "too premature. An awful lot of people are asking, 'Will you sell out?' I won't sell anything until looking at it and

129

seeing where it's going. I want to exercise some control over the sales. I don't want to come in and make a lot of extravagant promises to Atlantic City until I determine a little bit about the local feelings here." Griffin added a most significant comment. He said he wanted "a couple of years to learn about the community" before selling or developing any land.

Although the securities laws require disclosing all salient negative information to investors, Griffin's comments went unmentioned by Drexel in its prospectus for the $325 million of Resorts mortgage bonds. Since the second, third and fourth interest payments to bondholders were contingent on speedy asset sales, it was a highly significant omission. The Casino Control commissioners, who knew Atlantic City well and knew there was no clamor to buy Resorts land, never questioned Griffin or Drexel about this omission.

What Griffin said that day, though, proved to be true. By early 1992, Griffin had unloaded only one parcel of Atlantic City land, for $4 million.

There was yet another hard truth that no one dared ask about and it concerned why Griffin was buying Resorts International with all its liabilities—raw ghetto land, existing junk bonds, a fading Bahamas casino —instead of just acquiring the Resorts International Casino Hotel on the Boardwalk.

Just buying the asset seemed a smarter way to go, at least to Steve Norton, who had been a Resorts executive for years and who had a habit of speaking plainly, a quality not much revered in casino circles. Why pay a 63 percent premium over the twenty-two-dollar price that had already been established as fair? Norton also wondered, being unaware of the goings on at 900 Third Avenue.

Norton, a father of eight with a nervous twitch and eyes sunk deep in skin furrowed by years of worry, figured that buying just the Atlantic City casino would cost $200 million or so. Knowing the commission wanted to keep Resorts open, Norton figured the regulators would force Trump to accept such a proposal.

One day Norton started to tell Griffin the background of his thoughts, going along smoothly until he said, "There's a better way—"

"No there isn't," Griffin said, cutting him off and changing the subject.

130

Griffin's handlers also turned away questions about why Griffin wanted the whole company and not just the Boardwalk casino. Their strategy was to focus attention away from such trifling matters as having enough money to pay bills when they came due and to emphasize what casino lawyer Howard Goldberg called "the Merv factor." Goldberg played up how Griffin would bring glamour and big names to Resorts, promising innovative stage entertainment featuring television stars.

Griffin suggested, but did not quite say flat out, that his hit game shows *Jeopardy!* and *Wheel of Fortune* would air from Resorts. Why, NBC's *Today* would be broadcasting there for a whole week. And Griffin suggested that the American Broadcasting Companies would be producing shows at his hotel, noting that ABC chairman Thomas Murphy was married to the late Jim Crosby's sister, Elaine.

The idea that stars who supposedly were indebted to Merv for their big break would appear at Resorts, drawing players to the tables, was promoted as the most significant aspect of the deal, one that Griffin company president Michael Nigris emphasized in a letter to the casino commission.

But the talk of big-name stars and television shows was fantasy. ABC said it knew nothing of any production plans in Atlantic City. NBC's *Today* never came. Instead of the promised repayment of gratitude to Merv by big-name stars, when he got control of Resorts its showroom featured the crude humor of Rip Taylor, hardly a superstar. Merv even took to singing in his own showroom, which both saved cash and fed Griffin's need to be on stage.

At the beginning of the commission's hearings on the takeover Griffin said that he had been shown probably thirty financial projections for Resorts. In line with the "Merv factor" strategy, which included making sure only softball questions were lobbed at Griffin, he never claimed to have studied them. Besides, he said, spreadsheets paled next to his instincts that he could reverse the firm's rapidly declining fortunes. "Television is in the business to please the audience," Griffin testified. "A hotel, a casino, is the same thing. It's the people business. It's how to get them across your threshold and how to hold them there."

Goldberg crafted his presentation around such matters as how $10 million could be saved through efficiently assigning only the right number of chambermaids to clean rooms. He acknowledged that this saving was critical if Resorts was to be financially viable under Griffin.

At one point the commission went through a detailed discussion of just how the deal would work, including a host of money maneuvers designed mostly to preserve tax breaks.

Trump maintained that he could not understand why Griffin would do this deal. "Merv's the only guy I've ever done a deal with where I could not figure out why he would do it," he said. On the day the deal and the flow of money was laid out before the commission, Trump fretted. Leaving the hearing room he turned to an aide, Harvey Freeman, and said, "Now that they've explained it to him, he'll pull out."

Griffin did flinch. The bonds that Drexel's Dan Lee had proclaimed would easily sell at 12 percent found no buyers until the interest rate was hiked to nearly 14 percent. The higher rate would increase the annual interest burden by about half of the $10 million that purportedly was to be saved from efficient assignment of chambermaids, but the hearings were not reopened to examine this problem.

On November 16, eight months after Peter Aiello called from "Ernie's," the deal closed. Griffin owned Resorts and, for a day, the Taj, which then went to Trump for half what Crosby had squandered on it.

Griffin helicoptered to the Steeplechase Pier across from Resorts and rode a gray limousine the one hundred feet to Resorts' door, standing up through the sunroof opening with Eva and throwing kisses to his admirers, who crowded onto the Boardwalk.

Inside Resorts Griffin pushed his way past more adoring fans on his way to the same ballroom where he had spoken last June. He noted that he had once sung for his supper on a nearby amusement pier long since closed and ravaged by the elements. "It's been thirty-nine years getting to this hotel from the Steel Pier. This is a dream come true. I'm going to bring back this grand dame of Atlantic City and here's to all of you who are going to help me do it," he said, hoisting a fluted champagne glass filled with Mumm's to salute his employees.

Then Griffin took another dig at Trump when he was asked how it felt to owe nearly a billion dollars.

"Oh, I love debt," Griffin replied in his wide-eyed, childish way. "Somebody pointed out that I owe more debt than a lot of Third World nations. But next door at the Taj they owe eight hundred million dollars —and they have no-o-o cash flow."

Griffin was right. But before the Taj would open, seventeen months later, Griffin's Resorts would announce it could not make its interest payments and would seek refuge from its creditors.

Meanwhile, Trump was sailing toward his first date in Bankruptcy Court.

15

Taken for a Ride

A steady summer rain fell on the New Jersey shore, but still the patient crowd grew by the minute. Some brought umbrellas, while those who had tented newspapers had discarded the soggy pulp on the newly laid deck of the Frank S. Farley Marina, named for the late Republican political boss who ran Atlantic City and County in the two decades following World War II. Drenched or dry, they waited without a murmur for a chance to see a luxurious ship come in bearing its new owner.

Many had seen her as the *Flying Saucer* in *Never Say Never Again*, a 1983 James Bond film. She served as the floating headquarters of supervillain Maximilian Largo, an egomaniac of such burgeoning wealth that as Agent 007 watched a computer screen listing Largo's net worth at $4 billion, a correction flashed: $4.2 billion. Largo also owned a casino, where he challenged Bond at a game he had invented called World Domination.

Now the ship belonged to Donald Trump, another casino owner with an immense ego who had invented a game, this one named for himself, and who seemed to be on his way to dominating everything in Atlantic City and perhaps Manhattan as well, with all the daring buildings bearing his name and promises of many more to come.

This was the new owner's maiden voyage on the 282-foot craft, the world's sixth largest private yacht. The journey from New York began with a scare for Trump, who feared they were sinking until someone explained that it was just the anchor being drawn into his ship. Trump was not a sailor and admitted that waves made his stomach queasy.

When the waters calmed, the great white ship headed for the Atlantic City Inlet, cutting through a channel that separated two worlds, a channel dredged deeper just days before to accommodate her. Off starboard lay a clean white beach where waterfront land sold for ten thousand dollars per foot and perfectly sturdy little homes were routinely razed so opulent ones could be erected. Off port, though, the shore was blackened by the stinking muck that crews dredging the channel for Trump had dumped there illegally. Behind this fetid mess stood dilapidated houses that some occupants had acquired for as little as seven hundred dollars in the dark days before the casinos came to Atlantic City.

The boat arrived hung with a huge green banner heralding its new name, *Trump Princess*, in gold letters, the words separated by a crown. Its sleek side opened, revealing a gold-and-green velvet throne bearing Donald Trump, wearing his usual dark suit and sheepishly holding an umbrella, and the elegantly dressed Ivana, a maid holding her parasol. As an elevator lowered the throne to the dock, crewmen rolled out a red carpet and pointed the couple to a waiting electric cart. Trump waved the cart off and the couple marched triumphantly several hundred feet on the squishy carpet, past the yachts of the merely rich, toward the patient throng, which surged toward them.

Just as the inlet waters separated the wealth of Brigantine from the poverty of Atlantic City, a row of potted ficus separated the crowd. On the side where the Trumps would pass stood politicians and a few high rollers in finery that cost more than some of the dreary houses visible across the harbor. On the other side were the masses in their shorts, polyester shirts and rubber thongs. Suddenly a phalanx of teenage girls rushed up and pulled the leaves back, squealing with delight and jumping up and down as if The Boss, or had they been their mothers, The King, had graced them with his passing.

A half dozen bodyguards, some of them off-duty Atlantic City police whose weapons bulged under their raincoats, surrounded the Trumps, maintaining an opening that moved like the eye of a storm through the swirling fans. The adored couple pressed on toward the building across the street, Trump waving, his wife smiling. As they rode the escalator up into Trump Castle Hotel & Casino a new crowd appeared and others flowed out of the gambling hall to join in the endless applause. "Be our next president, Donald," one man shouted before Trump and his entourage slipped into a ballroom, where two lines of women in scanty sailor suits greeted them.

Inside Trump held a news conference during which he was asked three questions about the filth polluting the beach. The answers were classic Trump. He answered the first by denying any knowledge of dredge spoils dumped on the beach. He answered the second by saying that he had agreed to pay a fine. He answered the third by declaring the matter a nonstory.

Then he stepped off the dais to shake hands. Before reaching Trump, though, the local officials and their spouses had to pass the muster of a stout man in a pink silk blazer. One or two at a time they approached Paddy McGahn and, after paying homage for having been invited, waited for him to decide when their turn would come to have their hand shaken and their picture taken with The Donald and his missus.

The arrival of the ship and its owner in the tattered resort showed Donald Trump perfecting the art of being idolized. The crowds loved him for personifying the American Dream of success and the government officials basked in his glow. Trump's claim that the ship was his "personal yacht," suggesting it was an incredibly costly toy financed from his bottomless pockets, was uncritically repeated in print and television stories across the nation, adding to the Trump legend of unlimited wealth flowing from his deal-making artistry. For the rich kid from Queens who had taken Manhattan by audacious architecture, July 9, 1988, was a public relations triumph.

Trump's arrival and how it was treated in the news media illustrated a profound change in American values. Just a dozen years earlier, any man whose riches flowed from casinos would have been reviled as a vice lord, denounced from pulpits and editorial pages just about everywhere outside Nevada. But casino gambling had been decriminalized in Atlantic City and the major corporations—Holiday, Ramada and Hilton —that had come to dominate the business there and in Nevada had so thoroughly recast the public image of gambling, had so thoroughly glossed over its realities, that Trump was being treated as royalty, even urged to lead the world's oldest democracy, a suggestion he encouraged at every opportunity.

To the discerning eye, though, much more went on that day behind the glitzy image the Trumps projected, for these same events also demonstrated how much Trump had come to believe his own myth of being a modern Midas, able to turn dross into gold merely by affixing his name to a casino, an airline or even bare ground. In less than a year his spendthrift ways and foolhardy management would tarnish the carefully polished Trump image and press him to the brink of uncontrolled bankruptcy, a horror he escaped only because of the extraordinary leniency of government, a bailout from six dozen banks and the hundreds of millions of dollars lost by hardworking people whose pension money was invested in the Trump name.

Much of Trump's apparent wealth was illusory, the result of complex financial engineering that had come to resemble not the smooth-running money machine Trump endlessly hyped, but a Rube Goldberg contraption constantly in need of more cash to avoid collapse. It had been true almost from the start of his career. Now nothing showed this better than the *Trump Princess*, which added millions of dollars per year to the drain on his cash flow, plus $29 million in new debt since, as usual, he put no money down. He assumed these new obligations shortly before he was due to fulfill promises to pay down the balances on bank loans and on casino mortgage bonds—money he did not have.

The ship itself was a study in excess, from the foyer paneled with bird's-eye maple polished to a maize-colored sheen to the master stateroom shower, supposedly carved from a single block of onyx, with its twelve nozzles. Thick suede padding covered the hallway walls to dampen the rumble of the twin sixteen-cylinder, three-thousand-horsepower, turbocharged diesel engines, which gulped twenty-five tons of fuel daily and which, at best, could push the Italian-designed steel hull at a modest 17.5 knots per hour.

Ivana imposed odd restrictions that hampered its use as a device to draw high rollers. She wanted only white wine and champagne served on board in case anyone dropped their glass, which angered a few red wine drinkers among the gamblers given a ride, Trump Castle executive Christian Mari said. Ultimately that rule was rescinded. Mari and others also complained that it was difficult to get players on board. Ivana required that some guests remove their shoes and walk in stocking feet, though Casino Control commissioners and most gamblers were exempted from this rule. "Mrs. Trump does not want the carpets ruined," Captain Richard Cuckson explained, coughing lightly into his fist, as he stood beside two of the many maids who endlessly polished and cleaned every visible surface.

Minutes later Cuckson was interrupted in the salon by a call on one of the ship's 150 telephones. "Yes, madame," the British captain told Ivana, listening intently and giving polite assurances that all was well in hand. Cuckson explained that he was not exactly alone, mentioning that a writer was standing next to him taking notes, but the mostly one-sided conversation continued, Cuckson smiling ever so thinly.

"Yes, madame. . . . We have a high-roller party coming at two. I have the fashion models here now. . . . Yes . . . certainly, madame. . . . I appreciate that. We have eight people sleeping on board and thirty-one people aboard ship," he said, adding that "someone named Pauline" from Trump's Castle whose job was dealing with high rollers was to come over soon. "Thank you, madame. Most certainly," Cuckson said, waiting a moment to make sure Ivana had clicked off before gently putting down his handset.

The ship had been built in 1980 for arms merchant Adnan Khashoggi, a world-class gambler who had a habit of not paying his bills, as Steve Hyde had painfully learned at the Las Vegas Sands. Khashoggi claimed that the ship, which he named after his daughter Nabila, cost $90 million. Although Trump claimed to have spent $8 million refurbishing it, half of it on the interior, the fabrics and furniture were unchanged. Nor did Trump spend any money to remove the original logo, a black onyx triangle on a white background into which black stones are set in a design that looks like a wave and a whale, a play on the Arabic symbols for the name Nabila. While Nabila's name was a permanent fixture, Trump's presence was not. His name was visible mostly in the neat arrays of magazines on tables in every room, magazines that featured his smiling face and that inside treated whatever he said as gospel.

For fun the ship has its own disco with laser lights and a ten-foot marble circle for dancing, plus a movie theater with sofa seating for twenty that rivals that of any Hollywood mogul for luxury. Most of the eight double suites for guests feature color television sets that, at the push of a button, rise up from tables and can be tilted for viewing from the bed or the seating area. The ship can receive cable-TV signals from satellites and run two movies on its closed-circuit on-board network. Other buttons can dim lights or summon stewards for a glass of champagne. "This ship is a push-button dream," the captain said.

The spacious owner's suite included a long and narrow dressing room, made to look expansive by mirrored doors, behind which were enough closets to outfit a dress store. Above, on the highest deck and thus safe from prying eyes, was a sun deck with two chaise longues and a hot tub, a spot favored by Trump's mistress, Marla Maples, who frequently padded about the ship in string bikinis and bare feet.

Trump had bought the ship from its second owner, the Sultan of Brunei, who had foreclosed on Khashoggi when he failed to repay a loan. The Sultan was by far the richest person in the world, a man who owned his own country and who each year made far more money than even Trump claimed his empire was worth. Trump bought the ship the way the impulsive and profligate buy cars beyond their means: no money down and years of payments. Trump had two advantages, though, not available to most buyers.

One was his influence in Trenton, where New Jersey tax officials decided that Trump did not have to pay the 6 percent sales tax of $1.74 million on the $29 million purchase price. Instead, Trump only had to pay 6 percent of the monthly lease payment of about $400,000. The state's reasoning ignored the fact that Trump owned the company that leased him the ship.

Second, while the 1986 overhaul of the federal tax laws had taken away most deductions for boats, Trump did not pay for his "personal yacht" with his personal funds. While Trump bought the ship simply because he wanted it as a symbol of wealth, it was in fact a marketing tool for Trump Castle. Lose enough money and Trump would take you for a ride.

The Crystal Tower, the $110 million suite expansion that was intended to draw high rollers to the Castle, was still under construction. Trump needed a draw for high rollers and a luxury ship seemed like an interim solution.

The lease payments and all operating costs were charged to the Castle, which Trump owned in its entirety and which could deduct these costs on its tax return. The Castle would have turned a small profit in 1989 but for these costs. Instead, the Castle lost $6.7 million.

The *Princess* was not the only drag on profits. The Castle's Monte Carlo high-roller slots area opened just before the 1989 gambling season began. Separated from the hoi polloi by low marble walls, brass railings and etched glass, the Monte Carlo denoted an area for favored players, the kind willing to pay one hundred dollars per pull at their choice of three machines. Dozens of other slots priced at $25, $5 and just a buck stood arrayed before plush seats. The hosts, called Monte Carlo ambassadors, wore tuxedos. So did the ever-present cleaning man, who swept cigarette butts into what Trump said was a gold dustpan. The casino even provided phone jacks for those who wanted to play and work at the same time. And when the slot tokens turned hands black from heavy play, the ambassadors provided moist, hot towels.

It was the kind of service that appealed to players like friendly, dapper George Snyder III, who had been elected tax collector in the affluent Philadelphia suburb of Abington on a reform ticket the same year the Castle opened. Snyder liked the Castle slots so much that he and his pals, including the Abington police chief, were treated to suites and parties.

Snyder was a certified high roller. He lost eight hundred thousand dollars at Trump Castle, according to the Division of Gaming Enforcement. To lose that much a player typically would have to pump about $13 million into the one-armed bandits, including recycled winnings.

An indictment charged that the money Snyder lost, at least some of it, came from the taxes this reformer was collecting and then diverting to his own pocket. Five days *after* Snyder's alleged embezzling and gambling were exposed on the front page of the *Philadelphia Inquirer,* he was in the Monte Carlo slots arena gambling. He kept on gambling for months, until his indictment. Snyder, who pleaded innocent, as of this writing had yet to go to trial. The Castle never stopped him, or even asked if he was gambling with stolen public funds. It had no obligation to do so, noted Al Luciani, a veteran casino executive who helped draft the Casino Control Act. "A story in the newspaper that some guy is embezzling public money isn't any kind of notice at all," Luciani said.

"The casinos aren't required to pay any attention to that unless, perhaps —and this is only a perhaps—the guy is playing on credit. Then there might be an issue."

Snyder always brought cash when he played in the "highly regulated" casinos so there was never any question about the integrity of encouraging his play with lavish comps.

But the Monte Carlo arena, like the *Trump Princess*, failed to attract enough high rollers to pay for itself. In time, abandoning the Hilton marketing plan to chase high rollers proved disastrous.

Trump Castle barely turned a profit in 1987 and lost $3.1 million in 1988, but its cash flow created a mighty river of greenbacks. This is because net profits take into account deductions that appear on tax returns but that involve no cash outlay, notably depreciation on the hotel and its equipment.

In 1987, the Castle's cash flow was $23.4 million, rising to $33.7 million in 1988. Trump tapped this flow of cash during the Castle's first four years to withdraw $38.5 million of capital, a neat maneuver, since he had borrowed his capital contribution from a bank.

But in 1989 the failed high-roller strategy nearly dried up the flow of cash. The *Princess*, lavish comps for high rollers like Snyder, and the Crystal Tower overruns drained off so much money that cash flow slowed to a trickle—just $183,000 in 1989, which was less cash than flowed into the Castle every two days in 1988. Trump Castle was drifting toward Bankruptcy Court.

Before it got there, in 1992, there would be a few stops along the way where laws would be deliberately broken and the promise that casinos would be "highly regulated" would be treated like the polluted spoils dumped on the beach. And Trump would flout more rules. He would even be accused of cheating Castle players—with the sanction of casino regulators.

16

Other People's Money

The car creaking across the hot asphalt looked old before its time, its paint robbed of luster by the relentless Miami sun, its smooth metal skin wrinkled prematurely, the dings and dents a history of its driver's miscalculations. Because the owner couldn't afford the upkeep anymore, the once silent and powerful motor rumbled, devouring high-octane fuel while barely getting up enough energy to keep the hulk moving. The driver was about to have a chance encounter of the parking lot kind.

He tried to avoid those who knew his past: the kidnappers with long-barreled *pistolas,* the pals whose gambling debts he could no longer cover, the associate who had sued him to recover a million bucks, and the casino executives who, once upon a time, had encouraged his belief that he was invincible at the gaming tables.

At this very moment, stepping from another car outside the convenience store, the paper-thin soles of his Bally loafers dipping into a sticky residue of spilled Coke, was one of those executives who had encouraged the gambler to believe in his own myth. The casino executive, looking at the prematurely old man hauling himself out of the heap, checked his memory for a moment to make sure he was right. Then he felt surprise that Farayala Janna was alive.

Janna stood five feet nine, his short springy hair still jet black, though the muscled body looked puffy now, his swagger reduced to plodding, his lively grin worn flat. He was barely into his forties, when life should be grand for a man who was doing so well in his thirties that he took friends for a spin over the Netherlands Antilles in his new jet. But Janna's smile had lost its glow. He looked tired and beaten, old before his time. Janna seldom looked you in the eye, that being the custom among many Arabs, even those whose parents had left the troubled Middle East to find prosperity in Colombia after World War II, before it became troubled by cocaine. But now Janna's eyes seemed furtive as well.

When they came face-to-face, the casino executive and the man who had once been one of the five biggest gamblers in all Latin America, the executive knew he did not need to say a word about the unpaid marker. In Janna's line of work failure to pay debts was often treated as a capital offense. If Janna had any money the debt would have been paid long ago, the executive figured.

Once they exchanged surprise at their greeting, Janna looked down and then away, volunteering that he wished he could pay what he owed.

The casino executive knew the Lear jet was gone, that one of Janna's four children was deathly ill, that his Doris had left him. He was also sure that the Swiss bank accounts were empty.

Where had all that money gone? the casino executive wondered to himself. An even better question, the one he did not think about because in his line of work it is better not to officially know such things, was: Where had the money come from?

The answers to those questions would illustrate, better than any other story, that the promise that casinos would be "highly regulated" and insulated from the forces of evil was false. For Farayala Janna's riches to rags story showed that even the casino companies operating in supposedly squeaky clean New Jersey so lust for money that they will help the world's biggest drug dealers evade the law. Yet when the evidence was placed right under the Division of Gaming Enforcement's nose it never got a whiff of what was going on. Worse, the casino company's defense to civil accusations of wrongdoing was that the enforcement division had looked at its operations and had praised them for their integrity.

The story begins in Colombia, where Farayala Janna was born on the next to last day of July in 1950, the oldest son of Abraham Janna, who had emigrated from Palestine. Farayala grew up as handsome as an Arab prince. His face, clear-skinned and symmetrical, was dominated by frameless glasses with oversize lenses whose thinness revealed that his vision was only slightly flawed.

Janna lived in the Colombian industrial and port city of Barranquilla, where the coffee, cotton and oil that came down the Río Magdalena were loaded onto ships that sailed fifteen miles north to the eastern Caribbean and the world beyond. As the city grew to nearly a million souls, busy making concrete and textiles and developing their airport as a gateway for affluent South America to the Caribbean island resorts, Janna prospered. He told everyone he owed his good fortune to incredibly sweet deals with the Colombian government to construct housing and public buildings.

In the fall of 1979, Janna took a short flight to the desert isle of Aruba, just fifteen miles off the coast of Venezuela, near its border with Colombia. There he stayed at the Aruba Concorde, one of the many temples of chance opening around the world to cater to people like himself, people with an abundance of money. This newest, finest resort hotel in the Netherlands Antilles stood fourteen stories tall, its name suggesting both harmony and the elegance of supersonic travel.

Janna was not yet thirty, but he was already so rich that the casino manager, a tall, dark-haired man with a distinctive Germanic accent named Leon Samburg, gave him a fifty-thousand-dollar credit line. Janna played and paid. Soon Samburg gave him more credit on each trip, as much as $251,000, because Janna promptly honored his markers.

Janna, who often came with Doris and their four children, usually was assigned his favorite suite, formed by joining rooms 600, 601 and 602 to create two bedrooms and a living room with its own bar and a balcony view of the sun worshipers lazing around the Olympic-size pool below and on the sugar white beach a few steps beyond.

By June of 1985 Janna had come to the attention of the Colombian police. He was listed in their files as a suspected cocaine and marijuana smuggler whose base of operations was the Aruba Concorde Hotel. Janna often traveled to Aruba with an entourage and the Colombian police files listed some of them as suspected international drug dealers. A few months later Janna had prospered so much that he wanted to move into a more exclusive realm of world-class high rollers. Farayala Janna wanted to play with the whales.

Neil Smyth, the Caesars Palace executive in charge of Latin American marketing, listened carefully as the stranger in Florida introduced himself over the phone. Janna said he was the Colombian government's biggest contractor, a man of means who was staying just then at his second home in Miami Beach, but who wanted to spend the holidays in the Nevada desert, provided Caesars would extend him a quarter million dollars of chips on credit and give suites to his family and friends. It was the kind of lucky call that Smyth, who had once been Caesars' chief financial officer, got only every couple of years. Janna's proposal also entailed some risk, not to the future of Caesars World Inc., which won more than $2 million a day from its players in Nevada and New Jersey, but that this unknown player might lack the resources to pay back a quarter million dollars if he lost. Smyth had to worry, too, that the stranger might be trying to scam the casino.

Janna's choice of Caesars Palace was significant because Nevada casinos grant credit with few restrictions, unlike New Jersey casinos, which must prove a patron creditworthy through credit checks and analysis of credit applications. Janna simply referred Smyth to his banker at Southeast Bank in Miami. The banker reported that he held Janna in the highest regard and that his average checking account balance could cover the credit line with ease. On the basis of the banker's praise Caesars decided to take the risk. Smyth was unaware that the banker sometimes traveled with Janna on gambling sprees and that once the Aruba Concorde casino had paid the banker's $720 airfare to the Dutch isle. When Janna showed up on the Strip, in fact, the banker was among those who checked into Caesars Palace.

Janna and his entourage headed straight for the baccarat tables. Caesars has two baccarat areas. One is behind a low black marble wall right next to Nero's Nook, the bar famed for its classy working girls. The other, where Janna played, is up a free-standing staircase that swirls from the glassed entryway to the swimming pool to a room known as the Palace Court Casino.

In this private setting Janna promptly beat Caesars Palace for three hundred thousand dollars. Despite this win, Smyth believed, and the casino staff agreed, that Janna should be invited back because, while he fashioned himself invincible, he was a weak player.

"By that I mean he didn't always know what he was doing," Smyth recalled. "He was a man that imbibed quite a bit at the table so I felt that he could be a very desirable customer."

Anxious to see just how good a customer Janna might be, Smyth flew to Barranquilla and visited Janna's home. Smyth expected a grand hacienda with a high wall around it, a central courtyard and, given the political violence and kidnappings in Latin America, armed guards. Instead he was invited into a neat but plain home, not unlike the bland houses that fill the prosperous suburbs of American cities. Janna introduced Smyth around, displaying a personal intimacy with senior Colombian officials, and threw a little party to honor his American guest. Smyth then put on a party for Janna. Before leaving Smyth told Janna that Caesars would be delighted to extend him more credit.

Janna sought credit throughout the casino world, including Cable Beach and Resorts in the Bahamas, the El San Juan in Puerto Rico, the Desert Inn on the Strip and the Las Vegas Hilton.

Casino executives lucky enough to draw Janna to their tables greeted him warmly and treated him like a king because they regarded him, in the words of Rob Goldstein, as a born loser. Goldstein called him a "soft player," an industry term seldom heard by customers. It refers to gamblers who play until their money runs out. All it takes to beat a soft player is flattery, alcohol and enough hours at the tables for the house advantage to consume the player's bankroll.

"He was noted to be an extremely good customer since his gambling habits were such that he rarely won," observed Goldstein. "He is the kind of customer you want on a long-term basis, who has little or no chance to win because he was a poor player, poor money manager. His gamesmanship was poor. Long-term, the man was going to lose. We would like to have more of his business."

Goldstein got to know Janna because in 1986 the Pratt Hotel Corporation, the Dallas firm which owned the Sands in Atlantic City, won a contract to manage the Aruba Concorde after years of pursuing its owner, a billionaire Venezuelan banker named José Joaquín Gonzáles Gorondona, Jr., whom everyone called JJ.

The Aruba Concorde had been a cash till for JJ, but after seven years it needed a costly facelift and many more Caribbean casinos had joined the competition for gamblers. In summer 1985, the slowest season, four hundred of its five hundred rooms slumbered empty each night. The casino borrowed $5 million from Aruba Bank to get through the fall of 1985, but because JJ kept taking out cash it soon had a pile of overdrawn checks. That December the bank threatened to call the loan.

Chairman Jack Pratt touted his Sands staff as the best team to manage JJ's entire chain of Concorde hotels, boasting that "prudent casino credit decisions" resulted in markers so good that better than ninety-eight cents of each dollar was collected at the Atlantic City Sands. Pratt promised modern management, efficient cost controls and a marketing system that would bring in more profitable players. Much as Pratt wanted the business, when JJ showed him a budget that projected a $15 million net profit for 1986, Pratt told him: "If you can do that well, you don't need me."

A month later, with the casino in desperate straits, JJ awarded Pratt the contract. Soon Aruba had the Sands computer software, which could track its "premium player portfolio" of approximately 35,000 persons by the brand of Scotch each favored while also assigning just the necessary number of chambermaids to keep labor costs to a minimum.

Samburg was sacked without getting the $360,000 still due on his contract. The Pratt people said he had been imprudent in extending credit and was even worse at keeping track of markers, nearly $2 million of which could not be found. Jack Pratt's top aide, Bill Weidner, called Samburg a "managerial dinosaur." Samburg sued to get his job back or at least the money due on his contract.

The management contract gave the Sands team sole authority to decide who would get credit, even though it was JJ's money at risk.

The sharply tailored, perfectly manicured Goldstein was installed as the senior Sands staff member even though he stayed in Atlantic City.

He had started out helping his bookmaker father run junkets, like the one that brought him to dinner with Mitzi Briggs where, as the new owner of the Las Vegas Tropicana, she had denounced gambling as evil.

Goldstein said the Sands found a mess in Aruba, with $15 million in uncollectable markers, unpaid bills of $6 million and the electric company threatening to pull the plug. Gambling records were sometimes stuffed in shoe boxes and dealers cheated the house by helping players win, he said. Money was kept in a flimsy casino cage left open to wandering employees. The internal cash controls were so lacking that Goldstein concluded that the place was "waiting to be robbed."

The New Jersey Casino Control Commission had to approve the Sands operation in Aruba and enforcement division agents were sent down to check the place. They wrote a glowing report on the Sands' improving operations.

While the Sands management promised to clean up the operation and run it close to New Jersey standards, curious things began happening. The Sands managers stopped daily checking of the Aruba Concorde's slot-machine meters, which provide a way to monitor the amount of money taken from them, reducing the risk of skimming. Even more curious was the way credit was handled for Janna and his friends, like the four hundred thousand dollar marker that was prepared on May 1, 1986, at 8:11 A.M. for Gustavo Certain, a member of Janna's entourage and Barranquilla's mayor. (The term "marker" dates to the fifteenth century, when it was used to refer to one who kept score at a game. In time, it also came to mean the IOUs that marked how much a gambler was indebted for losing bets.) The chips were issued but the marker was unsigned and, therefore, worthless. A second four hundred thousand dollar marker was signed, but it had no bank name or checking account number. Worse, the signature was not even similar to the one on Certain's incomplete credit application, making that marker worthless in the opinion of an Arthur Young auditor who later examined it. This was not even close to the Sands operation in Atlantic City, where the regulations required complete and properly prepared markers.

Under Sands management Janna quickly became the Aruba Concorde's biggest player. João Miguel from Brazil wagered $1 million, repayable with inflated Brazilian *cruzados,* and plenty of players received credit in six figures. But no one else at the Aruba Concorde received credit on the level of Farayala Janna and his pals: at least five times in the summer and fall of 1986, the Sands executives in Aruba extended Janna $1 million or more.

Given that the Aruba Concorde's revenues from the casino totaled less than $18 million that year, extending more than $5 million credit to a single player created two enormous risks. One was that he would play and win, a risk heightened by the fact that he played with a group whose joint betting increased the potential win on each hand if they played together and virtually eliminated risk of loss if they played against each other. The second risk was that Janna would lose and not pay. This second concern was heightened by the fact that Janna's credit application was mostly blank, a sharp departure from New Jersey regulations, and his background was never fully investigated by the Sands managers.

But Janna's history of playing and paying made him appear to be a good risk. So long as he paid, Pratt Hotel stood to gain, since its ten-year contract paid it 2.5 percent of gross revenues plus 6 percent of net profits monthly.

There was another reason the Sands executives felt confident about extending so much credit. Janna showed them four pieces of stiff green paper, certificates of deposit in Swiss banks totaling $55 million. No one checked whether the Swiss millions were Janna's or not. The Sands team did not even try to write down the account numbers because they knew the money was untouchable under Aruban law.

Five months after the Sands started running the Aruba Concorde Janna flew to Atlantic City, where the Sands treated him as a "preferred player," a casino industry euphemism for a sucker with big money to blow that a casino hopes to keep away from the competition. Such players' credit lines and repayment histories are not shared with credit bureaus.

The Sands gave Janna a $2 million credit line on Memorial Day 1986. He lost six hundred thousand dollars, but did not pay off immediately, a delay whose purpose would later be questioned by Leon Samburg, who had been sacked when the Pratts were hired in Aruba.

During this Atlantic City trip Janna's friend Cesar Molina was given a one-hundred-thousand-dollar Sands credit line even though he had

149

maintained less than seven thousand dollars in his bank account. His Aruba Concorde credit application was mostly blank, not listing a job, income stream or assets that would indicate an ability to repay a six-figure debt.

Three days after losing at the Sands Janna ventured four blocks down the Boardwalk to Caesars, where Smyth was waiting. As part of the lure Smyth said he arranged for Caesars to rent a twelve-passenger van for a month so that a member of Janna's entourage, whom Janna said was a senior Colombian government housing official, could take his large family on vacation.

Caesars gave Janna $1 million credit. Janna lost $1,095,000, which he paid Caesars within ninety days, as New Jersey regulations required.

Janna's friends got huge lines of credit, too. Together they lost a half million dollars, but they promised their markers would be made good within ninety days, and they were. Molina's credit line at Caesars was for $420,000, though he apparently lost much less than that. Molina paid Caesars ninety thousand dollars on September 2, 1986, and Caesars marked his debt paid in full.

Smyth was ecstatic. He had lucked into a player willing to blow millions and millions, a player who brought along pals who lost as well, and they made good on their markers.

That view was shared by the Sands executives, who knew Smyth because he had been the Sands' chief executive very briefly in the early eighties.

As summer 1986 ended at the Aruba Concorde, credit manager Dennis Yin increased Janna's credit line to a permanent $1 million. Janna started to bet more and more. Like a coke addict going through ever more white powder, too much was not enough for him and his entourage.

As Christmas approached Janna made plans to spend a second holiday season gambling. He flew to Lake Tahoe. There, amid the snow-capped forests surrounding the cold clear waters of one of the planet's most beautiful settings, Janna hunkered down at the windowless casino's baccarat table accompanied by his father-in-law, José Abudinen, and attorney Jairo Esmeral. Janna wanted $2 million credit, but Smyth offered only half that much. Janna promptly lost it.

Janna asked for a second million. First, Smyth said, you'll have to come up with a half-million-dollar cashier's check. Janna did. Caesars won that money, too. Caesars then granted Janna the second million in credit and he proceeded to lose that, too. Abudinen and Esmeral lost another $1 million.

"When it came time to settle up," Smyth recalled, "Janna asked us to consolidate." He wanted his father-in-law's and attorney's markers assigned to him, putting him $3 million in debt, and their records cleared. That would be illegal in Atlantic City, but in Nevada Caesars could make such accommodations.

A marker is basically a counter check. Except in New Jersey, Caesars follows a little-known practice that helps increase its prospects of collecting in the event a losing player does not honor his debt. When Caesars presents a marker to a player it checks carefully that it has the correct signature, but it leaves blank the spaces for the name of the bank and branch and the checking account number. Caesars' theory is that high rollers have many bank accounts and leaving those three spaces blank gives it the option of depositing the marker against any account with enough money to cover it. All Caesars has to do is find a banker willing to share with it information about how much is in a given bank account.

Janna also asked for, and got, a 10 percent discount, another courtesy that at the time was illegal in Atlantic City, though commonplace everywhere else for high rollers. A few whales have even negotiated 20 percent discounts on their markers at Caesars, the Mirage and other Las Vegas houses that cater to a global clientele. Janna left three postdated checks in Tahoe, each for nine hundred thousand dollars.

Meanwhile, Janna and his party spent Christmas Eve and Christmas Day at the Aruba Concorde, where they took over two floors for round-the-clock revelry, fueled by his winning half a million dollars, according to Goldstein. Janna's unusual good luck caused a crisis.

"We were in very difficult shape financially," Goldstein said. JJ had put some cash into the Concorde earlier in December, but only a half million dollars, most of which went to payroll. The Pratt team had invited Janna and other South American players with about $4 million of credit for the holidays, but had less than a million dollars in the cage from which to pay winnings.

"It got to a point, when Janna was about to leave the property, that we could not pay Janna what we owed him," Goldstein said. "We offered him a check and he got upset and said, 'What about the rest of the people who are winning money here?' For some reason, he was concerned about the Concorde's image. He ranted and raved about how could we run a business where, 'We lose, we pay you . . . now when I win or my friends win I don't get paid. It doesn't seem fair.'

"Quite frankly, he was right. Ironically, Janna offered to put his winnings back on deposit [as] front money, which for a casino is a tremendous benefit. It allows you to have working capital if you have no money in your vault, in your cage. So Janna's group returned—Janna returned—some winnings, enabled us to pay off some South Americans" who were also winning, Goldstein explained.

Things quickly returned to the norm. "What happened the rest of the week was typical in a casino. We started beating the customers. . . . By the end of the New Year's period, we had a very successful month. We had revenue of $2 million. The earnings were very significant," Goldstein boasted.

Goldstein figured that Pratt Hotel was on its way to a great year running the Aruba Concorde in 1987. In fact, Pratt Hotel's relationship with the casino owner was about to come apart, thanks to the fired Leon Samburg.

Samburg had been fired as manager of the Aruba Concorde once before, back in 1982, after he got into a beef with an employee and slugged him, causing the Aruban unions to demand his head. To keep labor peace JJ discharged Samburg.

Samburg maintained a relationship with JJ, however, which paid off in 1984 when someone left a video camera on when the new managers added up the day's winnings. When JJ saw the videotape he fired the managers and hired the man who had sold him the video gear: Leon Samburg.

Samburg's second tour of duty on at the Aruba Concorde came after the oil bust had wiped out many of JJ's Venezuelan high rollers while JJ continued milking the casino for cash, leaving it with unpaid bills and checking account overdrafts.

Nearly a year after he was fired, on a morning when a cold front cut across Miami, whipping the Atlantic into a chilly froth, Samburg and his lawyer, Patricia Silver, began questioning JJ under oath as part of

152

Samburg's effort to recover his unpaid salary. They met in a building JJ had come to own only after a messy public hearing up in Tallahassee.

Dressed in an exquisite custom-tailored suit, JJ affected the outer polish of a Third World aristocrat. His father had represented Venezuela at the Bretton Woods conference that established the global monetary system after World War II. JJ had attended the finest schools and had earned a doctorate in economics in the fifties before going to work for Venezuela's largest bank, his father's Banco Nacional de Descuento. JJ had accumulated so many bank shares that when oil boomed in the seventies he became a billionaire, until the oil market collapsed, wiping out at least a third of his fortune. The Venezuelan government seized the bank in 1978, saying a quarter of its deposits had been loaned to companies controlled by JJ, companies not in the habit of paying the money back.

JJ fled to Florida to escape arrest on fraud charges. There he arranged to buy the small Dania Bank, which he wanted to rename the Caribank and grow into a chain. The Caracas government fought him, but JJ insisted the charges were only politics. JJ won approval to buy the bank, and when he eventually returned home a Caracas court dismissed the fraud charges. The leather chair where JJ sat this blustery January morning smoking a hand-rolled cigar and answering Silver's questions was in the Miami branch of Caribank.

The windowless conference room afforded no sense of the worsening weather outside, which was mild compared to the storm that Silver, a compact tornado of an attorney, would whip up once she got through her preliminary questioning. The rough weather began when she asked the erudite banker if he knew Janna.

"I have heard that name," JJ answered, blowing smoke from his cigar. "He is a customer of the casino and he has been since several years ago."

"Is he a blue-chip player?"

"Could you define that?"

Silver cared less about the answer than JJ's reaction. She focused her intense blue eyes on JJ's forehead, suddenly glistening in the air-conditioned room.

Silver's dual purposes were to make JJ realize that Samburg knew more about what was going on at the Aruba Concorde than JJ did and to

153

drive a wedge between JJ and the Pratts. Her hope was that JJ would realize that Samburg looked out for JJ's interests and should get his job back.

As her questions continued what struck Silver was how each time she said the name Janna, JJ sweated a little more. Silver realized anxiety gripped JJ, but why?

She had no idea who Janna was, other than a big player Samburg knew and whom the Pratts had granted millions in credit. She concluded that JJ knew Janna better than he was letting on and feared how far her questions would go. Silver had no idea that in this very branch of JJ's Caribank, on Brickell Avenue in Miami, or "money-launderers row" as some called it, Janna controlled a bank account. The name on the account was not his, though, but Hartsdale Resources.

Silver pressed on, asking if JJ was aware that in 1984, after Samburg had been fired the first time, a two-hundred-thousand-dollar Janna marker had been written off on the promise that Farayala and Doris would promote the Aruba Concorde among the players and fans of the Barranquilla soccer team named Junior.

"I do not know," JJ said, adding that he harbored no concerns. The look in JJ's eye, though, told Silver that as soon as the rich banker could escape the room he intended to learn more.

One after another Silver's questions dug a deepening well of doubt in JJ's mind about who was drawing liquid assets from his casino. Then, seven hours into her examination, Silver poured in a few words formulated to poison Pratt Hotel's relationship with JJ.

"Do you recall any discussions with Pratt Hotel Corporation concerning payments of debts Janna owed to the Sands in Atlantic City versus debts owed to the Aruba casino?"

"No," JJ said.

Silver shifted into deep sarcasm to signal JJ that she was not fishing, that she knew full well the predicates to her questions and that her purpose was to embarrass JJ into realizing he was not as well informed as his fired manager about conditions at the Aruba Concorde.

"You recall *no* discussions with *any* representative of Pratt concerning the allocations of monies of Mr. Janna toward payments of debts to the Sands in Atlantic City and the Aruba casino?"

"If Janna owed money to the Sands, he must have paid the Sands. If he owed money to the Aruba hotel, he must probably pay those debts to the Aruba Concorde," JJ answered.

"Were you aware, sir, that Mr. Janna won a substantial sum of money at the Aruba Concorde and those monies were used to pay debts at the Sands in Atlantic City?"

"I am aware," JJ replied, blowing more smoke, "that he had been a customer of the Aruba Concorde for some time, some years, and during the course of that relationship he must have won and lost several times. As to whether that money was used to pay debts of Mr. Janna to the Sands, I do not know."

Minutes later, when the deposition ended and Silver and Samburg walked into the windy afternoon grinning, JJ began angrily demanding that subordinates find out what in hell was going on in Aruba and whether money his casino lost to Janna had gone north to pay Janna's marker at the Atlantic City Sands.

The phone began ringing in the Aruba office of Joap Poot, the quiet Dutchman who was the Concorde's outside auditor. He quickly carried JJ's concerns to Doug Pattison, the Pratt Hotel Corporation's chief financial officer at the Aruba Concorde. As Pattison recounted it in a memo to Rob Goldstein, Poot was directed by JJ and his aides to investigate "the unusual coincidence" that Janna lost money at the Sands and then won a similar amount in Aruba.

"They believe that Mr. Janna is being utilized by PHC to extract cash from the Concorde," Pattison wrote.

Poot also was to find out if "key employees are receiving money from players to hold checks," which would suggest imprudent credit decisions, and whether "cash has been taken from the drop boxes and slot machines."

Pattison said Poot advised him that the Sands team "would not be managing the property for much longer. In my opinion, these accusations are a serious threat to the on-going relationship between PHC and Concorde."

As Poot and Pattison spoke something far more serious was taking place at the Aruba Concorde, something that had begun the day before at the Caribank branch in Miami. Something that should have set off alarm bells at the New Jersey Division of Gaming Enforcement.

17

See No Evil

Casual gamblers open their wallets at the tables to buy chips, their greenbacks stuffed into a drop box with a paddle to prevent theft by dealers. High rollers are different. Because they play with more money than even the fattest wallet can hold, high rollers arrange for their bank to wire their money to the casino cage or they bring a check, depositing it into a front money account bearing their name. A front money account allows a big player to leave money on deposit at the cage whenever he or she takes a break to play golf, eat or sleep. But front money accounts can also be put to other uses.

On January 22, 1987, Farayala Janna wired $665,000 to his front money account at the Aruba Concorde. He sent $50,000 from an account at JJ's Caribank in Miami, plus $615,000 from nearby Sun Bank.

Janna did not gamble, though. Instead, the Aruba Concorde casino wrote Janna four checks the next day, one for $50,000 and three for $205,000 each, returning all the money to Janna. All four checks went back to Florida. The small check was deposited into an account Janna controlled at Southeast Bank in Miami. The other three were deposited into one of Janna's accounts at the Miami branch of the Bank of Credit and Commerce International, a bank later shown to have been the world's largest conduit for illegal money from drug dealers and arms merchants, as well as for the Reagan administration's arms for hostages deal known as Iran-Contra. At the CIA they referred to BCCI as the Bank of Crooks and Criminals International.

Janna could have simply written checks himself if he wanted to move money from one account to another. He could have accomplished the fifty-thousand-dollar transfer from Caribank to Southeast Bank by walking a few paces down Brickell Avenue instead of sending the money on a journey of several thousand miles. What Janna was doing was washing the money through the Aruba Concorde, creating a paper trail which made it appear to any nosy government agent who did not dig too deeply that the checks were for gambling winnings.

The object in laundering money from criminal enterprises, such as selling drugs, is to make money appear to be the fruit of legitimate enterprise. Accomplishing this requires washing the money through an institution. While paper sacks full of cash raise questions about their origins, a check from a business, a bank or a casino makes money appear to be payment for services, the proceeds of a loan or winnings from a lucky day at the tables.

Laundering fails to wash away the stain of criminality, however, if the money can be traced back to its original and illegitimate source. To make it difficult to prove that the dollars coming out clean went in dirty, money launderers often engage in numerous sham transactions, washing dirty money through several accounts and mingling it with clean money in hopes that, if the government gets suspicious, enough complexity will be added to the wash to introduce an element of reasonable doubt that anything criminal took place.

The records in this transaction, however, showed a single cycle wash, one that made it easy to trace every step as the $665,000 flowed from the two Miami banks, was wired to Janna's front money account at the Aruba Concorde, and then was withdrawn the next day in four checks, all endorsed on the back by Farayala Janna.

So where did the money originate? The two accounts Janna took the money from were in the name of Hartsdale Resources. And what was

Hartsdale Resources? It was an arm of the Medellín drug cartel, according to U.S. Treasury Secretary Nicholas Brady.

By the time the U.S. Drug Enforcement Agency seized the various Hartsdale Resources accounts at Miami banks in 1989 the money in them was all gone. An investigation into a Los Angeles–based money-laundering operation had tipped the drug lords to the DEA inquiry. But bank records seized by the feds showed that the Hartsdale Resources accounts were used to wash tens of millions of cocaine dollars.

The DEA established Hartsdale's purpose from bank records seized after the Panamanian dictator, General Manuel Noriega, was arrested following the United States invasion of that country in December 1989. The DEA's Operation Polar Cap froze 680 bank accounts, of which Hartsdale Resources at Sun Bank was the second largest. Treasury Secretary Brady called Operation Polar Cap "the largest law enforcement undertaking involving bank account seizures in U.S. history."

Operation Polar Cap focused on Colombian business people who bought cocaine dollars on the black market at a discount, laundered them by passing them through business enterprises, banks and casinos, and then sold the cleansed money back to the Medellín cartel.

Janna was well known to law enforcement by 1987, when the Hartsdale Resources money was washed through the Aruba Concorde. The Colombian national police had been keeping files on Janna's cocaine and marijuana smuggling since 1985. The U.S. Drug Enforcement Agency had a file on Janna, too.

The question arises whether the Sands executives knew, or should have known, that Janna was a drug smuggler and a money launderer. The best authority on that issue is Jack Pratt, chairman of the hotel company bearing his name, the company which owns the Atlantic City Sands and which managed the Aruba Concorde.

Pratt Hotel Corporation, Pratt testified when these very questions were raised in a closed door arbitration proceeding, operates "very extensive corporate security in Atlantic City that's made up of ex-FBI and ex-U.S. drug enforcement agents, so before we do any transaction with any company or individual, they have to pass our clearance. And if there's the slightest red flag in their background or their financial ability, then that's our alert not to transact business with them."

158

The corporate security force, however, with all its FBI and DEA connections, somehow failed to learn about the file on Janna—identifying him as a cocaine and marijuana smuggler and money launderer—that the Colombian drug police (whose salaries DEA pays) opened in June 1985.

The U.S. Justice Department did not reveal that Hartsdale Resources was a money-laundering account until 1989, but the Sands team in Aruba knew in May 1987 that Janna was brokering cocaine dollars. Their source was none other than Jairo Esmeral, Janna's lawyer, according to Dennis Yin, the credit manager who hiked Janna's credit line to $1 million, and Doug Pattison, the chief financial officer installed by the Sands.

Despite this, Rob Goldstein, the top Sands executive for Aruba, said there was no money laundering that he knew about.

He explained that $615,000 of the $665,000 that passed quickly through the Aruba Concorde was part of a favor Janna was doing for the cash-starved casino. The casino had lacked the cash to pay Janna his winnings at Christmas, Goldstein said, so the three $205,000 checks were to pay his winnings. Goldstein, under oath, said the checks were postdated and Janna was told to hold them until he was given the okay to deposit them.

"Janna got tired of waiting. He put the checks in for deposit. When he did, the checks bounced," Goldstein later recounted under oath. Janna then decided to advance the Aruba Concorde $615,000 to make the checks good, Goldstein testified.

That Janna would entrust his money to a casino that could not pay him because he was embarrassed by the casino's problems was a curious explanation for the quick flow of dollars from Miami to the casino and back to Miami.

Records from the casino and Janna's bank account revealed a very different story. The records showed that none of the four checks written to Janna on January 23 were postdated and that none of them bounced. And they showed that in mid-January Janna was paid more than the amount he supposedly left on deposit at Christmas to help the casino.

Among the checks Janna received from the Aruba Concorde in early 1987 were these:

Date	Check Number	Amount
January 9	151	$500,000
January 13	154	171,000
January 13	155	18,758
January 13	156	240,000
January 23	166	205,000
January 23	167	205,000
January 23	168	205,000
January 23	211	50,000
February 1	206	205,000
February 1	207	205,000
February 1	208	205,000
March 3	227	204,000
March 3	239	205,000
Total		$ 2,618,758

Just as the four January 23 checks washed the Medellín cartel's Hartsdale Resources money through the Aruba Concorde, the three February 1 checks came after Janna wired another $615,000 from Florida to the casino and got it right back the next day without gambling. Two of the casino checks to Janna, numbers 207 and 208 dated February 1, did bounce, reducing the net proceeds to Janna to $2,208,758.

But there was more, including checks to members of the Janna entourage, such as the seventy thousand dollars paid on January 13 to Guerra Salim, who deposited the money into BCCI's Ft. Lauderdale branch.

The fast flow of checks into and out of the Aruba Concorde was not the only evidence that Janna was using the casino to launder money for the Medellín cartel. During this time cash began flowing out of the Aruba Concorde like fast-melting snow from the Andes, where coca plants are processed into another kind of snow that also tends to disappear quickly. A lot of the cash flowed toward Janna, though there is no record showing that all of it reached him.

The Arthur Young accounting firm, in a report to JJ, said that during the nineteen months when Sands executives ran the Aruba Concorde "an excessive amount of questionable and unsupported cash payouts were made from the casino cashier's cage." There was $203,500 in cash to Janna, including $12,000 cash taken from the cage one day to pay for a jet charter, followed by a second withdrawal of $12,160. On another occasion $59,000 was paid out for a jet charter even though there was no invoice showing a jet had been hired or that Janna's Lear jet had been used.

An additional $37,200 was paid from the cage to casino manager Mike Barozzi, who often signed both to take the money from the cage and as the ultimate recipient. Barozzi says every cent was used legitimately. So does Pratt Hotel. The Arthur Young auditors also reported on $400,900 in "additional unsupported or questionable cash payouts" during the Sands' tenure at the Aruba Concorde. The Sands contends that paper receipts existed and must have been removed.

Smyth, meanwhile, was having problems that spring collecting the $2.7 million debt from the holiday gambling spree at Lake Tahoe. Janna's first nine-hundred-thousand-dollar check, dated March 1, 1987, cleared. Later that month Janna called to say that his Panamanian bank account had been intervened and his second check was no good. Soon he called Smyth with a new story, about some second party on his account, and that's why his account was intervened. Smyth didn't believe him.

Janna called again. "Well, the problem is still the same in Panama," he told Smyth. "But I have been kidnapped and I have to pay a large ransom."

Smyth figured that was a whopper, too, but he decided to call Caesars' marketing rep in Medellín. The Colombian newspapers, Caesars' man in Medellín reported, had indeed carried stories that Janna's father had been kidnapped by guerrillas. Smyth decided that Janna was telling the truth about being kidnapped.

At the Aruba Concorde Janna's credit remained as good as gold. On March 9, the Sands team made Janna their agent to recruit players from

161

Colombia and to collect their markers. "Players referred to us by Janna are unique," Dennis Yin wrote in a memo announcing Janna's appointment, "in that he will guarantee settlement of their accounts" with 50 percent due immediately, half the balance in thirty days and the rest in sixty days.

The Sands team began talking to Janna about his buying the Aruba Concorde, turning the sixth and seventh floors into private apartments for permanent partying.

In mid-April Janna came and gambled more. Then came April 28. Janna was due in two days for some big play and the Sands managers decided it was time to collect what was listed on the books as "deferred salary—advance." Credit manager Dennis Yin pocketed two checks totaling forty thousand dollars and three others received nearly fifty thousand dollars.

Janna and his entourage arrived April 30 and played heavily. Early on the morning of May 2, Janna quit while he was ahead. The cage exchanged his chips for four checks totaling a half million dollars. Before dawn Janna was back at the tables. He wanted $2 million credit, double what was authorized. Reuben Schwengle, the casino shift manager, did not demand that the checks be returned. Instead he gave Janna the full $2 million credit. When it was gone Janna asked for another $2 million. Schwengle gave that to him, too. Janna lost it.

At 9:30 A.M. credit manager Dennis Yin came down from his room to the casino. Schwengle told him he had lost control in the heat of the moment and had given Janna $4 million credit earlier that morning. Yin was more than surprised; he was shocked. But neither Yin, who felt he had no authority, nor anyone else disciplined Schwengle, who was not even chewed out, and Schwengle's authority to approve credit continued. What worry did the Sands executives have? They logged the $4 million as winnings, listing in the books an account receivable that would hike their monthly management fee by at least one hundred thousand dollars. If Janna paid, the Sands fee could grow by as much as $240,000 because the firm received 6 percent of net profits. And if Janna did not pay it was JJ's loss, not Pratt Hotel's.

Janna promised to pay $1 million a week to retire the $4.1 million he owed, but made no payments. Esmeral, his attorney, explained to Doug Pattison and Dennis Yin about the DEA tying up Janna's bank account.

The Sands in Atlantic City soon suspended Janna's credit. But in Aruba the Sands team did Janna a huge favor.

In late June the Sands agreed to let Janna sign a new marker for nearly $2.5 million to replace a stack of markers from Janna's family and friends. Their markers were then destroyed. But the new marker that Janna signed did not list a bank, branch or account number. Instead, in these spaces Janna wrote his name and hometown, making the marker worthless. And because all the old markers were destroyed, there is no way to collect the money owed.

Meanwhile four checks the Sands team wrote to Janna on May 2 took their cooperation with Janna's money-moving to a new level. The checks were written not to Janna but to his surrogates. The first was for two hundred thousand dollars and it was made out to Ahmed Dahruj, who cashed it at BCCI in Panama. The second check, for $120,000 to the El Ruda Trading Company, ended up at Philip Morris in New York as payment for a shipment of cigarettes. It bounced because the casino stopped payment on it, along with an eighty-thousand-dollar check made out to the Caribbean Import & Export Trading Company.

But the fourth check, which cleared, was the most interesting of all. Check number 764 was for one hundred thousand dollars, payable to Hartsdale Resources. Janna endorsed it. It cleared. The Sands team had now not only taken in money from the Medellín cartel, they had sent money to it.

While JJ would not learn of these money-laundering transactions for months, the inquiry he launched after hearing Patricia Silver's questions quickly yielded results.

JJ collected affidavits from six dealers and one assistant manager who alleged that the Sands executives in Aruba allowed Janna to break the rules and win money.

The video camera recorded Janna one time placing his two-thousand-dollar bet after the white ball settled between two of the frets that separate each number on the roulette wheel, guaranteeing himself a seventy-thousand-dollar win. Another dealer swore that late on the night of April 30 Janna was allowed to touch the blackjack cards, marking them by creasing the corners. "This is not the first time that this gentleman is allowed to break this blackjack rule without management doing anything about it," dealer Servasio Semeleer declared. Another

163

dealer, Juan O. F. Vrolijk, said that Janna "is known to break all existing game rules at any game he is playing" while "management does nothing to correct this."

The cheating allegations were denounced as scurrilous lies by Roberto Rivera-Soto, the Sands general counsel. He said the seven no doubt gave the affidavits to save their jobs.

JJ sent Jack Pratt a long letter that July complaining of management shortcomings and broken promises, along with a videotape of manager Mike Barozzi in a drunken fight with his brother, who blocked him from slugging a young woman. In August JJ had the locks changed and ordered the Pratt executives out.

Pratt Hotel then sued JJ, claiming it had not been properly notified that the contract was being terminated. The private arbitration hearings focused on the issue of whether JJ gave Jack Pratt proper notice before breaking the contract.

The Sands team's main line of defense to all integrity questions raised at the arbitration hearing was to cite, again and again, reports written by the New Jersey Division of Gaming Enforcement, reports that praised the Sands group for the integrity it had brought to the Aruba Concorde operation.

The testimony and many of the exhibits from the hearings were sent to the Division of Gaming Enforcement by JJ's lawyer, Nick Ribis, who was also Donald Trump's casino lawyer. Ribis, seeking an advantage in the dispute with the Sands, and no doubt hoping to weaken the Sands as a competitor to the Trump casinos, pointed to the flow of money in and out of the casino for Janna's benefit, to the huge sums of cash that had vanished, and to the testimony by Pattison that showed the Sands people had been told that the DEA had frozen Janna's bank account.

Ribis went to the New Jersey Division of Gaming Enforcement with evidence that the Sands was doing favors for the Medellín cartel, evidence questioning whether the Sands could meet the integrity test required to operate a casino in Atlantic City. But even with hard evidence put right under the enforcement division's nose, no one there got a whiff of what was going on. Barth Aaron, the prosecutor assigned to the Sands, and Anthony J. Parrillo, the division director, came to the same conclusion: they had authority, but they lacked proof. They never sent investigators to Aruba again, nor did they put any of the key witnesses under oath. They said they saw nothing wrong, absolutely nothing.

"I don't see how we can do anything," Parrillo explained. "First, I understand that some of the records are missing in Aruba. Second, the Sands won the arbitration, so how can we bring a case against them?"

Sands executives, who talked candidly about the Aruba Concorde case, insisted that they were unaware of Janna's drug ties at the time they gave him credit, and thus no regulatory issue existed.

The Sands won on the narrow issue of whether JJ gave proper notice before canceling the contract. The arbiters ruled that he had not.

Janna continued to play at the Aruba Concorde, though at a much reduced level. But JJ's new managers had grown suspicious of him. In December 1988 Rich Fortin of the casino security team tapped Janna's phone calls and filed reports on what he said. In one conversation Janna kept telling two men at his Miami home to "be cool, be cool" and promising he would be there the next day with whatever it was they expected.

He seemed squeezed for cash. He borrowed $1 million from Daniel Fernandez in Colombia, leaving a postdated check to cover the loan. The check bounced. Fernandez sued, but his lawyer never could collect the debt. Janna said he was broke and his daughter was deathly ill, a story the lawyer believed because Janna seemed always to be in the children's wing at a Miami hospital.

Soon Janna lost one of his waterfront Miami homes. Then he lost the second. The Rite Aid drugstore chain won a judgment against Janna for a $1,140 check he wrote for Florida lottery tickets. The check bounced. He told Smyth that Doris had left him. Smyth quit trying to collect Janna's Caesars Tahoe markers and then retired in 1989.

The last time a casino executive saw Janna was in the convenience store parking lot where he looked like any other poor schlub trying to make ends meet and saying he wished he had the money to pay his debts. Janna later returned to Colombia, where he went into hiding. He said by telephone—after bombs exploded outside his home and the tiny fabric store he listed as his business on his casino credit application—that it was not safe for him to be in public. He would not say why. But he said he was never a drug trafficker or a money launderer.

The regulators, who saw nothing wrong with drug money subsidizing a casino company, faced other issues testing their diligence—issues that involved "little people," not high rollers with millions of dollars. The first test began with a roulette player who said Trump Castle deliberately cheated him out of eight hundred dollars.

18

By the Book

Bob Signore longed to be walking on the beach enjoying the warm, gentle breeze at the Jersey Shore one August evening in 1987. But the rest of the family wanted to get out of their summer place. Asko Sullivan, his favorite uncle, yearned for some action at Trump Castle. Reluctantly, the soft-spoken Signore tagged along. Signore, a slight man in his thirties with a mustache, had trained as an accountant, so while he did not gamble he understood numbers enough to know the family would probably lose all their stakes. At least, he figured, with all the state regulations anyone who gambled at Trump Castle would lose their money honestly. He figured wrong.

Alone, Signore wandered through the half acre of Trump Castle slots, pulling the smooth handles here and there to try his luck. The slots just did not feel right to Signore, so eventually he ambled over to the roulette wheels to watch his uncle. Asko Sullivan played Trump Castle and the Claridge often enough to be a rated player, wise to the ways of being comped to dinner or a suite to soothe the pain of losing hundreds or even thousands of bucks on the gaming floor.

Sullivan was a big, jovial man whom Signore admired for his integrity and toughness. Sullivan was a political figure in the Philadelphia suburbs, something of a reformer, who owned a heating and ventilating

167

business. What Signore admired most was how Sullivan had stood up to the corrupt roofers union local, which had paid off a score of Philadelphia judges to ensure that its goons would escape jail after beating up contractors who would not pay off union boss Steve Traitz and his buddies. Sullivan never paid, nor was he beaten, but he had said he was threatened.

Watching Sullivan place his chips on his favorite spots on the grid of thirty-six numbers plus zero and double zero, Signore tried to discern the rules of the game. But he wanted more than a rough understanding of roulette before risking his money. So he walked over to a booth at the edge of the casino floor and took a brochure called "A Guide to Games at Trump's Castle Hotel & Casino."

The two-page spread on roulette featured a colored illustration of the betting table showing how thirteen different bets work. Signore studied the illustration and watched the dealer pay wins and take chips when players lost. At first he couldn't quite grasp the game. But soon his eyes opened wide. The dealers were not paying by the rules, at least not by the rules in the official Trump Castle gaming guide.

The book showed that when a chip is placed on red the player won if the roulette ball landed on black. But the dealers paid on red only if the ball landed on red. The guide also showed that even paid off on odd. And it showed that a chip on 13 and 14 paid if the roulette ball fell into either 11 or 12. In all, Signore calculated that six of the thirteen illustrated bets were wrong. Signore motioned for his uncle to take a look. Sullivan couldn't believe it, but as he studied the booklet he, too, saw the mistakes. Sullivan realized that he would not be taken in, but a novice without his nephew's inquiring mind, especially one who did not speak English and relied on the illustrations, might well be.

The casinos were supposed to be the most highly regulated industry in the country, more regulated than nuclear power plants. The state Division of Gaming Enforcement prided itself on its image as the toughest regulatory agency the country had ever seen. As Sullivan listened to his bright nephew, he says, headlines from the newspapers flashed through his mind. He recalled how one casino complained that it had to spend hundreds of thousands of dollars because a cement wall where armored cars pull up was a fraction of an inch shy of specification and some punctilious regulator thought a few dollars might slip through the opening. Bally's Park Place claimed it once had to spend a quarter million bucks on new carpeting because the regulators decided that there was not enough contrast in colors where the casino carpet was sewn to the hotel lobby carpet. Sullivan figured that all the mistakes in this booklet, the official book of rules, could mean serious and expensive trouble for Trump Castle.

Go tell the casino manager about it, Sullivan advised his nephew, and after you explain to him what you found suggest that Trump Castle return the favor by buying us all dinner.

Signore was so unwise to casino ways that he went not to a casino official, but to the Casino Control Commission booth, where he was told he needed to talk to an employee of the casino. Signore waited for half an hour before the shift manager came. The man listened to part of his story and then dismissed him, his complaint about the mistakes in the official gaming guide and, especially, the idea of being comped.

"How much did you gamble, sir?" Signore reports being asked.

"I didn't gamble," Signore said, trying to add that he wanted to learn the game first and was studying the guide when—

"Sir, we only comp players," was the response.

As the manager in the sharp black suit walked off, Signore felt humiliated at the treatment and outraged that Trump Castle didn't give a damn that its gaming guide had the rules all wrong, that novices could be cheated.

Well, maybe, Signore thought, he should not have listened to his uncle about asking for a comp. But damn it, the written rules are wrong.

All the way back to the family's summer house on Long Beach Island that night Signore stewed and tried to figure out how to prove his point. The next morning he hit on a plan.

The following night Signore returned to Trump Castle. His uncle and a friend came along, but they entered the casino separately. Signore sat down at the roulette table and bought a stack of fifty-dollar chips. He also pulled out the official "Guide to Games at Trump's Castle Hotel & Casino" and a piece of paper. He made a show of looking at the guide for advice, explaining to the dealer and the other players this was his first time at a roulette table. On the paper he wrote down each bet. On his nineteenth bet, when the ball fell on 17 black and the dealer reached for his chips, Signore spoke up.

"What are you doing?" Signore asked.

"You lost, sir."

"No, I didn't."

"Sir, you bet red and even and it came up black and odd, so you lost."

"No I didn't. I did bet red and even. And, yes, it did come up black and odd. I should win," Signore said. "Look," he implored, "just look at this official Trump Castle official gaming guide." The dealer's lips suddenly sealed tight.

Another player said he wanted to get on with the next spin. A supervisor came, then the supervisor's supervisor, the pit boss. "Sir," she advised, "this book might have mistakes."

"That's not my problem. I played by the rules," Signore said, waving his official gaming guide. "I want to be paid by the rules."

The pit boss refused.

"I'd like the Casino Control Commission here. Now," Signore demanded.

"Sir, they will not come to the table," the supervisor replied. It was a lie. No such policy exists. But the casinos use it as a ploy, like signaling guards to stand around with arms folded when they want to intimidate a player who asks hard questions. The pit boss kept saying she would not discuss Signore's complaint.

Finally one player at the roulette wheel piped up. "Hey, why don't you give the kid a chance. Maybe he has a point." It was Sullivan. But when the complaining player grabbed his chips and left, the supervisor told Signore he could play quietly by the rules—the real rules, not those in the brochure—or guards would show him the door.

Signore took his chips to the Casino Control Commission booth, a den of bureaucratic lethargy where many disgruntled gamblers have learned that no one wants to lift a pen to write down a complaint, much less act on it. Signore explained what had happened, while his uncle remained at the table playing roulette and quietly observing.

"Oh, sir, you are not playing by that book are you?" the commission inspector asked.

"Yes, I am."

"That booklet has errors in it. Someone reported it last week."

Signore listened in amazement, thinking, *You are telling me you know there are errors in it and you're the same person who handed me this booklet half an hour ago? This makes a lot of sense.* But what he said was, "In that case, I'd like my money back. I'm out two hundred dollars, but according to this booklet I should have won six hundred dollars. Trump Castle owes me eight hundred dollars." The bureaucrat said she had no authority. She did call the casino shift manager on duty, James McDermott, and when he showed up twenty minutes later Signore showed him the guide.

"Sir," McDermott said, "you really haven't been harmed. The odds are the same. It really doesn't make any difference because the odds are the same. I am sorry, there will be no restitution."

Then McDermott turned his back on Signore. But instead of just walking away he headed for the roulette table where Signore had played. He asked the dealer for her stash of rule books. He flashed them to several other employees and suddenly the room was alive with action as they searched through the acre and a half of casino recovering the offending guides. Signore could not believe how many there were or how many places they came from. They were behind tables, under podiums, stacked on shelves. There were hundreds and hundreds of them and he watched as McDermott stuffed them into a container like so much trash.

Finally commission inspector Louise O'Donnell wrote a brief notation of the incident and Signore left, almost vindicated. All he had to do now was get the state to return his money. After all, he reasoned, by removing all those official gaming guides Trump Castle had confirmed he was right.

Deborah Signore thought her husband was nuts. It was not a big deal, Deborah said, and besides, you could get hurt, even killed, fighting these people.

Signore thought that was ridiculous. The casinos were regulated industries. They do not kill people. This is not the mob, he said, this is Donald Trump. And besides, he said, waving a copy of the Casino Control Act, the law said that the overriding principle of casino regulation is honesty. People, the law says, can trust the "credibility and integrity of the regulatory process and casino operations."

"They're cheating people," Signore told his wife. "If the state knew it would stop it."

171

But the state already knew.

More than a year earlier, in 1986, a state Division of Gaming Enforcement agent had spotted the same mistakes and recommended that new guides be printed. The guides had been in use since Trump Castle opened in 1985. Before the first one was distributed proof sheets had been submitted to the regulators. But the toughest regulatory agency the world had ever seen had failed to notice that nearly half the roulette bets in the Trump Castle guide were wrong. And when the mistakes were first found the regulators did not order the brochures thrown out, but said the casino could keep distributing them.

Signore's complaint was rejected by Fred Gushin, the enforcement division lawyer who had approved continued distribution of the inaccurate guides. Gushin was hated by the industry, which perceived him as too tough on cases involving women and minorities and when the casinos bent rules to accommodate the whims of high rollers willing to drop fortunes at the tables. Now Gushin asserted that "no one was cheated here because while the gaming guide contained technical errors, the game was played according to the rules approved by the commission."

Besides, any citizen who consulted the "official roulette rules approved by the commission" would not have been misled, he insisted. Just how would a citizen obtain these rules? Gushin said the Casino Control Act required casinos to make those written rules freely available to anyone. "All you have to do is ask for a copy of, uh, well, uh," Gushin said, his voice trailing off as he realized he was saying the rules were in the very brochure Signore was complaining about.

"But, still," Gushin said, recovering his argument, "there was no cheating because Trump Castle played the game according to the rules. If they had cheated anyone, we would have filed a complaint against them immediately."

Signore hired a lawyer and wrote letters to the commission and to lawmakers seeking new gaming guides, an apology and restitution of his money or, at least, forfeiture of the eight hundred dollars by Trump Castle to the state or, better yet, his favorite charity. Sometimes he also asked for his legal fees.

Mostly the regulators ignored him. But Dennis Daly, a commission lawyer, was struck by the inaction on Signore's complaint and asked questions around the commission's office in Lawrenceville. Major Lloyd

172

Hall of the New Jersey State Police wrote Daly a letter in January 1988 saying Signore's complaint lacked merit because when he played roulette he already knew the official gaming guide had errors. Hall also wrote that Trump Castle had placed corrective stickers on the gaming guides. Daly passed the major's letter on to Signore, who figured that ended his quest. It didn't.

Three weeks later Signore decided to swing by Trump Castle and take a look at the corrective stickers. At the Casino Control Commission booth he found the gaming guides uncorrected and without stickers. Signore was livid.

He started writing letters again. When they were ignored he filed a lawsuit charging Trump Castle and the Casino Control Commission with fraud. Nearly three years after he found the mistakes, Signore thought he was about to get his day in court. He showed up early at the modern red-brick courthouse in Atlantic City, as did a lawyer for the state and another for Trump Castle. The judge dispatched them to a windowless room with plain white walls where two local lawyers, Dara A. Quattrone and Michael R. Mosca, tried to settle the case.

Trump's lawyer, Steven D. Scherzer, could not figure out why he was there. It struck him that Signore had a point, even if he had pushed it to ridiculous lengths, and that the amount of money at issue was not worth his time when the casino could have just written an eight-hundred-dollar check to a charity of Signore's choosing. But Scherzer knew Trump would never write a letter of apology, so he was there working on the clock to defeat Signore. Deputy Attorney General Franklin Widmann represented the regulators. Projecting an air of august contempt for Signore, he had a simple view of the case: not only was Signore not cheated, because he knew the brochure was flawed, but Widmann said the state was under no obligation to enforce any particular law. He also had an interesting defense of the faulty guides, arguing that the gaming guide's illustrations showed only "sample bets and did not say you would win, or lose, if you placed them."

Mediator Quattrone frowned at Widmann, but told Signore that while morally he was right, legally no fraud occurred because he knew the guide was flawed.

"I guess we're going to trial," Signore said as he stuffed his papers into a folder and walked out.

Two months later Atlantic County Superior Court Judge John G. Himmelberger called Signore's case. He dismissed it, but not before lecturing Signore.

What gives you the right to act as public advocate? the judge asked, searching for an analogy to explain what angered him about Signore's conduct. He likened the plaintiff to a guy standing on a street corner who watches someone run a red light day after day and then gets it into his head to step off the curb so he can sue for medical damages.

Your honor, it's not like that, Signore said. It's more like I'm standing on the corner with a police officer and he's not doing anything. Secondly, I didn't do anything wrong, I played by the rules they gave me. I had no medical injuries.

Maybe, Himmelberger conceded, he hadn't come up with a good analogy. Case dismissed.

None of this surprised Gregory Imperiale, an attorney who had seen how the regulatory system worked from another vantage point. Imperiale was not the kind of lean and finely tailored lawyer the casinos hire. He wore white shirts, but the cuffs slopped onto his pudgy palms and his polyester ties hung only halfway down his enormous belly. The floor of his modest office in suburban Northfield was a mine field of G.I. Joes, Nerf balls and plastic garbage trucks because while he wrote briefs his children often played at his feet. His speciality was representing casino workers.

"There's two standards," Imperiale said. "One is for the people who work in the casinos. The other is for people who own them. To those of us who work in this area, it's obvious the commission caters to the owners." How else could one explain the case that most outraged Imperiale, the case of Diane Pussehl, Martin Friel and Joseph A. Carfagno.

Friel started out as a dealer and worked his way up through fierce competition to become a pit boss, supervising craps and blackjack dealers to make sure the money was all accounted for and neither they nor patrons cheated the house. At age thirty-two he was making sixty thousand dollars a year, about double what dealers who worked year-round collected in pay and in tokes, as tips from players are called.

Just before midnight on December 30, 1986, Friel spotted a purple gaming chip on Harrah's green and rose carpet. He motioned to Carfagno, twenty-nine, the floor person who worked under him super-

174

vising the tables. Carfagno in turn motioned to cocktail waitress Pussehl, who gracefully knelt down, scooped up the chip and pocketed it. Later that evening, filling her tray with drinks at the service bar, Pussehl handed Carfagno one hundred dollars cash and told him that she would give Friel the same amount the next time they met. When her shift ended Pussehl drove home.

Pussehl had just drifted off to sleep when the telephone rang. It was Harrah's security and they demanded she return to work immediately. Friel, it turned out, had not been the only person to notice the chip. It was also espied by a woman who was known to the casinos as a forager, someone who came not so much to play as to poke between slot machines looking for loose change. Money and chips are found in casinos all the time. On a typical day more than ninety thousand people pass through Atlantic City's casinos, so chips, coins and cash get dropped everywhere. The spokesman for one casino noted that "the guys who sweep up find chips all the time. I think everybody in the industry believes if it's in the pit it goes back on the table, but if it's on the floor it's found money."

But before the old woman could even get close to the five-hundred-dollar chip the tall and slender cocktail waitress had recovered it. Harrah's security and state police detectives grilled Pussehl. She told them she had found chips and cash before in the casinos and turned them in. Records showed that she had. But this time two members of management told her to keep the chip, so what had she done wrong? She said she gave one hundred dollars to Carfagno because he was management and she felt pressured to share the booty.

The detectives were not impressed. Harrah's fired Pussehl, Friel and Carfagno.

Pussehl was stunned by how the state agents treated her. When the interview ended they told her to bring the chip to their offices, which opened at nine in the morning.

Be there right at nine, Pussehl heard one agent order her. If you get there at five after we're coming to your house and we're going to search every inch of it. We don't need a warrant.

To Gushin, the Division of Gaming Enforcement lawyer who prosecuted licensing violations, this was an important case, not at all like Signore's gripe about being cheated. Gushin is a nervous man whose hand continually strokes the thinning strands of black hair he sweeps over his balding head. He cares passionately about equal justice for minorities, whom he believed most casino executives despised. And Gushin was so punctilious about his personal integrity that he would not accept a cup of coffee from a casino executive or even a reporter.

The case was sent to a state grand jury, which quickly handed up indictments. But when the trio came to court the judge threw the felony theft case out. The state tried to prosecute them for misdemeanor crimes. A judge rejected that, too, just as Imperiale had expected. "Say you find a one-hundred-dollar bill on the ground," Imperiale noted. "You are not required to turn it in unless you know or can reasonably be expected to know whose it is. This chip was in a common area and there was no way to establish that it belonged to anyone. Case closed."

But Gushin was not done. There had been only one high roller playing with purple chips that night, the casino's records showed. Gushin reasoned that the trio knew whose chip it was and should have returned it. Maybe they had not committed a crime, but to Gushin they were conspiring thieves who should not work in a casino. He filed to revoke their licenses as casino workers on the grounds that they lacked the requisite character and integrity that the law required of both casino workers and owners.

Faced with the loss of their livelihoods Pussehl, Friel and Carfagno demanded an administrative hearing. The stakes in such a contest are not equal. The state simply billed Harrah's for its time and expenses, including them in a lump sum bill sent each casino monthly to cover the costs of regulating it, but not disclosing just what the money was used for. The three unemployed workers impoverished themselves paying their legal bills, knowing that even if they won they could never recover these expenses.

Administrative Law Judge Jeff S. Masin ruled that the state had no case. In part that was because Harrah's lone five-hundred-dollar-chip high roller that night said he had not lost any chips, a statement that spared him from any risk of being called as a witness. But Masin found a more fundamental problem. In his twenty-two-page opinion Masin ruled that there was no way to prove that Harrah's had ever advised the employees of a policy requiring that found money be turned in. To avoid such problems in the future, Masin suggested that casinos be required to adopt written policies on found money and to adopt a mechanism to prove each employee had been informed of the policy, perhaps by signing a copy of the policy manual.

But his sound recommendation to create a new regulation that would resolve doubt about whether casino workers acted honestly was ignored by the Casino Control Commission. Instead, when Masin's report came before the commission with its recommendation for reinstatement, Commissioner Carl Zeitz delivered a tongue-lashing in which he made it clear that he believed the trio had not acted honorably. "Whether or not there was a policy and whether or not you knew it, you should have picked up the chip and turned it" over to someone in higher authority, Zeitz said. Then he voted with the other four commissioners to let them keep their licenses.

Later, Harrah's made every employee sign a letter saying found chips would be turned in. Months later, restored to her job, Pussehl still fumed at the thought of what had happened and at the hardships the state's action caused her. "It's unbelievable what they can do to you," Pussehl said. "They can try to destroy you."

Imperiale felt the case symbolized what was wrong with regulation. Casino owners sold hundreds of millions of dollars worth of bonds that any fool could see would never be paid back, and neither the commissioners nor the Division of Gaming Enforcement ever suggested there was anything dishonest in this. But little people like Pussehl, Friel and Carfagno made easy targets for the kind of overzealous enforcement that would polish the state's image as a tough regulator. "All my client did was point his finger at a chip on the floor. That's it. For that he lost a job that pays maybe sixty thousand dollars a year, he was out of work for eight months, and to reenter the industry he has had to go back to an entry-level job as a dealer at another casino," Imperiale said. "It's an outrage."

But there were much more ominous outrages involving children and the casinos.

19

Sweet Sixteen

At the edge of Harrah's casino in Atlantic City one game catches the eye, the Big Six wheel. Spinning constantly, the wheel exerts a hypnotic effect that draws people, an effect enhanced by dealers who invite passersby to step up and give their luck a try. When someone reaches into his wallet for a bill a knot of people often gather to watch the player lay his money atop $1, $5, $10 or $20 bills embedded in a table. If the wheel stops on the corresponding blade the bettor wins. Slim chance. While baccarat gives the house an advantage of slightly more than 1 percent, and in blackjack the advantage can be less than one half of 1 percent, the Big Six wheel gives the house a whopping 10 percent plus advantage.

Dan Chapman, like many people venturing onto a casino floor for the first time, was drawn to the Big Six wheel. But even this virgin gambler quickly realized the Big Six wheel was a sucker's game and moved on to the roulette table.

Only about one in fifty casino visitors plays roulette, not because they fear that the wheel is rigged, like the one in *Casablanca*, but because from the house's perspective the odds, while not so obese as the Big Six wheel's, are plenty fat. There are eighteen red numbers, eighteen black numbers, plus two green spaces (numbered 0 and 00). Bet red and there are twenty losing compartments the ball can fall into—the eighteen blacks plus two greens—but only eighteen red slots. That makes the odds twenty chances to lose and eighteen to win, which means the house enjoys a 5.3 percent advantage.

Still, Dan took a liking to roulette, which unlike blackjack and craps requires no skill, making it a perfect choice for novices. For most of one day in March 1989, he put down his wagers and watched the little white ball spin clockwise until it settled between two frets on the wheel, which spins counterclockwise. Because Dan bet steadily cocktail waitresses soon appeared providing drinks gratis, a courtesy which dulls the temptation to quit before the house advantage reduces a player's stake to zero.

When Dan finally went up to his room for the night he called room service for more drinks. As the night wore on Dan started feeling sick. He was unaccustomed to alcohol and the dizzy sensations overpowering his body made him so scared that he picked up the phone to call his mother.

Dan was fourteen years old. Casinos draw teenagers anxious to test the adult world the way a magnet in the sand attracts iron filings. Children roam freely at the Circus Circus casinos, which cater to families on a tight budget and feature trapeze acts and arcade games just off the casino floor. One cannot walk from the Circus Circus lobby in Las Vegas to the hotel towers without passing through the casino. And while discreet brass signs advise that those under twenty-one are not to linger, a glance down the long banks of slot machines will often turn up teenagers pulling the handles. Sometimes children in grade school can be seen trying their luck, often with a parent or older sibling standing at the next machine.

Although the casino industry maintains it wants to keep children out, the real problem is neither the young people who want to be grown up nor the casinos anxious to turn them into steady customers. The real problem is government. The regulations controlling every legal gambling hall in the United States—from Connecticut to Colorado, from Reno to Minnesota—actually encourage casino owners to let teenagers gamble. Neither the government nor the casinos have ever considered changing those rules, for reasons that will soon become clear.

On the boardwalks along the Jersey Shore, in suburban shopping malls ringing New York and Philadelphia, and in the parking lots of Las

Vegas hamburger stands teenagers readily pop open their wallets to show off their frequent-gambler cards from Harrah's, Caesars, Trump Plaza, Resorts and other gambling halls.

Debra Kim Cohen became the most infamous underage gambler in America in the eighties. Debra was just thirteen when she learned how to play at Resorts International in Atlantic City. Her grandmother brought her and neither the casino nor the inspectors assigned to the casino floor threw her out.

By sixteen Debra was a veteran at Caesars in Atlantic City. The pit bosses and floor persons watched the slim, five-foot, four-inch girl with dark hair carefully enough to rate her play, and thus her profit potential, but Caesars maintains it had no idea how young she was. Debra was a profitable piece of business, wagering thirty dollars a hand at the black-jack tables. Caesars plied her with comps: gourmet dinners of lobster and champagne, plus front-row seats for her and her teenage girlfriends at a Poynter Sisters show. When the Poynter Sisters rested their voices Debra invited her girlfriends to spend the night in her suite, another gift from Caesars. But the girls said their parents wanted them home, so Caesars sent them in a limousine.

When Debra's father first heard about her gambling he figured stopping it would be easy. But she had won big on her second casino visit and was hooked. She was now a compulsive gambler and, like many, a rebellious teen who would not listen to her father.

Cohen adopted a new strategy. He went to Caesars, told them his daughter's age and asked that they bar her. "They just laughed at me," he said.

The response infuriated Cohen, a veteran detective in the Atlantic City Police Department who, like most resort town cops, believed in cutting people a lot of slack, but not if they flouted their disregard for the law. Cohen hired an attorney, who drafted a letter putting Caesars and every other casino on notice that his daughter was well under the minimum age to gamble. The letter was sent registered mail, along with a current photograph of Debra.

"This is supposed to be the most highly regulated industry in America, so I figured that would put an end to it," Cohen said. It didn't.

Debra was soon a rated player not just at Caesars, but also at the Atlantis, Harrah's, Resorts and Trump Plaza. They all plied her with drinks and some gave her suites, too. Her habit was getting completely out of hand. Debra stole two thousand dollars, a wedding gift to her father and his second wife, and blew it at the tables. Her five-thousand-dollar college fund disappeared the same way.

Cohen went back to Caesars and begged them to bar his daughter. "I was told, 'It's your problem, don't bother us. We are sick of dealing with your problem.' "

Desperate, Cohen turned his daughter in to the Division of Gaming Enforcement. She was arrested and later pled guilty, receiving a five-hundred-dollar fine—suspended on the condition that she attend Gamblers Anonymous meetings—and a year's probation.

"What I did was wrong," Debra told the judge, "but the casinos weren't right, either." She said she never was asked about her age, never had to lie, and that lots of other kids were gambling and the casinos knew it.

Standing next to his daughter, Cohen said he was outraged that the casinos were not being prosecuted. Based on the industry's own figures it was turning away more than a quarter million underage gamblers a year at the doors and tossing another twenty-seven thousand a year—seventy-five a day—off the gambling floors.

Cohen suggested that the casinos got a much better deal from the government than bar owners, who were sometimes shut down for thirty days for serving liquor to minors, even minors who had produced expertly faked IDs. Debra and her friends got all the booze they wanted and so, it appeared, did thousands of other kids.

Since 1977, in response to growing public sentiment against youthful drinking, New Jersey has passed tougher laws requiring bar owners to check IDs and strengthening the principle that the bar is responsible for making sure an ID is valid. But not one of these reforms has been applied to the casinos.

No Atlantic City casino has ever had its liquor license suspended. Total fines for letting teens gamble, ten years after the first casino in town opened, totaled just fourteen thousand dollars. In Nevada it is the same story of lax enforcement.

Debra's case generated an outcry from the public, filling letters-to-the-editor pages with angry blasts at the casinos. Chuck Hardwick, a Republican lawmaker who was speaker of the New Jersey Assemb

181

and was about to run for governor, joined the criticism, calling for toughening the law punishing casinos that let juveniles gamble. Detective Cohen, figuring he had a powerful ally, called Hardwick's office. Cohen called and called and called. He wrote letters. Neither Hardwick nor his staff ever responded and no legislation was ever introduced to get tough on casinos that let children drink and gamble.

The outcry did force the enforcement division to file a complaint. At hearings on the violations Caesars and four other casinos said they were reluctant to challenge people at the casino entrance for fear of offending someone who was twenty-one or older. Caesars eventually paid a ten-thousand-dollar fine and made a ninety-thousand-dollar tax-deductible donation to compulsive gambling programs. The four other casinos were fined a total of eight thousand dollars and donated seventy-two thousand dollars.

At Caesars' 1988 license renewal the enforcement division brought up the Cohen case as well as illegal payments to selected high rollers and to travel agencies. Deputy Attorney General Mitchell A. Schwefel complained of a "continuing and disturbing pattern" of misconduct that, by the most charitable interpretation, demonstrated that Caesars "lacks sufficient and effective controls to ensure proper corporate behavior in a highly regulated industry."

The commission said it would not consider these matters, however, because they had not been fully adjudicated in the state's administrative hearing system.

Caesars lawyer Lloyd Levenson did admit the casino had a problem obeying the law. "Compliance has to come," Levenson said, or else its license might be in jeopardy. To stop lawless behavior, Caesars had a solution. Levenson said Caesars was thinking about hiring a compliance officer who would tell the casino's executives if their behavior was improper. Then Levenson revealed Caesars' true view by saying this job would probably go to a law school student.

The commissioners, however, were satisfied that Caesars had confessed its sins, even if it did not admit to any, and voted unanimously to renew the lucrative gaming license.

During the time when Debra's case focused public attention on the problem hordes of other teenagers, including Joseph Bevan, continued wagering. He gambled at Harrah's, Resorts, Showboat and Trump Cas-

182

tle enough to have his play rated ninety times. The casinos weighed his play and decided how much to give him in the way of booze, meals and other perks, but none of them checked his age. In the fierce competition for his business Bevan asked for credit, and on April 15, 1989, a day when millions of Americans were laboring over their tax returns, Harrah's gave Bevan a twenty-five-hundred-dollar line of credit. Only after Bevan failed to pay a marker did Harrah's dig deeply enough to find out that he was only nineteen. Bevan was arrested for underage gambling and indicted because the check he wrote to pay his marker bounced.

Maurice Childs drove up from the District of Columbia frequently and gambled until April 30, 1989. That night he hit a fifty-thousand-dollar slot jackpot. Resorts asked Childs for identification because it must report transactions of ten thousand dollars or more to the federal government. Childs was only nineteen, so he was arrested for underage gambling.

Resorts kept the jackpot, and therein lies the problem. In New Jersey, Nevada and the ten other states where casinos are legal, so long as kids are losing money the casinos have no incentive to throw them out. And if they win the casinos suddenly take a keen interest in their age because if the player cannot prove he or she is twenty-one then the casino gets to keep the money.

Detective Cohen later sued Caesars, claiming its actions had worsened his high blood pressure and aggravated an ulcer. His real intent was to get someone to tell Caesars that its conduct was not only wrong, but outrageous.

The trial was held before Judge John G. Himmelberger, who had lectured Bob Signore for having the temerity to sue Trump Castle because it played roulette by a different set of rules than it handed out to novice gamblers. Cohen asked for a two-week delay, saying he had had trouble finding a lawyer without a conflict of interest because every one he approached did some work for the casinos. The day before the court appearance, one finally agreed to take the case, but he needed time to prepare. Himmelberger refused the request, forcing Cohen to act as his own counsel.

Attorney Levenson said Caesars was not at fault for Cohen's ills and, besides, he told the jury, why wasn't Cohen suing every casino where

183

his daughter played? Levenson also argued that to win Cohen must prove his daughter suffered a physical harm.

After hearing Cohen's case Himmelberger delivered another lecture, focusing this time on Cohen's claim that Caesars laughed when he asked them to obey the law and keep his underage daughter out. "Are we so thin-skinned these days that if someone laughs at you, it causes us severe emotional distress?" Himmelberger asked. He threw the case out.

The dismissed jurors hung around the modern brick courthouse in Atlantic City to meet Cohen. They told him they admired him for what he had done and one of them added that it was a good thing for Caesars that Himmelberger dismissed the case because they were going to award him money to teach Caesars a lesson.

"I had hoped the judge would do something to make the casinos protect young people, to make them stop thumbing their nose at the law," Cohen said.

Five months later, on December 12, 1990, Debra Kim Cohen got off work and started playing blackjack at Trump Plaza. She was twenty, still too young to gamble in a casino, although under New Jersey law she was old enough to be a cocktail waitress. You can't legally drink in New Jersey until you are twenty-one, but you can serve liquor at age eighteen. At eighteen you can also gamble with the state by playing the lottery.

Debra had been there for five or six hours when her boyfriend, bartender Jack O'Brick, got off work and came looking for her. He asked Debra to leave, but she wouldn't quit playing, so O'Brick told Regina Welch, who was supervising the blackjack tables, that the most notorious underage gambler in town, the girl whose case made such a ruckus on TV, was wagering. Welch did nothing, she later testified, because she claimed she could not see anyone fitting the description O'Brick gave her. O'Brick's story was a bit different. He said security showed him the door.

But O'Brick came back, told a Casino Control Commission inspector about the violation, and Debra was arrested.

No one, not even Detective Cohen, believes every underage gambler can be kept out. The Atlantic City casinos created public service announcements warning teens that they can be arrested for gambling. But

184

Akio Kashiwagi, the boldest gambler in the world, wagered $14 million an hour for days at a time in casinos from Australia to Atlantic City. But Kashiwagi played games away from the table, too. He owed at least ₵10 million in credit, known as markers, to one of Donald Trump's casinos, to the Las Vegas Hilton and to other gambling halls at the time he was hacked to death with a samurai sword at his Kashiwagi Palace near Mount Fuji in 1992.

Kyodo Photo Service

Jess Marcum dreamed up the "freeze-out" game to lure Kashiwagi back to Trump Plaza after he had won more than $6 million there. Marcum, a physicist who helped invent radar, was a lonely atheist in the temples of chance because he did not believe in Lady Luck. He had endeared himself to casino owners by inventing a lucrative new bet, one he admired Kashiwagi for being too smart to make.

Courtesy of Lois Marcum

Benjamin "Bugsy" Siegel invented modern Las Vegas when he built the Flamingo gambling resort as World War II ended. The opening was a disaster, and Siegel was soon shot to death at the Beverly Hills home of his mistress, Virginia Hill, whom he called the Flamingo. Mobsters ran Nevada gambling for the next three decades, but today the Flamingo is owned by Hilton Hotel Corporation, which, along with other publicly traded companies, dominates the business. Below is the Flamingo as it looked in 1944, and as it appears today.

Las Vegas News Bureau

Courtesy of the Flamingo Hilton

Lester "Benny" Binion ran illegal casinos in Dallas before joining the postwar migration of gamblers to Nevada, driving west in a Cadillac with suitcases of cash. One regulator opposed giving Binion a casino license because he had killed two men, but state tax commissioners roared with laughter as Binion told the tale. In his eighties he bragged, "I'm still able to do my own killings."

Above right: William Fisk Harrah was the pioneer who changed gambling forever by catering to customers with curtains and carpets and by not allowing skimming of casino winnings. Harrah won Securities and Exchange Commission approval to sell stock even though he had charged the cost of hookers for high rollers to a "customer satisfaction refund" account.

Left: Michael D. Rose steered the Holiday Corporation into gambling when it bought Harrah's in 1980, causing Holiday's president and two directors to resign. Rose later sold the namesake motel chain to create a gambling concern called the Promus Companies.

Donna Connor

Al Glasgow, the wit of Atlantic City, used to drink mob lawyers under the table before becoming one of Donald Trump's most trusted advisers. When Glasgow heard that Kashiwagi had been murdered, he quipped, "See what happens when you don't pay your markers?"

Donald Trump put his then wife Ivana in charge of his Trump Castle casino even though she had no management experience. He blew a fortune having Ivana compete for high rollers against his own Trump Plaza casino while ignoring Harrah's next door, which earned a million dollars a week in profits. To attract high-stakes play to the Castle, Trump offered rides on the world's sixth-largest yacht, the *Trump Princess,* but its $861,000 monthly cost just drained money.

Steve Hyde was the Mormon accountant who briefly made Trump Plaza the high-roller heaven his boss wanted. Ivana nearly forced Hyde out. After Hyde was killed in an October 1989 helicopter crash, the Trump casinos plunged into disarray and all three ended up in bankruptcy proceedings.

Michael Milken and his imitators raised money for the casinos on a scale the mob never could. His early casino deals made everyone rich, but the Atlantis casino and Merv Griffin's Resorts were financed with such bad junk that they hurtled toward bankruptcy. Milken pleaded guilty to six felonies, one related to Steve Wynn's Golden Nugget casino company, and is now serving a ten-year sentence at a Club Fed in California.

Wide World Photo

Philadelphia Inquirer/*Gerald S. Williams*

Merv Griffin and his companion, Eva Gabor, triumphantly ride a hundred feet across the Atlantic City Boardwalk on November 16, 1988, the day he bought Resorts from Trump in Mike Milken's last big junk-bond deal. Griffin's takeover began as a stock manipulation, one of many run out of The Griffin Company president's office. Griffin said that he was unaware a reputed mob associate had a desk in the president's office at The Griffin Company.

ACQUISITION OF RII BY THE GRIFFIN COMPANY

FLOW OF BONDS

Griffin's takeover of Resorts from Donald Trump was the looniest casino
junk-bond deal of them all, involving more than one billion borrowed
dollars. This chart shows the complicated flow of money needed to complete
Griffin's side of the deal and preserve various tax breaks.

Farayala Janna received millions in credit at casinos in Atlantic City, Nevada and the Caribbean before he welshed on debts and bombs exploded outside his home and business in Colombia. Janna controlled the second-largest known bank account of the Medellin cartel, but when regulators were shown evidence of how an Atlantic City casino company helped him launder drug dollars, they did nothing. Janna got out of one debt by having a Colombian soccer team wear jerseys promoting the Aruba Concorde Hotel's casino.

El Tiempo

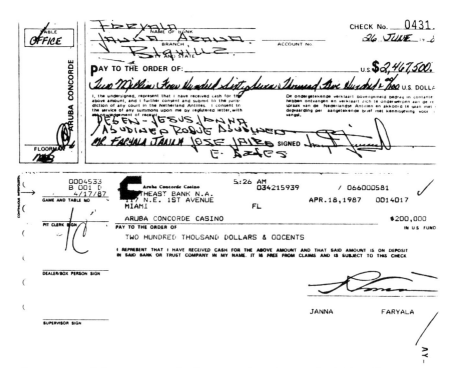

Janna signed this counter check, or marker, for nearly $2.5 million to replace earlier markers he and his pals had signed. The other markers were then destroyed. This marker is worthless because Janna wrote his name and hometown of Barranquilla where the name of his bank, its branch and his account number belong. Pratt Hotel executives accepted this marker a month after they suspended Janna's $2 million credit line at the Atlantic City Sands casino.

Bob Signore argues his case that Trump Castle cheated him because its gaming guide was riddled with errors. New Jersey regulators knew about the mistakes, which cost Signore eight hundred dollars, but instead of ordering them fixed, let the Castle continue using them, then falsely told Signore the brochures had been corrected. Signore sued Trump Castle for fraud. The judge who threw the case out lectured him for having the temerity to question the integrity of casino regulation in New Jersey.

Philadelphia Inquirer/*Marty O'Grady*

Press of Atlantic City/ *Scott Stetzer*

Debra Kim Cohen, shown here in court when she was almost twenty, started gambling in Atlantic City casinos when she was thirteen years old. Her father, Police Detective Leonard Cohen, pleaded with casinos to stop giving his daughter liquor, limousine rides and suites, because she was underage. "They just laughed at me," he said.

Stephen Cooper, whose firm advised the Misfortune 500 on coping with creditors, testified that the Atlantis Casino Hotel would emerge from bankruptcy proceedings to become a robust Boardwalk competitor. It went bust a year later.

Wide World Photo

Deputy Attorney General David Arrajj grilled Cooper about the $3.7 million fee his firm was paid by the Atlantis's corporate parent while Atlantis creditors received three cents on the dollar. Arrajj was one of the few regulators left with any sense of the bulldog a decade after gambling began in New Jersey with the promise that casinos would be "strictly regulated."

Philadelphia Inquirer/Michael Bryant

Jeanne Hood fought casino regulators' efforts to shut down the Atlantis Casino Hotel, which, like its mythic namesake, was sinking beneath a rising tide of red ink. Hood enraged Atlantis workers when she refused to ask a bankruptcy judge for permission to pay a scheduled raise worth a quarter million dollars, then arranged a quarter-million-dollar bonus for herself.

Wide World Photo

New Jersey Casino Control Commission Chairman Walter N. "Bud" Read played a game of regulatory poker with the renegade Atlantis and Hood, but in the end succeeded in shutting the casino down. Casino executives thought Read did not approve of gambling, but he voted for nearly all of their financial deals and did not stop Donald Trump's feigned raids until all but two competitors were weakened by them.

Las Vegas News Bureau

Steve Wynn bragged that he was Michael Milken's first big customer, and even after Milken went to jail he could not bring himself to say a critical word about the man who made him rich enough to have his own DC-9 jet. Wynn gave high rollers bragging rights by personally handing out keys to suites.

Jack Bona was never charged with a crime, but the unsuccessful casino developer spent nearly two years in the Atlantic County jail in a dispute with Wynn over a piece of land. Wynn's lawyers claimed Bona hid $30 million and had a secret life flying into the ayatollah's Iran, but the records they relied on turned out to show little more than Thrifty car rentals that earned Bona extra frequent-flier miles. He is shown on the Boardwalk on the day after his release.

Philadelphia Inquirer/*Mark Stein*

Courtesy of Mirage Resorts

Wynn's Mirage casino on the Strip is to casinos in the nineties as Disneyland was to amusement parks in the fifties. It features a man-made volcano, Siberian tigers, a seaquarium where dolphins frolic and, lest anyone forget its elemental purpose, a giant aquarium behind the registration desk where sharks lurk.

Philadelphia Daily News/*Michael Mercanti*

Donald Trump talks at Merv Griffin in April 1990 during the grand opening of the Taj Mahal casino, which lacked a swimming pool and other amenities because Trump was on the edge of financial collapse and ignored memos warning about cost overruns.

Trump outside the Taj, which cost a billion dollars but lacked any of the pizzazz that drew high rollers from around the world to Wynn's Mirage, which cost $630 million.

Philadelphia Daily News/*Wayne Faircloth*

Philadelphia Inquirer/*Akira Suwa*

Mitzi Briggs once had $44 million, but she was forced to work as a hostess at the Carving Cart restaurant after she bought part ownership of the Tropicana in Las Vegas. First the Kansas City mob skimmed the winnings. Then Ramada bought the property, but refused to make the payments. A judge found Ramada displayed "corporate arrogance" and ordered Ramada to pay $35 million, but by then Briggs was so broke she had sold her interst in the lawsuit to the man shown next to her, Ed Doumani.

Courtesy of Steamboat Casino Cruises

Actor Howard Keel, right, who played the gambler in the 1951 film *Show Boat*, became the first American to legally bet on a riverboat when the *Diamond Lady* opened at dawn on April Fools' Day in 1991. Vanna White and owner Bernard Goldstein cut the ribbon while a dime store Mark Twain held a microphone. Davenport, Iowa, politicians who had fought riverboat casinos all either retired or were voted out of office.

Marvin B. Roffman accurately predicted that the Taj Mahal would be in bankruptcy soon after it opened. Robert Trump threw him off the property, and Donald Trump not only demanded he recant but tried to edit his forced letter of apology. Unable to tell a lie, Roffman refused and was fired by the Janney Montgomery Scott securities brokerage. Janney and Trump both later paid him big settlements.

Fred Trump had his lawyer buy $3.5 million worth of chips so his son Donald could make the December 1990 mortgage bond interest payment on Trump Castle. The director of New Jersey's Division of Gaming Enforcement was tipped in advance about the loan but kept it to himself.

New Jersey News Photo

Casino Control Commissioner Valerie Armstrong voted against renewing Trump's casino license once, saying he lacked integrity. Later she asked if the Division of Gaming Enforcement knew about Fred Trump's loan in advance and was told it did not. She complained about a double standard in regulation that benefited Trump, but cast the crucial vote in 1990 to renew his license.

Commissioner W. David Waters Jr. called the enforcement division's handling of the illegal loan "an outrage" and complained that "around here integrity has come to mean you haven't been convicted of a felony." When his term expired he was not reappointed to the Casino Control Commission.

Steven P. Perskie sponsored the Casino Control Act as a New Jersey legislator in 1977. But after he became chairman of the Casino Control Commission in 1990, he refused to enforce its provisions against Donald Trump and voted to renew his license even though Trump did not meet the act's financial stability requirements.

the financial incentives that encourage the casinos to let teens gamble remain.

It would be easy to create powerful incentives for casinos to challenge youthful patrons. Every time an underage gambler is caught on the casino floor, gambling or not, Cohen favors a one-thousand-dollar fine, believing that sum is high enough to encourage diligence at the entrance. Repeat offenses should result in progressively larger fines with a casino that behaves as Trump Plaza did when it threw out O'Brick facing a fine of up to $1 million and a place that acts as Caesars did, laughing at a parent while continuing to give comps to a juvenile, losing its license.

Another simple reform would also cut down on teen gambling and drinking in casinos. At present a casino wins whether a teen gambler wins or loses. Instead, when an underage gambler loses, the state could seize the money, including any previous losses shown by player-rating records. Likewise, when a juvenile wins, the state could seize the money instead of giving it back to the casino, as happened at Resorts.

Taking the profit out of underage gambling by seizing the money casinos now pocket is an idea that Caesars and other casinos oppose. This reform has never been considered by the regulators.

While casinos could ply teenagers with liquor and engage in a host of financial abuses with little or no punishment, there was one thing that the regulators could not abide. That was the prospect of a casino with so many debts that it might not pay off gamblers who made winning bets.

20

A Rising Tide of Red Ink

Stephen Cooper fidgeted in the witness chair as he waited for the first question from David Arrajj, a portly, wisecracking deputy attorney general who was one of the few people left in the entire New Jersey casino control system with a bit of bulldog in him. Cooper, a short, balding man who had stumbled on his way to the witness chair, tugged at his brown suit, rubbed one tasseled loafer against the other and gnawed on an empty Styrofoam coffee cup.

Cooper is a work-out specialist, one of the leading consultants to the Misfortune 500. When Eastern Airlines, Allegheny International, retailing giant Campeau and other companies hooked on junk bonds lacked enough cash to pay their bills they paid big fees to Zolfo Cooper & Company of Manhattan and Red Bank, New Jersey, for advice on holding off creditors while they worked out their problems.

This April morning in 1989 Cooper's client was the Elsinore Corporation, owner of the Atlantis Casino Hotel in Atlantic City, which in late 1985 took refuge from its creditors in U.S. Bankruptcy Court, where it welshed on debts to just about everyone it owed except Zolfo Cooper. Some creditors, like Hugh Hefner's Playboy empire, which had been partners in the casino until he was denied a gaming license, ended up

186

with nothing. Many vendors never saw more than three cents on each dollar the Atlantis owed them. But while the Atlantis failed to pay nearly $2 million in Atlantic City property taxes, money that had to be made up by raising the taxes paid by every other property owner in town, Zolfo Cooper was paid every penny it billed because no one was more essential to keeping the Atlantis in business than Steve Cooper.

One year before, sitting in that same plain wooden chair in the spacious plain modern room where the Casino Control Commission met a few miles outside Trenton, Cooper had provided the crucial expert testimony needed to renew the Atlantis license for another twelve months. He said the Atlantis was about to emerge from bankruptcy proceedings, which it did in September, and with its troubles behind it would become a robust competitor in the Boardwalk jungle. A new $7 million line of credit would insure that the Atlantis could make it through slow periods, such as the long winter months and, his financial projections showed, finances would improve steadily.

But even as Cooper testified in 1988 the casino's pile of unpaid bills was mounting. In the coming year it would grow from $643,000 to more than $4.5 million. By the time Cooper again took the witness chair it was easy to see why he might fidget at the prospect of questions about what he had said with such certainty a year before. Now, as Cooper sat waiting for Arrajj's first question, the Atlantis was losing money at the rate of more than five thousand dollars each hour the casino remained open.

Arrajj's job was to shut down the Atlantis. Standing outside the hearing room, a cigarette affixed to his right hand like an ashen-tipped sixth digit, he chortled at the prospect of grilling Cooper. There won't be any fantasies passed off as expert testimony today, Arrajj cracked. Grinning, Arrajj marched into the hearing room to confront the nervously twitching Cooper.

"Just how much money had the Atlantis paid Zolfo Cooper?" Arrajj asked.

"I don't know, off the top of my head," Cooper answered, slipping his index finger inside his short collar and running it around his neck.

"Ballpark?"

"I don't know, off the top of my head," Cooper repeated.

"Does $3.7 million sound right?" Arrajj asked.

"I could verify that," Cooper said, hunching his shoulders and adjusting his position in his chair, "but I don't choose to speculate."

Arrajj let the issue drop, moving on to other questions about the Atlantis. But when Atlantis attorney David M. Satz, Jr., the former U.S. Attorney in Newark, got his turn he tried to put a better face on the issue instead of leaving it alone.

Please tell the commissioners, Satz said, about all the work Zolfo Cooper performed. Cooper explained that for three years a half dozen people, the equivalent of two or three people full-time, were used to "evaluate operations, evaluate cash needs, evaluate marketing, evaluate staffing and on and on." Satz did not ask for more details, but even these vague answers revealed that each full-time consultant cost four hundred to six hundred thousand dollars per year at a casino that could not pay its bills for food, liquor and electricity or meet its mortgage.

Sensing an opportunity to score more points, Arrajj jumped up. Just how much did these well-paid experts know about the business that paid them so well, he asked. What Arrajj's grilling dragged from Cooper could be summed up in two words: not much. Over and over Cooper had to say he just was not familiar with an issue or had only scanned a contract and could not answer questions about it or that he was not familiar with a document at all.

Arrajj tried, but failed, to extract an admission that Zolfo Cooper's main advice came down to this: if you lack cash to pay your bills, write the checks but don't mail them immediately.

Bruce McKee had been doing just that for months. McKee was the Atlantis' chief financial officer, the lowest paid in town even though he had by far the toughest job juggling bills his casino could not pay. McKee performed miracles from an office in the softly lit executive suite until Cooper came along. Cooper banished McKee to a distant space where anonymous clerks stamped invoices and added up columns of numbers. It would be good for morale, good for the troops to know the top people are with them, McKee remembered Cooper telling him as he was ushered out of his own office. Then Cooper took it over.

But Cooper was not the only one aboard the slowly sinking Atlantis who rearranged deck chairs and stuffed his wallet. And Arrajj would have no easy task shutting the Atlantis down, even if he was dealing with corporate renegades who were challenging the state's authority

188

and were prepared to eviscerate the Casino Control Act if it would keep them in business for one more summer gambling season.

It is one thing for a company to report a net loss when the red ink is for accounting charges such as depreciation. It is quite another when a business loses hard cash. In 1988, the Atlantis lost $76.6 million, mostly because it wrote down the value of its building by half. But it also had negative cash flow. A casino should be a cash-rich enterprise, yet nearly $10 million had flowed out of the Atlantis.

Richard LaVasseur, vice president for marketing at Elsinore's Four Queens in Las Vegas, came back to Atlantic City and was amazed at the lack of promotions. In Las Vegas casinos gave away special gaming chips to lure players, chips that could not be used at any other casino. LaVasseur wanted a similar plan at the Atlantis. Conventional wisdom held that the Casino Control Commission was so rigid that it would never allow specialty chips, that casinos had to give patrons coins or scrip good for meals and drinks or forget it. The coin giveaways were costly. Atlantic City gambling halls gave $170 million in quarters in 1988, enough to pave one lane of the Garden State Parkway for seventy-four miles, more than half the way to New York. LaVasseur wanted to stop people from collecting their fifteen or twenty dollars in quarters at the Atlantis and then walking out the door to another casino.

Harry Jay Levin, the Atlantis general counsel, figured out a way around the conventional wisdom. An affable, bearded thirty-four-year-old trademark specialist who favored three-piece suits that hung like tents when he chain-smoked and threatened to burst their buttons when he quit, Levin was a little appreciated strength at the Atlantis, as he would be later at Donald Trump's Taj Mahal.

Levin had made himself an outsider the day he was hired by going through the files, as was his duty, and discovering that four Atlantis executives were not properly licensed. Levin immediately went to see Jeanne Hood, who had taken over as Elsinore president.

"I'm reporting this to the Division of Gaming Enforcement immediately," Levin told her. Hood protested, but Levin said prompt disclosure would prevent a disaster if the regulators discovered the problems on their own. He vowed to work everything out with the regulators. Levin did, but Hood never trusted him with any corporate secrets or with any of the personal financial and historic details she had to disclose to casino regulators to qualify for her license.

Hood did press Levin to move ahead with LaVasseur's tokens plan. "We have to bring in more business without spending more money," she said. Levin figured that the Atlantis could offer tokens for its slot machines provided that the tokens went into a separate hopper and that any winnings were paid in cash. He sold the idea to the casino commission staff, who liked and trusted him, and eventually the commission adopted the plan. Levin expected Atlantis marketing would implement the "hot spots" as one part of a marketing scheme, but he was wrong. Hot spots *were* the marketing plan.

On July 4, 1988, the Atlantis declared its independence from coin giveaways. Players who wanted quarters could get sixty of them by riding a bus to Caesars, Trump Plaza, Showboat and the other casinos. Players who wanted to watch the reels spin twice as long could ride a bus to the Atlantis and get 120 tokens. Players could also get half tokens and half scrip, a deal the sharp players quickly recognized as the most lucrative in town because they could play the slots and get a free meal instead of choosing one or the other from the competition.

Hot spots drew lots of people like Louise Palidori, who picked up a bus on the corner near her Philadelphia home almost every morning for a trip to Atlantic City. "Now I'll get a hundred and twenty tokens instead of sixty quarters and I can play longer before my money runs out," she said while boarding a Greyhound bus for home one windy afternoon. That day, she said, she had not played with a single coin of her own. Palidori was one of many retirees who came almost daily, playing with the casino's money until it ran out and then sunning themselves on the Boardwalk until their buses left. For these customers, hot spots were a godsend.

Steady gamblers who understood the numbers realized that hot spots could be a nice little way to get the Atlantis to subsidize them. Because the Atlantis' quarter machines paid back almost 90 cents on the dollar, a player theoretically could put in 120 tokens, win back 108 quarters and walk out the door with $27. That meant that after playing with the plastic money the player would still have as much money as the other casinos offered in coin, $15, plus an extra $12.

Robert Latimer, a jovial enforcement division agent who loved to ferret out nuggets of truth hidden among the mountains of computer printouts and ledger sheets the casinos kept, studied how well hot spots worked to conserve cash and bring in new business. His digging showed that plenty of players must have done just that. The casino commissioners later adopted Latimer's findings as fact: hot spots brought in $1 million of new business at a cost of $2 million.

The only hope remaining for the Atlantis was that an end to the bankruptcy proceedings in fall 1988 would remove doubt in gamblers' minds about whether they would get paid their winnings. It did not. And Hood's claims that she had slashed costs also appeared hollow when Latimer's digging showed that the Atlantis spent almost $22.94 on each bus patron in 1988, up from $17.41 the year before.

Arrajj knew what had to be done and he gathered up the facts to get permission to, for the first time, shut a casino down. As spring approached, Peter N. Perretti, Jr., New Jersey's attorney general, announced that he wanted the Atlantis put out of business. Cash was flowing out of the place at the rate of twenty-seven thousand dollars per day. Absent a fresh infusion of cash from its owners, Perretti declared, "the Atlantis cannot meet the financial stability, integrity and responsibility requirements of the Casino Control Act."

Perretti's recommendation launched a comic show that belied the frequent boast by New Jersey officials that they ran the most highly regulated industry the world had ever seen. On a cold day in March the Casino Control Commission began license renewal hearings that effectively showed how ill-prepared it was to control a casino, especially one intent on being a renegade.

Satz, the former U.S. Attorney who represented the Atlantis, began by asking the state for a six-month license. Never mind that the Casino Control Act said a license "shall" be for two years, Satz wanted a license until the end of the summer gambling season. A shutdown then would mean that Elsinore could try to wring some profits from the casino, but it would also mean putting sixteen hundred people on the streets just as the job market began entering the winter freeze.

Satz said he was confident the Atlantis could meet the Casino Control Act's financial stability test, although he offered a curious new twist to the existing definition of stability under which bills should be paid as they came due. "Given the ability to defer payments to professionals and the bondholders, we will continue to be stable for a six-month period," he said.

His comments foreshadowed how three other debt-ridden and cash-starved casino owners—Donald Trump, Merv Griffin and Bally Manufacturing—would deal with financial instability. In essence Satz was proposing the equivalent of Chapter 11 protection from bills coming due by negotiation with creditors, a sort of privatizing of bankruptcy proceedings.

The commission wouldn't buy it. On a 4 to 1 vote the commissioners rejected the six-month license idea and then they adjourned so the Atlantis could run to Bankruptcy Court for relief. Bud Read, the retired real estate lawyer who chaired the commission, knew he was playing a game of poker, waiting to see who would bluff best and who would fold. Elsinore knew it had to shut down the Atlantis at some point, Read figured, but he feared that the casino would persuade Bankruptcy Judge Rosemary Gambardella that regulators were capricious and, asserting federal supremacy, she would order the Atlantis casino license renewed.

What Read did not know was that Elsinore had not figured out what to do. Hood failed one day even to show up for the hearings. Satz said she was "exploring options." Hood never did give Satz and Harry Levin a clear path to follow.

Chairman Read could have ended the entire proceedings on the first day. The issue Read decided not to use then was Drexel's investment in Elsinore. The brokerage owned 5 percent of Elsinore's stock and 9 percent of its bonds, enough to force Drexel to be licensed. But in February the commission had banned Drexel because it had admitted to six felony charges, one of them involving Golden Nugget. Elsinore had done nothing to purge Drexel. At least for the moment, Read set this critical issue aside.

The hearings soon devolved into a three-sided game among the commissioners, the Atlantis and the enforcement division, who made up the rules as they moved along. The only firm—though unspoken—rule of this game was that no inquiry would be made into how the regulators had conducted themselves in the past, into the wisdom of past commission actions approving the Playboy note, the high-interest Drexel bonds, the low-interest loan to the Pritzkers, the failure to investigate Playboy's claims of fraud and that Elsinore upstreamed cash to take care of the

Pritzker interests at the expense of everyone else. It was a rule that all three parties would adhere to strictly, even when a major failing by the regulators, who had been unaware of two secret casino deals by the Pritzkers, made front-page news later in the hearings.

Suddenly, into this regulatory circus rode Ernest English, who had once sparred a few rounds with Mike Tyson and who had made a name for himself a few months earlier when, tired of pushing a wicker rolling chair along the Boardwalk to earn his daily bread, he launched a fleet of golf carts to ferry folks. He found a partner, who put up the money to secure all one hundred authorized permits for motorized rolling chairs —the ordinance said nothing of wicker, so modified golf carts seemed to fit the law—and within weeks the pair had collected a half million dollars in fares. Soon English was fantasizing in public about enclosing the Boardwalk in a giant plastic bubble, a $40 million dream supported only by hot air. But the story made headlines coast-to-coast, emboldening English.

During the second week of the Atlantis hearings English announced he would buy the Atlantis. Chairman Read gave him an audience. English arrived in a limousine that day, though he often rode a New Jersey Transit bus to attend Atlantis hearings. Later he would be evicted from a motel for not paying his rent. But in the midst of the Atlantis follies, that the state's chief casino regulator would take time to grant him an audience seemed sensible, a sideshow to the circus in the hearing room.

Meanwhile, Latimer, the numbers cop, dug up more damaging information. The Atlantis was required to keep $3 million in the bank. But to make sure it had enough cash on hand to pay winning gamblers over Presidents' Day weekend, traditionally one of the year's busiest, it had dipped into this reserve for three quarters of a million dollars. Latimer also came up with an internal document showing $4.5 million in bills coming due in April, while the casino had enough cash to pay only half that amount.

The coming weekend marked April Fool's Day. It was not a good time for the Atlantis, which drew too few fools to its tables to cover the coming week's bills. On Monday morning the Atlantis, which instead of making money had become a cash eater so voracious that it was devouring more than twenty-four dollars each minute it remained open, gobbled up the last scraps of credit in its larder. Hardly six months after it had emerged from Bankruptcy Court with a fresh start, the Atlantis had consumed the entire $7 million credit line that Cooper testified was designed to take it through the winter and any slow summer weekends. And the start of the summer gambling season was still two months away.

When the hearings resumed in Lawrenceville—with Hood back in town, but still without a plan—Arrajj asked her what had happened.

McKee had prepared a slip requesting the last $117,000 and Hood said she signed it.

"What was the money used for?"

"No particular reason," Hood said.

Arrajj then began picking away at Hood's credibility as he had earlier with Cooper's. Like Cooper, she appeared to know little about her own company. Again and again Hood could not answer basic questions about finances and contracts, once saying she would need "a refresher course" to understand the tax-sale arrangement that resulted in Elsinore loaning the Pritzkers $20 million at about half the interest rate it paid for the money. She called out to advisers for help with details and once said Harry Levin could answer a question for her. Read put a stop to this, saying Levin had not been sworn in as a witness. Levin, who had not said a word, shrugged and smiled for the audience.

Satz, the Atlantis' own attorney, unwittingly extracted the most damaging testimony. He asked his client about how things appeared when she took over the Atlantis, just before it filed bankruptcy in November 1985. Hood said she knew the popular belief among casino executives was that the Playboy never had a chance, that its three-tiered casino was inefficient and unattractive, that it lacked adequate parking and that the massive blank walls on Florida Avenue made it hard to find. But she said when she arrived at the Atlantis she ignored all that.

"I have a certain persistence, and I wasn't going to believe that had to be so," Hood said. "I was going to try and make it at least marginally profitable until we could resolve the reorganization, restructure the corporation and sell the property. . . . I now have concluded . . . that all those flaws have an extreme effect on how we conduct the business there and the profitability of the company."

She also conceded that the Atlantis had no hope of proving financial stability for two years. "But I feel very confident going through September 30," she told Commissioner E. Kenneth Burdge.

Read concluded he had what he needed to establish that her testimony the year before, when Hood and Cooper said the Atlantis was poised to earn substantial profits, consisted of only wishful thinking and that Hood had demonstrated a disregard for facts. He set a vote on the license for later in the week and adjourned.

The next day Marvin E. Jacob struck back. Jacob was a stout New York bankruptcy lawyer, a leading member of what some called the vulture bar, and he regarded himself as the supreme expert on debtors in possession.

Jacob arranged a hearing in Camden, before Judge Gambardella, a hearing that dragged on late into the night as he expounded on his view of her powers to disregard the casino commission. Jacob said it was obvious what the commissioners were up to in Lawrenceville. They planned to deny renewal, to name a conservator and to take title to the Atlantis. But that would make the Atlantis bonds due immediately and neither the Atlantis nor Elsinore had that kind of cash, so chaos would reign.

Jacob slicked his black hair back as severely as he shaped the arguments he put forward. Like his suit and shirt everything was black and white with no room for shades of gray. His voice boomed as he attacked the casino commissioners and Arrajj as connivers, his tone leaving no doubt they were unworthy of his contempt.

While Jacob worked for Elsinore, he seldom talked of its interests. He never focused on Elsinore's unconditional guarantees to pay some Atlantis obligations, and he said nothing about Hood's real fear that Elsinore's board could be subjected to shareholder lawsuits. Instead Jacob spoke of the poor, forlorn creditors, especially Michael Milken's junk bond addicts, whose interests, he declared, were blithely ignored by the casino regulators.

Jacob also produced an affidavit from Leonard C. Tranchitela, an Atlantis vice president, who testified that if a conservator were named "there would be employee vandalism." Employees would suddenly become thieves, the affidavit said, and "anything movable would be subject to the risk of being stolen" by employees with no loyalty to the conservator and, evidently, their conscience.

But the real problem, Jacob argued, was the lack of integrity shown by the regulators. He charged that they did their devious work "by ambush."

John Zimmerman, the commission's deputy general counsel, who rarely appeared in court, took the podium and in a voice so quiet attorneys cupped hands to their ears, defended the commission. He appeared personally wounded by the ambush remark, saying that if anyone engaged in ambushes it was the Atlantis. After all, the Atlantis knew for months what issues it would face in licensing hearings yet arrived with no plan and then put forth at least three radically different proposals.

Arrajj, ever the scrapper, was not so polite when he took up the issue of whether a casino license had to be for two years. He said Jacob had lied when he told the court that the state wanted to interpret the mandatory word "shall" in the Casino Control Act as the permissive word "may." Then Arrajj stuck the knife in. While Jacob was professing concern for the wounded bondholders, Arrajj said, one Atlantis proposal anticipated skipping a looming May 1 interest payment to bondholders —a payment Gambardella had earlier ordered in approving the Atlantis reorganization plan.

Gambardella rejected Jacob's request to bar the casino commission from voting on license renewal. But then she joined the game of regulatory chicken, setting a hearing for the following week, after the commission's vote. The lawyers all went home for a night's sleep and a day's rest.

Friday morning Bud Read was ready. He had drafted a twenty-one-page opinion savaging Atlantis management for incompetency and unfounded testimony to justify its previous license renewals. He challenged its integrity for temporarily moving three quarters of a million dollars out of its restricted bank account. The plastic tokens, "the latest in a series of failed marketing strategies," should have been quickly dumped and the blind adherence to them reflected poorly on management's abilities, he said. The rest of the commission went along, with Frank J. (Pat) Dodd, the former state senate president whose declared interest was to champion casino interests, casting his vote reluctantly. Then Read moved to appoint a conservator, prompting hours of debate that ended at sunset with a 4 to 1 vote of approval. Dodd dissented.

196

In the audience watching all this was Nick Ribis, Donald Trump's gaming lawyer. Trump was not the only outsider interested in the Atlantis. Golden Nugget chairman Stephen Wynn flew into Atlantic City aboard his private jet—a DC-9 like Hefner's—to look over the Atlantis. The two casino moguls had very different ideas in mind. Trump wanted beds, Wynn wanted bets.

The nearest casino to the Atlantis is Trump Plaza, three hundred paces up the Boardwalk. At the time Trump Plaza was the busiest casino in town and its hotel often had to turn away serious gamblers, many of whom had switched after Wynn sold the Atlantic City Golden Nugget in 1987 and returned to Las Vegas. Trump coveted the five hundred Atlantis rooms as an annex to Trump Plaza. He figured he could buy the property for much less once its casino closed because no one else could afford its $36 million annual operating cost, which came to more than three times what it could generate as a hotel alone, even assuming 100 percent occupancy. Besides, he wanted a place to stash Marla Maples and a permanent apartment at the Atlantis offered the best mix of access and privacy.

Wynn saw the Atlantis as a low-cost way to reenter the market. By buying the Atlantis for a fraction of the $183 million spent on construction and improvements, then acquiring the Convention Hall annex for parking and construction of a single-floor gaming area, Wynn figured he could make a substantial profit.

Meanwhile, a new embarrassment for the Pritzkers and the regulators appeared when the *Philadelphia Inquirer* revealed that in 1984 they had used a front to buy two Puerto Rican casinos. Nevada's foreign gaming law requires casino owners to get advance permission from regulators before purchasing casinos outside the state. Violating any Nevada law would also put the Pritzkers in violation of New Jersey law because their license required them to comply with all Nevada laws.

The Pritzkers had always acknowledged that they bought the two broken-down old Rock resorts, which they renamed the Hyatt Dorado Beach and the Hyatt Regency Cerromar, in July 1985. But records in a lawsuit brought by Paul A. Dopp, the former owner of Butler Aviation, revealed an earlier deal. Dopp had sued because the Pritzkers were trying to force him out as their minority partner.

In November 1984, with the deadline looming for a deal Dopp had put together but that he lacked the capital to complete, he arranged a seat on a Braniff Airlines jet, an airline the Pritzkers owned, and sat down next to Jay Pritzker, the family patriarch, for the trip to Chicago. Within hours after landing Jay Pritzker dispatched lawyers to Puerto Rico, who quickly reported back that it was a great deal. Then Jay Pritzker had a heart attack.

While the Pritzker patriarch lay in a hospital, his fate uncertain, the Nathan Shapiro family stepped in and bought the casinos. The Shapiros were longtime business associates of the Pritzkers.

Anthony J. Parrillo, the New Jersey gaming enforcement director, had been unaware of the Pritzker deal until just before the story broke in the newspaper. Mike Rumbolz, the former Nevada Gaming Board chairman, said he was never told about the use of the Shapiros as a front.

The morning the story broke, Elsinore and the Atlantis returned to Gambardella's courtroom, no longer free to pose as innocent victims of casino regulators whose rules they had always scrupulously obeyed.

In court Jacob stood and renewed his attack on Bud Read. "He is sitting as Judge Gambardella. He is negating your entire plan," Jacob declared.

Arrajj just shook his head. "I don't understand why we are here," he kept telling the judge.

Gambardella focused on something else, though. What, she asked, was the Atlantis going to do about Drexel, which owned five percent of its stock and nine percent of its bonds and yet had been disqualified by the casino commission from doing business in Atlantic City because of its admitted criminal conduct? This was the issue that Read had let slide on the first day of commission hearings. Gambardella then postponed making a decision for two days, until the casino commission voted on who would be named conservator of the Atlantis.

The next day, back in Lawrenceville, Arrajj hammered away at the Drexel issue. Then the Atlantis put Jacob on the stand, where he said he told his client to ignore Drexel and not pay it any interest or dividends. Hood promised to follow the advice. Chairman Read called a recess. He worried that Gambardella might just buy the argument that the Drexel issue was now dead and that she might order the gaming license renewed, eviscerating state control of casinos. When the commissioners returned to the dais they blinked.

198

The commission voted 4 to 1 to name Joseph Nolan, the treasurer of the American Bar Association and a former New Jersey Bar Association president, as conservator and directed him to take title when the Atlantis license expired the next day. But they also agreed that while Arrajj had made a persuasive case that Drexel could influence the Atlantis and that alone would disqualify the casino, the decision whether to let the Atlantis continue to operate should be left to Judge Gambardella. In effect, the commission ceded to the federal official the power to determine the future of casino regulation in New Jersey in an era when it was clear more debt-ridden casinos would be seeking refuge in Bankruptcy Court.

As Harry Levin put it: "It's Rosemary's baby."

Gambardella did not want this particular squalling baby, though. The next day, in an opinion that took her more than an hour to read, she said, "This court will not at this time interfere."

Hood, pale and shaking, said nothing as she left the courthouse surrounded by lawyers and executives who helped her into a limousine. She had vowed to close rather than submit to a conservator, so it seemed to be the end of the Atlantis.

It wasn't.

When the license expired at midnight Hood had decided to stay open under conservator Nolan's aegis. Just before midnight she sold the Atlantis, for $63 million, to Donald Trump. Afterward, Nolan fought the deal, insisting he could get a better price. But the commission said he was not hired as a real estate broker and let the deal go through.

On May 22, four days short of the eleventh anniversary of legal gambling in Atlantic City, a casino began shutting down for the first time. As the dealers were let go, one table at a time, they stormed down the Boardwalk to Duke Mack's bar where they denounced Hood and downed whiskey. A half hour before the required 4 A.M. closing time, the games ended, the slots stopped whirring and the Atlantis, like its mythic namesake, disappeared beneath a rising tide of red ink.

When the sun rose over the sea in the morning Donald Trump seemed to be the only winner in the Atlantis debacle. In addition to his two existing casinos and his Taj Mahal, where workers hurried to finish construction, he had bought up the abandoned Penthouse casino site between Trump Plaza and Caesars, taking a potential competitor out of the picture. Now he had taken over another casino, the Atlantis, removing it from the market while keeping its hotel rooms to serve Trump Plaza. Not many fully appreciated it, but from that day forward Atlantic City's destiny would be tied to Donald Trump's.

Meanwhile the burden of huge debt payments that drowned the Atlantis were overwhelming another Boardwalk casino.

21

Bet on Merv

All morning, rain came down like waves from the sky, flooding parts of Absecon Island a foot deep. Even carrying a stiff umbrella and trying to walk on the high spots could not ward off the cold water as the fast-paced men with sleek attaché cases streamed into Merv Griffin's Resorts casino hotel, the eighty-two-year-old Boardwalk grand dame once known as Haddon Hall. They walked into the lobby, their shoes filled with water, their cuffs dripping, hoping to find a dry haven. Instead of a smiling doorman they were greeted by waterfalls cascading from the ceiling into an obstacle course of white buckets, a squad of maintenance men racing to replace each with an empty one before it overflowed onto the red-and-gold carpet.

Merv Griffin could not have asked for better weather to make his point to the men and women who had come that day not to play in the casino, which was nearly deserted because this was the Tuesday morning after the new Miss America had left town, but to play a real-life version of *Let's Make a Deal*.

In August 1989, just nine months after he closed his deal to buy Resorts from Donald Trump, Griffin had announced that Resorts would not continue paying interest on either the $325 million of Drexel bonds sold to finance his purchase or on the $605 million of Bear Stearns bonds

201

Resorts owed before Griffin came along. The Drexel junk addicts had received only one interest payment before Griffin cut off their cash. Owners of Resorts bonds paying 16 5/8 percent interest, which a year before sold for $1,060 each, could get only $395 the day before Griffin announced the suspension of interest payments. They quickly fell toward $200. Griffin's message to bondholders was this: the more than $11 million per month Resorts owed them in interest and principal had to be diverted to fix up the place or else the bonds would trade at next to nothing because no one would patronize such a run-down casino hotel.

The suspension of interest payments came after Griffin announced that in April, May and June of 1989 Resorts had lost $27.9 million, more than twice as much as it had the year before under Donald Trump. That meant that on the very days when the Casino Control Commission was moving to shut down the Atlantis because it was losing nearly a buck a second, Resorts was losing $3.54 with each tick of the clock.

Griffin explained the stunning second-quarter losses by saying that Resorts was in much worse shape than he had realized when he bought it. Just as he had failed to realize that an electric shock had made the duck dance in Las Vegas, Griffin had seen only what he wanted to see at Haddon Hall. He had noticed the back walkways that allowed maids to scurry unnoticed by the guests. And he reveled in the opulent suite that he occupied when he stayed there. The other dreadful conditions that no guest could miss somehow escaped Griffin's scrutiny.

Trump boasted that he had shown Griffin a few renovated rooms and that Griffin had not asked to see rooms picked at random. Had Griffin shown such diligence he would have seen hundreds, priced at $150 a night, more suited to a Skid Row dump than a glamorous resort. Griffin also evidently failed to inspect all the costly and unseen systems that make a hotel work: the boilers and chillers, the wiring and ductways, the plumbing and elevators. Some of the elevators were so old, so jury-rigged that their jerks frightened many riders. Left unsaid was how the experts Griffin retained, the appraisers and attorneys and underwriters, could have failed to notice such things and to factor them into the numbers presented to the Casino Control Commission and to the prospectus for the Drexel junk. For that matter, how did such basic facts escape the casino regulators who supposedly investigated the deal thoroughly before the commission certified its financial stability? That certification indicated their finding that for at least one year after Griffin bought it Resorts could pay all of its bills as they came due.

The bondholder meeting that rainy morning drew an odd assortment of six hundred people. Many were from the Atlantic City suburbs, like the retiree in an orange plaid polyester sport coat and brown plaid pants who was in such a panic that he could not grasp the directions to the men's room. He said a broker told him years ago to put half his retirement nest egg in the Resorts bonds that had been paying more than 16 percent interest. Retirement had been sweeter than he had expected, but now, how were he and his wife going to eat? Most of the bonds, though, were controlled by the mutual- and pension-fund managers who, along with the vulture capitalists looking over what might soon become a corporate carcass, poured through Griffin's 189-page proposal. As quickly as they came up with numbers they reached for their pocket phones, issuing orders to buy or sell Resorts bonds depending on how they valued the bankruptcy plan Merv was proposing.

Griffin did not attend, of course. No way were the executives, lawyers, work-out specialists and underwriters going to let the bondholders, especially the often unsophisticated retirees filled with panic or rage, get a chance to confront the personification of the Merv Factor, the capitalist who had left at least one of them in fear for his next meal.

The deal Griffin offered was simple. The Bear Stearns bondholders could expect no cash for five years and then less than half what they had been paid because they would be given new bonds with a face value about one third of the originals. Until 1994 they would be issued additional bonds in lieu of cash interest. The Drexel customers, who held first mortgages on Resorts casinos in Atlantic City and Nassau, would get about twice as much.

From Griffin's perspective it was a brilliant proposal because it immediately set the two groups of bondholders at each other's wallets, fighting over whether the mortgages were valid or whether the deal with Trump involved a fraud in which money due the Bear Stearns bondholders had been wrongly diverted to Trump and other stockholders. Knowing this Griffin had set aside two meeting rooms, one for the Drexel crowd, composed entirely of sophisticated money managers, and the other for the Bear Stearns crowd, which included many retirees.

Griffin's team had one last bit of bad news. They said Griffin, having put in $50 million cash plus the $10 million letter of credit, was sewing his pockets shut, just as Jay Pritzker had done at the Atlantis when it began to sink under the burden of its debts. Griffin would not put up another penny, Resorts president David Hanlon declared. Hanlon also said he had given no thought to reducing his own pay. His contract called for $4.9 million in his first twenty-six months with Resorts plus 5 percent of Resorts stock.

Harsh as these terms were, Griffin knew he had little fear that the bondholders would force him out of Resorts. First of all, his name was in fact a valuable asset that drew some gamblers. Second, removing a debtor in possession, which is what Griffin would become as soon as Resorts filed in Bankruptcy Court under Chapter 11, is a long, costly and uncertain process that could destroy the company. Finally, Griffin proposed these terms with an ace up his sleeve: the New Jersey Casino Control Commission.

Two days after Griffin announced suspension of the interest payments the commission decided to take Griffin's side in the looming fight with bondholders. Without debate or a single question to attorneys arguing the case, the commission unanimously accepted Griffin's contention that not paying the $52 million in interest due bondholders over the coming fourteen weeks was irrelevant to whether he qualified to convert his temporary casino license into a full license. That decision signaled bondholders that they did not have a license to run a casino, that it was Griffin alone who held the license, and without that license their bonds were worthless.

Daniel Heneghan, the perceptive casino writer for the *Press* of Atlantic City, scolded the commissioners in his column, saying that to ignore Resorts' financial condition is to "pay mere lip service to the requirements of the state's casino law . . . the commission apparently bought the argument that it shouldn't allow itself to be used during negotiations with the company's bondholders. Would the bondholders use the situation for their advantage? Sure. But so would Griffin/Resorts. In fact, it would be easy to argue that Griffin/Resorts already has."

Instead of the all-seeing eye that "strict regulation" implied, the commissioners agreed to look at Griffin's situation in discrete little pieces. Howard Goldberg, Griffin's casino lawyer, could never have gotten the entire Griffin matter past the commission in one piece. But by presenting a series of little issues, their order carefully orchestrated to ensure no fatally damaging fact would arise until a series of rulings made it irrelevant, he could steer Griffin through the Casino Control Act.

From the day the game-show mogul first petitioned them for a license the commissioners had shown their willingness to go along to win Griffin both as a prospective source of glamour in Atlantic City and as a counter to Trump. They had swept aside the stock manipulation that had fathered the deal, rationalized Griffin's decision to retain Mike Nigris for nine months as head of his noncasino businesses, and dismissed Griffin's past association with casino-stock swindler Nate Jacobsen. They had also let Drexel peddle the junk for the deal even after it was clear it would be indicted for fraud.

The handling of the Drexel matter illustrated how breaking issues into discrete pieces worked. In the fall of 1988 Resorts was the only major junk deal Drexel had going. It was sued by the SEC for civil fraud and was busy negotiating the terms of its indictment and Michael Milken's separation from the firm. Drexel's indictment was automatic grounds for expulsion from the casino industry, but the commissioners waited until February 1989, three months after Griffin's deal closed, to find it unfit and expel it from the New Jersey casino industry. When Dan Lee attended the Resorts bondholder meeting he came not as a paid adviser to Griffin, but as a representative of Drexel clients and Drexel's own portfolio, which included millions of the Resorts bonds for which it had not found buyers.

What neither the commissioners nor Griffin's people wanted to talk about was all the evidence that showed they must have known that the deal was doomed to end up in Bankruptcy Court. There was plenty of evidence beyond the fact that the projected cash flow fell $108,000 per day short of interest expenses.

Two weeks after Griffin closed his deal with Trump on November 16, 1988, Hanlon had begun cutting costs furiously. The Treniers, who had performed in Resorts' lounge since it opened, had their contract abruptly canceled because their nine-thousand-dollar weekly fee was too high. So did other entertainers, all replaced with the cheapest talent Hanlon could find. But for months Hanlon kept his polo team on Resorts' tab and he delayed selling its helicopters, which he often flew as copilot. By April, after Drexel had already acknowledged it would be indicted for securities fraud, Hanlon traveled to the last Predators' Ball, the annual Beverly Hills conference for corporate raiders who drew their sustenance from Michael Milken's manipulations. Anthony J. Parrillo, the enforcement division director, gave Hanlon permission to go provided he spoke in a side room. There Hanlon stunned the audience by saying Resorts had a liquidity crisis, the first admission that the deal closed just six months earlier was foundering.

Even though the commissioners had certified the Resorts deal as financially stable, they knew that it probably would fail, as one of them later admitted. "We knew that Resorts could not make it with all that debt," the commissioner acknowledged after leaving office. "Everyone knew the debt would have to be restructured and I believed there was a good chance Resorts would go out of business. But look at it this way. If we approved Merv's deal then Donald would finish the Taj, which everybody wanted, and Merv would keep Resorts open at least until the Taj opened, because it would take a couple of years for [Resorts] to use up the extra cash it banked from the Drexel bonds. It looked like it would take a couple of years, not months.

"So anyway, by approving this we saved four thousand jobs at Resorts until the Taj could open, which was going to mean another five thousand or six thousand jobs, so that even if Resorts folded after that we didn't throw a lot of people out of work. Nobody wants their gravestone to read: Here Lies a Public Official Who Destroyed Four Thousand Jobs."

And the bondholders, what of them? "Drexel's clients are sophisticated," the former commissioner said. Yes, but the money they invest is often held in trust for people's retirement. "That's just not our problem," the commissioner said. As for the original Resorts debt holders, the commissioner said that, too, was not the commission's problem.

Resorts did not fold, in large part because Griffin's statement that he would sew his pockets shut was only a negotiating ploy. The terms of the bankruptcy plan were mostly worked out in advance, prepackaged for Judge Rosemary Gambardella to review and sign with few hearings. "This is the harbinger of what restructurings will be like in the future," observed Tom Gallagher, the Gibson Dunn & Crutcher attorney who supervised the deal with Trump and for a time acted as Griffin's chief executive. He was proved right, as other companies burdened with too much debt from the eighties followed the pattern set in this case, negotiating the terms and voting for them before asking the Bankruptcy Court to rubber-stamp them.

Griffin agreed to give the bondholders nearly 80 percent of Resorts stock. He paid $15 million and gave a letter of credit for $11 million to buy the balance of the equity, on the condition that he control the board of directors for several years. Some of the money that would have gone to interest went into fixing up Haddon Hall.

By 1992, Resorts had sold only one major parcel in Atlantic City. The Bahamas complex that the company claimed was worth $300 million had produced only a single offer, for $160 million. And the new bonds that were issued to replace the old debt traded at only two thirds of their face value, which was less than the old bonds were worth the day Griffin said Resorts could not pay its bills as they came due.

Resorts' emergence from Bankruptcy Court a year later got little attention in the press, not because it was preordained, but because it was overshadowed by another casino bankruptcy filing right next door.

22

Dolphins in the Desert

When Steve Wynn's $630 million dream come true opened in Las Vegas, an unusual national television ad introduced it. The too rich and too thin appeared for split seconds, zipping up a skirt, descending in a wrought-iron elevator, racing a Jaguar with its top down through Beverly Hills, taking off on the Concorde, all hurrying to reach "A New Destination in the World."

What viewers hardly saw was the Mirage itself, a giant gold box trimmed in ivory, with three thousand rooms and suites rising for thirty-eight stories behind a storybook tropical lagoon and the world's only man-made volcano, a fifty-four-foot mountain dotted with mature palm trees, water cascading down its artificial rock sides. After dark the volcano erupts on the quarter hour, flames and compressed steam dancing in the night air while lights and bubblers turn the waterfall and then the lagoon into a boiling red sea. Crowds gather to watch the free show and, when it erupts, hundreds on the sidewalks interrupt their journey through the neon forest to behold what Wynn has created. Under the porte cochere, made of fake palm tree beams, Mirage customers enjoy an unexpectedly delightful sensation. Beyond the lagoon, across the wrought-iron fence adorned with smiling dolphins, they can observe the cars jamming the Strip but without hearing the whining engines, blaring radios and startling horns that would remind them of urban life. The gurgling water screens out these sounds and magically transports them into another world, as distant from the odor of exhaust fumes as the Strip is from the rest of the planet.

Passing through the main entrance—a wall of glass doors on perfectly balanced hinges, each bearing the Mirage logo of five palm trees in vibrant purple, tangerine, orange, hot pink and jade—guests enter another fantasy world. Across a narrow strip of marble that serves as a threshold, a little boardwalk gives them safe passage through a jungle beneath a hundred-foot-high glass dome. Babbling brooks and tropical mists enchant the guests; real orchids blossom amid palm trees that seem alive but are only cellulose carcasses embalmed with fire retardants. Beyond this lies the casino, carpeted with an acre and a half of orchids that invite guests to traipse through them, while those in a hurry stay on the curving pathways of pink and black that flow past the gaming tables toward guest rooms, meeting rooms, shopping and the free-form pool out back whose border meanders for nearly a half mile. In the heart of this red-felt jungle Wynn has erected a mahogany lodge reserved for his high rollers, with shuttered panels that can be open for the masses to look in or drawn tight to protect a famous player's identity. Off to the left, past the poker parlor and the fast-food court that looks more like an upscale eatery, stands a long wall of reassuringly thick glass, through which the never-ending crowds study a pair of Siberian tigers, their stripes black and white, as they sleep or frolic or swim in the moat.

Past the tigers, doors lead outside to a pair of moving sidewalks. They cost $430,000 and may seem superfluous, since they carry people just one hundred feet. But they are Wynn's statement of confidence in his creation, for just beyond them his property ends before a gaudy fantasy image of a Roman temple, rich with marble and brass, guarded by a smiling centurion who welcomes every passerby. Behind him a moving sidewalk rises through the Roman temple, passing above giant square pools of cool, clear water, continuing on beneath a canopy for a quarter-mile. But it goes in only one direction, carrying players away from the Mirage and toward Caesars Palace. Wynn's sidewalks carry people into his casino and back out, a courtesy not extended by his rival in the competition to win the hearts and pocketbooks of the people.

Behind the Mirage, which from the sky resembles a giant Y, beyond the pool with its own island in the center, past the private villas with their own little pools or putting greens, Wynn created another extension of his tropical paradise, a seaquarium featuring performing dolphins in the desert. Wynn also built an eighteen-thousand-gallon aquarium that stretches the entire length of the hotel desk where, as a silent reminder of the elemental purpose of this vast wonderland, sharks lurk.

Steve Wynn's Mirage is indeed a new destination in the world, for the Mirage is to casinos in the nineties as Disneyland was to amusement parks in the fifties. The joints the mob built in Las Vegas relied on neon outside, a few ornaments inside and revues featuring nearly naked dancers to create their adult Disneyland. The Mirage has no neon, but it is themed right down to the railings formed by molding plastic to resemble carved ivory, and the only place to see a bare breast is in your own room. It is a world away from the Castaways, the forgettable joint it replaced, the place where Michael Rose started out in the hotel business as a front-desk clerk.

In December 1989, its first full month, the Mirage won $40 million from its players, a new world record that surpassed the $38 million Caesars Atlantic City won in August 1988. So long as the crowds keep coming to Las Vegas, Wynn is virtually assured of success at the Mirage because it is a must-see attraction, the best in town. And even if hard times should strike Las Vegas, Wynn faces little risk of losing the parent company. That's because the junk bonds Mike Milken sold to finance it contained a little-known escape clause. Once the Mirage's cash-flow equaled 1.5 times interest costs for nine months running the corporate parent's guarantee that the bondholders would get their interest was wiped out. This guarantee evaporated on October 1, 1990, the earliest possible date. In the unlikely event that the Mirage sinks into bankruptcy, bondholders could claim the building, but at the risk of losing the magic touch of its creator to maintain and expand the fantasies which draw the crowds.

The Mirage prospers because Las Vegas operates on a different economic model than Atlantic City. "The only way for Atlantic City to succeed is to become another Las Vegas, but those idiots in New Jersey won't do that," Wynn argues. "You have to offer more than slot machines and blackjack. Gambling can't be the whole cake."

At night, seen from a jetliner, the Strip's neon used to blaze in the desert dark. Now the flashing signs are almost lost amid all the lights that fill Las Vegas Valley, for now more people live here than in San Francisco. By day the once tan desert has changed even more, and mostly to one color: green. All those greenbacks brought in by plane and car and train provide a market for seventeen golf courses (including one exclusively for Mirage high rollers) and for tens of thousands of lawns. All that greensward has made Vegas the capital of water use, 375 gallons per capita per day, double the rate in Phoenix, four times the rate in Philadelphia. It is one of many superlatives. Off and on for three decades Las Vegas has had the distinction of being the fastest growing metropolis in the United States. As the nineties began, as recession swept most of America, Las Vegas boomed. Another hundred people arrived in Las Vegas every day, another one thousand homes and apartments were built each month and plans were made to build seventy-seven schools by the end of the decade.

The old come, too. The Del E. Webb Corporation abandoned the casino business to go back to its roots in construction. At Webb's newest Sun City, part of a Howard Hughes development called Summerlin, three out of five buyers pay cash, many investing profits from homes bought long ago in Southern California. West of the Strip, where the desert slowly rises toward the Spring Mountains, on land the mob is said to have favored for burying the bodies of luckless gamblers who failed to honor their markers, developments with names like Moonlight Bay and Desert Shores rise around artificial lakes while the entrance to Canyon Gate is a man-made waterfall.

While both Las Vegas and Atlantic City are known for their casinos, the eastern resort's only real product is gambling. Hardly anyone goes to the beach. The streets are not safe for anyone whose clothes and jewelry mark them as rich. There are no movie theaters, although the Showboat casino does offer that popular blue-collar sport, bowling. Atlantic City's casinos do provide some headliners and low-budget revues and lounge acts. But its product is cash and to get people to buy it, to play at games where they will usually lose, the casinos must lavish rolls

211

of quarters, free rooms and other comps on their customers. To sell cash requires heavy discounting.

Las Vegas sells entertainment, sells an experience available nowhere else on the planet. It comps only the best customers, while charging for its rooms and meals and drinks and shows. The gambling halls, the places where the casinos market money, fatten the bottom line. Las Vegas and Atlantic City, in the late eighties, won about the same amount of money from players. But while cash sales of rooms, food and beverages added only about 10 percent to Atlantic City's revenues, they nearly doubled revenues in Las Vegas. So while Atlantic City sells only the steak, Las Vegas sells the steak and the sizzle. And the Mirage is the best sizzle around.

In a way the New Jersey Casino Control Commission and its favored licensee, Donald Trump, made this gaudiest of Las Vegas gambling palaces possible. Donald Trump's raid on Bally Manufacturing, which the commission could have stopped, resulted in Bally offering $440 million for the Atlantic City Golden Nugget. The nearly $200 million that Wynn took back to the Nevada desert provided the down payment so Milken could sell enough junk to build the Mirage. Without the Golden Nugget windfall even Wynn acknowledges the Mirage might have remained just an illusion shimmering dreamily in the future.

Money alone, though, could not have created the Mirage, for even much larger sums could be squandered on a building lacking its magic touch, as Donald Trump would soon prove. Wynn is a master showman, a P. T. Barnum whose genius lies in his ability to see what the people want in entertainment even as he slowly loses his own vision to the degenerative eye disease retinitis pigmentosa.

Steve Wynn works from a ground-floor Mirage office that is specially lighted to enhance his limited vision. He sits behind a white marble desk, his back to a corner where two long glass walls meet. From across the room a black-and-white photograph of his late father, a compulsive gambler who brought his boy to Vegas when he was just ten, looks over what his son cannot see: the white sofas, the vibrant white, purple, teal and coral carpet, visitors seated around the room. On another wall is a color portrait of Elaine, the former UCLA cheerleader he married, divorced and then, after continuing to live in the same mansion for four years, remarried. She smiles, as do their two daughters, all with shoulders bared.

When he is in the mood Wynn can sit in this stark throne room and talk from dusk to dawn, ordering in one plate of proteins and greens after another, nibbling a bit and then asking a guest to take it away. He likes to wear bright-colored polo shirts, the better to show off his muscled physique and to highlight his capped white teeth. And as he tells stories for hour upon fascinating hour, mimicking the voices of Caesars chairman Henry Gluck, Resorts chairman Merv Griffin and a host of others, he also pulls confidential documents out to show how much he knows not just about his own casino, but about the inner workings of the competition.

He has secrets to tell about boxing impresario Don King, with whom he has sparred for dominance over Buster Douglas, and about "that lightweight phony Donald Trump."

Wynn is a complex man whose powerful emotions sometimes get him into trouble, causing him or others to waste vast amounts of money and time. The passion, the drive that built the Mirage is mixed with feelings that often run wild, showing loyalty beyond reason, devouring others' fortunes without mercy and relentlessly pursuing those who cross him.

His loyalty to Milken, the man who made him rich beyond his dreams, is eternal. Even though one of the six felonies to which Milken pled guilty involved Wynn's company, then called Golden Nugget Incorporated, Wynn cannot say a single critical word about his hero in public or in private. Wynn says, and no evidence disputes him, that he did not know of the illegal deal between Milken and Ivan Boesky to help Wynn out of a failed raid on MCA, the giant entertainment conglomerate. Golden Nugget bought nearly 5 percent of MCA on Milken's advice. It picked the wrong company to go after. That was not because Lew Wasserman, MCA's chief executive, was then the most powerful man in Hollywood, but because he was the studio chief who had made Ronald Reagan a millionaire and just then Reagan was in the White House and the federal government's Manhattan prosecutor, Rudolph Giuliani, was moving in on Milken and his manipulations. When Golden Nugget dropped the raid MCA's stock price fell. Milken admit-

213

ted he arranged to have Boesky sell the stock off slowly to minimize the loss to Golden Nugget, promising later to pay Boesky back.

When the Mirage opened, Milken was there even though by then Wynn had concluded that his friend would have to go to prison. Milken had the good grace not to stand front and center—next to Governor Bob Miller and all the other politicians—but to position himself just outside the focus of the news cameras.

Wynn also can explode like his volcano, dismissing subordinates as fools. Or he can be as soothing as the waters flowing into the Mirage lagoon, cajoling subordinates into doing their best. He can focus on fine details, like when he told Rob Goldstein to have the curb at the Golden Nugget painted white every week so it did not look scuffed. And he can be blind to what would motivate others to do what he wants. Like Mike Flores.

In the vast parking lot that feeds the Mirage stands an old stucco apartment house, a simple, two-story survivor from the fifties built around a courtyard with a little swimming pool. Wynn wanted the one-acre site, partly to get rid of it, partly so he could build an outdoor coliseum to stage prizefights and other events that bring in bettors. Flores wanted to sell, but not at the $1 million price he was offered. Wynn thought it was a real premium, given that he had paid seventy-five thousand dollars an acre for the rest of the site. But Flores not only owned the last parcel, which usually commands a stiff premium, he also had a cash cow pouring more than one hundred thousand dollars a year into his pocket. Flores was also a bit offended that Wynn sent a lawyer to negotiate, but that snub was forgotten when Flores said he was offered four front row seats at the Roberto Durán–Sugar Ray Leonard fight. Flores quickly bragged to his dad and two buddies that Wynn was treating them all. But the tickets didn't come. Finally, Flores called and was told the tickets were gone, that he had not paid the four thousand dollars for them. Furious, Flores went to see Ralph Englestad, owner of the low-roller Imperial Palace across the Strip from the Mirage. Englestad owns much of Bill Harrah's old car collection now, including a Mercedes that belonged to Hitler. He also was fined once by the Nevada Gaming Control Board for hosting a birthday party honoring Hitler. Wynn, a supporter of Israel, hates him. Englestad recognized an opportunity and paid Flores $1 million for an option on the site. "He made a mistake," Wynn said of Flores, "because now I won't buy his piece at any price. NOT AT ANY PRICE." That means Wynn won't rid himself of an eyesore or get his coliseum, either.

Wynn's single-mindedness was also demonstrated when his Atlantic City Golden Nugget sued Schmuel Aboud of Queens, New York, over a twenty-eight-thousand-dollar marker and ended up changing the law on serving free drinks to gamblers.

Aboud had won $395,000 in damages from an auto accident in 1985 and decided to visit Atlantic City to celebrate. He quickly learned why the casinos are known as slayers of fortunes. He checked into a one-thousand-dollar-a-night suite for no charge because he brought along twenty-seven thousand dollars for gambling. The Golden Nugget provided a limousine, a butler and complimentary tickets to the shows for Aboud and five friends. Two days later his money ran out, so the Golden Nugget flew him by helicopter to New York to draw another twenty-seven thousand dollars from his bank. But when Aboud returned to his suite, back pain began to set in, the same pains for which he won the damages. Ever helpful, the Golden Nugget brought in a doctor, and later another one. They prescribed Percodan, a powerful painkiller.

Bottle of pills in hand, Aboud returned to the gaming table, where he was given a free cognac to wash down the pills, even though the Percodan bottle sat on the table, and even though mixing it with booze can be lethal. Eventually Aboud became so woozy he fell facedown on the table, but not before he had signed a twenty-eight-thousand-dollar marker. At three in the morning, Aboud testified, a host called and he was not in a friendly mood. Aboud said he was told to get down to the tables and gamble or else vacate the suite.

Steven Goldman, Aboud's attorney, said the Golden Nugget was on a "fishing expedition. They spotted a fish, they baited the line, they reeled him in and they did not let go" until he had lost a quarter million dollars. Golden Nugget argued that Aboud's lawsuit was intended to get him out of paying a "just debt." Besides, the Golden Nugget said it had no records showing Aboud had lost that much money and neither did he.

Golden Nugget's attorney, Stephen Dratch, noted that drinks are dispensed freely in the casino and that "unless these cases are cut off at the pass, there will be a flood of these."

U.S. District Court Judge Mitchell Cohen did not see things the Golden Nugget way. In a written decision he held that "a casino has a duty to refrain from knowingly permitting an invitee to gamble where that patron is obviously and visibly intoxicated and/or under the influence of a narcotic substance." New Jersey's dram-shop laws, he added, apply to casinos, meaning casinos can be held liable for personal injuries caused to persons whom they allow to get drunk. Still, the jury decided Aboud was partly responsible and must pay the $28,000.

The New Jersey Casino Control Commission had no such regulation and had ignored a long history of the casinos getting players drunk not just to weaken their skill at blackjack, but to get them to sign markers wiping out their assets. And while neighborhood-bar owners saw their licenses routinely suspended for repeatedly serving liquor to juveniles, no New Jersey casino lost the right to sell and give away booze for even a minute, no matter how many teenagers got drunk on casino cocktails.

But Wynn's pursuit of people like Aboud paled in comparison to what he did to Jack Bona, who spent nearly two years in the Atlantic County jail even though he was never charged with a crime.

Bona's firm paid Golden Nugget about $2 million for a 1983 option to buy land next to the Atlantic City Golden Nugget and to repeatedly extend that option. Bona wanted to build a one-thousand-room casino called the Dunes at the south end of the Boardwalk, right within view of the students at Atlantic City High School, but he never seemed to have the money to close the deal.

Bona had been a small-time real estate broker until he moved from Brooklyn to San Diego, where his fortunes changed. In 1979 he earned less than eighteen thousand dollars. By 1986 he was worth $26 million. The money started rolling in when Bona realized he could make a fortune converting apartments into condos. Before long Bona and a partner had borrowed $180 million from San Marino Savings and Loan in suburban Los Angeles at a time when five San Marino directors owed six hundred thousand dollars to Bona and his partner. The $180 million was not paid back and San Marino folded, with the taxpayers picking up the loss. Bona said all the money was spent on failed real estate ventures,

216

some of which involved Morris Shenker, who then ran the Las Vegas Dunes and who had a long and intimate history of dealings with mobsters and their favorite cookie jar, the Teamsters Central States Pension Fund, before he died. It was the unbuilt Atlantic City Dunes, in which Shenker was a key figure, that gobbled the rest of the fortune.

On the last day of the last extension of his option for the Boardwalk parcel Bona put his company into bankruptcy, tying up the site for four years. Wynn grew so livid that "I woke up at night screaming." He hired Martin L. Greenberg, who had quit as a state senator to become a Golden Nugget executive before it was sold, and his Greenberg & Margolis law firm to get him some justice. Attorneys Clark R. Alpert and Steve Pasternak set out to prove that the bankruptcy filing was done in bad faith. After they succeeded at that they dusted off a hoary legal doctrine known as *capias ad satisfaciendum* that most attorneys last heard about in law school. It means to deliver the head, or body, in satisfaction of a judgment and was used under English common law to throw debtors into prison. Alpert and Pasternak argued in court after court that Bona had hidden assets, tens of millions of dollars in hidden assets, and that arresting him was the only way to make him pay up. Their briefs never mentioned a 1663 decision on the *capias* doctrine that demonstrated its cruelty when an English judge declared that "if a man shall . . . lie in prison for debt . . . he must live on his own, or on the charity of others; and if no man will relieve him, let him die in the name of God, says the law; and so say I."

The first time Alpert and Pasternak revived this ancient idea and took it to a judge he turned them down. But in 1989, in Cape May Court House, New Jersey, Judge Peter Thomas, who said he knew next to nothing of bankruptcy law, told the bailiff to put Bona in the slammer. For nearly two years Bona endured a living hell, kept in a lockup built to hold men for only brief periods, where men gone mad screamed into the night until tougher inmates beat them into silence.

Alpert and Pasternak, meanwhile, filed reports with the court claiming that Bona had a secret life, that his Eastern Airlines frequent flyer records showed he had repeatedly flown in and out of Tehran after the shah was deposed and that he had been to secret U.S. military bases. And they filed a "forensic audit" purporting to show Bona had hidden at least $30 million.

217

"I'm in debtors' prison," Bona said after a year behind bars, a guard watching him as carefully as if he were one of the rapists, bandits or other violent criminals with whom he was incarcerated. "This is unreal. This is America in the twentieth century, not Dickens' England. How can this be happening? I have no assets. They say there's fifty million dollars missing. There isn't. It's gone, all gone. But how do you prove a negative? How do you prove you don't have millions of dollars hidden somewhere? You can't. But the only way I can get out of prison is to prove I don't have hidden assets, and since I can't prove that I may spend the rest of my life here. It's crazy. This is outrageous."

That prospect seemed plausible, especially after Judge Prudence Abram of U.S. Bankruptcy Court in Manhattan wrote a scathing fifteen-page opinion about Bona's lack of credibility with her and his lack of disclosure about just where all the money from San Marino Savings had gone. "Bona's incarceration is not incompatible with the proper administration of the bankruptcy case," she wrote in denying his request to be freed from jail.

The idea of Bona locked away and forgotten appealed to Wynn. "Is he still in jail?" Wynn said. "I'd forgotten all about him."

Alpert and Pasternak soon enlisted the agency created to bail out the savings and loan industry, the Resolution Trust Corporation, even though Bona had settled with its predecessor, the Federal Savings and Loan Insurance Corporation, which had not sought criminal or civil prosecution of Bona.

Al Glasgow figured that hard as it might be in the joint, Bona was probably smart to keep his mouth shut, even if it angered Judge Abram and others in black robes. "If Morris and the boys got the savings and loan's money," Glasgow observed, "your choices would be to keep your mouth shut or they would shut it for you permanently."

Bona's luck began to change when it turned out that the "THR" on his frequent flyer records indicated not a trip to the ayatollah's Iran, but the rental of a car from Thrifty, and that the other codes referred not to secret military bases, but to Marriott's Seaview Country Club a few miles outside of Atlantic City. Finally in 1991, after twenty-three months in jail, Judge John Callinan in Atlantic City reviewed the entire case. He found the actions of Golden Nugget's attorneys to keep Bona locked up "unseemly" and in a scathing fifty-three-page opinion set Bona free. He noted that Golden Nugget's grievance was over a land deal gone sour and said that if Bona should have been jailed at all then a few days was the most that could be justified. Later the Resolution Trust Company joined the criticism, saying Wynn's lawyers had acted in direct violation of the RTC's instructions and urging that they be brought up on professional disciplinary proceedings. Alpert and Pasternak denied any wrongdoing and said there was no basis to recommend discipline.

Bona was not a player, but the story of what happened to him circulated widely among high rollers and explained why, as Al Glasgow put it, "a lotta guys who will stiff casinos all over town make sure Wynn's joint gets paid. Steve can be a great friend, but he can also be an enemy who never forgets, who waits until he has his chance to make you regret not paying."

Bona was not alone in having vast sums of money that were suddenly gone. Donald Trump's profligate spending was about to knock over his elaborate house of cards.

23

What Hath Gaud Wrought?

As Resorts hurtled toward default so did the Taj—and Trump knew it. Walt Haybert, the gentle accountant he put in charge of the Taj's finances, sat down in his dark office in the collage of temporary buildings that served as Taj headquarters on Brigantine Island, six miles from the Boardwalk, and analyzed spending against the budget. Haybert warned Trump in a memo that at current spending levels the Taj would go $108 million over budget. Haybert hoped the memo would result in an end to the lavish spending spree, a thoughtful scaling back of the project, or else would prompt Trump to put in more money.

Trump had no cash to put in, though. The $63 million Griffin paid him for the Taj management contract was gone. Although Trump had paid that same sum for the failed Atlantis, which he renamed the Trump Regency, none of the money went there. Trump borrowed every penny for the purchase price plus the modest sums he spent to replace the lumpy mattresses and worn carpets. He even charged the monthly mortgage payments on the loan, adding them to the balance owed Manufacturers Hanover until the debt soared to $81 million. Even if the Atlantis ran at full occupancy every day it would barely generate enough revenue to pay the mortgage interest. Why the bank, which foreclosed in 1992, made such a stupid loan was a mystery.

Instead Trump used some of the Griffin money to plug other pressing financial holes and lost most of it in a feigned raid on American Airlines that his brother Robert said cost him some money, too. The deal fell apart when the market realized he was not a real raider and the stock of the airline's parent dropped like a jet out of power.

It appeared that Trump had $75 million invested in the Taj, but that, too, was borrowed. First Fidelity Bank of New Jersey made the loan, which was guaranteed by Trump's management fee for the next decade. The fee gave Trump 1.75 percent of the Taj revenues.

Haybert's memo did prompt Trump to seek more money. He persuaded NatWest, the British bank, to lend him $50 million for furniture, fixtures and equipment. That solved almost half the problem Haybert initially foresaw, but because the orders for chandeliers and carpets and art, and the innumerable costly change orders and mistakes, had continued, he projected that even with the First Fidelity money the casino would go more than $100 million over budget. Then tragedy struck.

Steve Hyde, Taj president Mark G. Etess and Jonathan Benanav were flying in a chartered Italian helicopter back to Atlantic City from a Manhattan press conference promoting a boxing match when the main rotor and transmission broke loose and flew off on their own. The copter fell like a rock for a terrifying half mile, crashing into the pine trees that separate traffic on the Garden State Parkway. The three executives and the two pilots died instantly. It was a major catastrophe for Trump, who knew little about how his casinos actually operated and whose management style bred intrigue among his senior staff. Hyde had been a solitary, calm and competent force in this chaos, slowly building an organization of the best people he could persuade to work for Trump by promising them great pay, contracts and himself as a buffer.

The loss of Hyde was more significant to Atlantic City than the arrest a few weeks earlier of the mayor, four current and former city councilmen, and ten others on corruption charges. The arrests, arranged by the casino intelligence squad of the state police, destabilized the black political establishment in Atlantic City, which the casino executives in private all denounced, one saying that Mayor James L. Usry was incompetent even at incompetency. Two years later seven of the first eight defendants brought to trial were exonerated by the judge or acquitted by the jury and evidence would show that the state knew it had no case against two

221

of the defendants but prosecuted them anyway. Usry plead guilty only to the least serious charge against him, one of the few successes in a prosecution that was largely a disaster for the state police and the attorney general's office, which publicly admitted to serious flaws in its own conduct. The political life of Atlantic City, such as it was, would go on after the arrests. But without Hyde's steady hand in the Trump casinos, the cash machines that financed the vaunted Trump lifestyle desperately needed a firm hand, one that Trump trusted and would largely leave be. With the Taj opening, one of every four casino jobs would be in a Trump casino, making his welfare the region's.

Trump sent his brother Robert down to be his eyes and ears. Robert had an easygoing style and a taste for simple things like the Thursday meat-loaf special at a greasy spoon called Gilcrest's Cafe, but gaming was not in his blood the way it was in Hyde's. Haybert was named president of the Taj and he continued the stream of warnings that money could run out before the Taj opened.

As the new year began the wild spending on the Taj began to draw the bank account dangerously low. Vendors, used to the Trump slow-pay method, waited longer and longer for their money. Irwin Tobman, who sold the Taj its seventy multicolored fiberglass minarets, demanded payment with such urgency that he was invited down from New York. Tobman walked into a Taj construction office and was shown a check for the full amount due. "Just as soon as the money's transferred to the checking account we'll give it to you," Tobman reports being told.

Trump's construction chief, Tom Pippett, Robert Trump, Haybert and even Donald pleaded with contractors to make the promised April 2 opening, saying the checks would be forthcoming. Making the opening was critical because the first two Taj bond interest payments, totaling $94.5 million, had come from the proceeds of the Taj bonds that Merrill Lynch had sold at a stiff 14 percent interest. Making the third payment, due May 15, depended on starting up the cash flow that Griffin had joked about the day he took over Resorts.

The Taj Mahal was proving to be an unexpectedly fitting name for Trump's biggest casino. The name was taken from the beautiful mausoleum that a Mogul dynasty emperor built to honor his late wife. The Taj Mahal in Atlantic City was quickly entombing what was left of the

Trump fortune. He purchased the Eastern Airlines Shuttle for $365 million in borrowed dollars and only later realized that he was stuck with a fleet of jets more than twenty years old that guzzled kerosene. He paid way too much for the Plaza Hotel in Manhattan. And like all developers he was leveraged, making him vulnerable the moment the economy stopped growing, as it did just as he went on his spending spree. He owed $1.3 billion to the junk bond buyers for his three casinos and an astounding $1.9 billion to six dozen banks, with Citibank's syndicate due more than $1 billion. And he knew that without some new deals he could not pay his bills as they came due.

A key sign of Trump's troubles came on March 20, 1990, when Neil Barsky, the savvy *Wall Street Journal* reporter who was one of the few journalists not taken in by the Trump myth, wrote a routine story about the Taj opening set for thirteen days later. Included in it was the latest version of a quote by Marvin B. Roffman, the sagacious Philadelphia gaming analyst who had said again and again that the Taj was a bad investment and would have a hard time getting through its first winter. "When this property opens, he will have had so much free publicity, he will break every record in the book in April, June and July. But once the cold winds blow from October to February, it won't make it. The market just isn't there," Roffman told the *Journal*.

Trump exploded in fury. When Roffman showed up that morning for a tour of the Taj, Robert Trump told him to get off the property and never come back. Back at Janney Montgomery Scott, Roffman was greeted by a letter from Trump that demanded he recant or the brokerage would face "a major lawsuit."

Janney cochairman Edgar Scott, Jr., a Main Line scion whose mother, Hope, inspired *The Philadelphia Story*, came to Roffman's cramped office and spoke to Trump by telephone.

"Janney Montgomery Scott has been in business since 1832 and to the best of my knowledge it has never publicly apologized to anyone," Roffman heard Scott say. "What is it you want, Mr. Trump?"

"I want you to call Norman Pearlstine [the *Journal* managing editor] and tell him that son of a bitch Neil Barsky misquoted you and you're going to get that guy."

He also wanted a letter saying the Taj would be the greatest success

223

ever. Scott ordered Roffman to sign a letter of tacit apology. Roffman bowed. But that night Roffman's conscience got to him and he decided that he could not tell a lie.

The next morning he went to advise Janney's brokers to dump the Taj bonds, but research director James Meyer barred him. "I can't let you," Roffman said he was told, "because if word ever gets back to Donald Trump that you are badmouthing his bonds you'll get fired."

Roffman went to his cramped office where the telephone was ringing. It was Norma Foerderer, Trump's assistant.

"Norma said Donald wanted two changes in my letter," Roffman recalled. "He wanted me to say I had not the hope, but every expectation, that the Taj would be a great success and he wanted me to take out a reference to the 'traditionally slow period' in winter and to mention 'the possibility of a slow period.'

"This was worse than outrageous because not only was Donald demanding I write things that were not true, he was asking me to mislead Taj bondholders and I believed that would violate the securities laws," Roffman said.

After fretting for several hours, Roffman faxed Trump a new letter, but instead of including the changes Trump wanted, Roffman withdrew his retraction. Scott fired Roffman. Both Janney Montgomery and Trump would later pay Roffman hefty settlements that enabled him to buy a palatial suburban home and start his own money management firm. But ten weeks would pass before the reason would emerge for Trump's vociferous response to a quote that was not news and that later would be proven stunningly accurate.

A week after the Roffman incident, and three days before the Taj opening, the Casino Control Commission breezed through licensing Trump in less than an hour of jovial exchange between Trump lawyers and the commissioners. No one asked a question about the unpaid bills from contractors or all the unfinished work, about how a hotel could meet the first-class standard in the Casino Control Act without a swimming pool, a gymnasium or a theater. The commission did ask the enforcement division to look into a complaint from the Atlantic County Board of Chosen Freeholders and the Brigantine City Council that Trump had violated a state permit in paving over an old dump to create a Taj parking lot. Everyone knew nothing would come of it.

Meanwhile, a ten-minute walk up the Boardwalk, entertainment director Colin Wilson had arranged a pep rally for the seven thousand Taj workers, most of whom showed up. They filled the Mark G. Etess Arena, which resembled a giant warehouse with its high ceiling and bare cement floor. Soon this concrete box would host Elton John, the Moscow Circus and Billy Joel because it was the only semblance of a theater available at the Taj. Eight cocktail waitresses stood on chairs wearing black spandex tights and white shirts on which they had written in gold letters T-A-J M-A-H-A-L. Others displayed a banner, liberated from a local bar, that proclaimed "It Ain't No Mirage."

Then the lights died. Amid hoots and shouts the employees twirled phosphorescent light-sticks above their heads that created swirls of red, green and blue in the dark. Suddenly a Max Headroom–style genie appeared on the giant television screen, his face and eyes moving abruptly in a visual stutter. Fabu, short for fabulous, implored "members of the fabulous Trump team" working at "The Eighth Wonder of the World" to remember from their training that the "one key ingredient to success is ESP—Excellent Service and Performance."

When Fabu urged everyone to stand and clap their hands while performers in costume danced on stage, Taj casino manager Bobby Yee and General Counsel Harry Levin ran onto the stage to join in. In the front row Blaine Trump moved gently to the music while her husband, Robert, danced in place by swiveling on his knees. Next to him Taj highroller handler Bucky Howard thrashed about wildly. Harvey Freeman, the detail man who made Trump's deals work, stood still, politely appearing to clap. Next to him was The Donald, stiff as a corpse, his lip curled, clapping his hands out of time with the simple rhythm. When an aide approached, Trump seemed relieved to be led away from the madness. Soon green laser beams projected a Bengal tiger running across a white curtain at the back of the darkened stage. As the loudspeakers blasted out "Eye of the Tiger," the image focused down to the tiger's head, then to its giant eye. The curtain rose to show Trump, emerging as if from a genie's puff of smoke, an array of pencil-thin green laser beams fanning out from behind him as four thousand Taj employees screamed "Donald! Donald! Donald!"

"Thank you very much, folks," Trump said, his stilted voice contrasting with the party atmosphere he had paid to create. "You really are

225

great—boy, a lot of payroll. I asked someone, 'Am I paying them today or does it start Monday?' and I was told it started two weeks ago. That's okay."

Having dampened the enthusiasm, Trump left the stage. But his words were filled with truth. Trump was barely able to meet that payroll and the shortage of funds was obvious inside the building. The long second-floor hallways leading to the New Delhi Deli and the ballrooms were supposed to have marble columns. Instead they had been hastily covered with pink wallpaper. Many rooms were a mess, with hanging rods laying on closet floors, curtains that would not close and keys that did not match the doors weeks after the grand opening.

The casino itself was a mixture of plain and fancy. Over the table games, barrel vaults lined with brass and mirrors held giant chandeliers so heavy that extra beams were needed to support them. But half the ceiling was plain, gray acoustic tile, evidence of the cost overruns that Haybert warned about. Even with his dire warnings to conserve money, however, waste and expensive mistakes could be seen everywhere. In the lobby seven gorgeous Oriental carpets had been unrolled so they could be set into large openings in the white and black marble floor. But someone had failed to coordinate between the stone masons and the carpet weavers; men with sharp blades had to slice off the rich borders. Then there were the white statues of Chinese lion dogs. Two of them were stationed at the entrance to the huge baccarat and high-roller area, which was sunk into the floor on one side of the casino, a setting for the show-off gamblers who liked a crowd. When high-roller recruiter Bucky Howard saw the lion dogs he yelled that they had to go. One of the staff tried to calm Howard, saying he apparently didn't know they were symbolic guardians of wealth.

"That's right, you idiot, and what putting them there tells any Asian player is, they are there to guard Donald's money, so get them the hell out of here before this place opens," Howard ordered.

Trump had promised real elegance. No faux marble, no *Trump l'oeil* views, none of that plastic posing as ivory that Steve Wynn used at his Mirage. But except for the chandeliers the place was mostly fakery and dross. At the main entrance to the Taj stood six white elephants that Trump said had been carved from stone; they were fiberglass, and even before the place opened a tusk on one had cracked, but no one repaired

226

it for weeks. The six elephants, plus a trio on the Boardwalk, seemed fitting symbols for this oversize, over budget white elephant that would drain money instead of produce profits. This was a pauper prince's palace. The giant space built above an arch over the Boardwalk, planned as a nightclub where customers could look down on the passing throng, remained a hollow shell.

Round-the-clock efforts by the contractors allowed the Taj to open April 2 for a test run, but it was a disaster. The Taj covered more than two and a half acres, the size of Trump Plaza and Trump Castle combined, with three thousand slot machines. But instead of many change booths and an army of people making change, it relied on untested machines, most of which quickly jammed. Worse, they frequently shorted the customers. The casino cage was too small even for a casino half its size, as one of Castle president Ed Tracy's aides had warned in another ignored memo. To control the flow of money between the cage, which is the casino's bank, and the gaming floor, money must be handled in precise amounts. Thus if $1,001 in quarters is needed on the casino floor, exactly 4,004 coins must be obtained, signed for and delivered, where they are signed for again. The system quickly broke down on the first day, and no one knew how much money was out or who had signed for it. On the second day the casino did not open until late afternoon and then only because the regulators agreed to set aside the mass of money from the first day and count it later. Four days later a sack that propped open a door inside the cage was examined. Inside was four hundred thousand dollars. One Taj executive watched a man walk from the cage, his coat bulging as if he had just put on ten pounds. But the executive decided not to add to the chaos by questioning him. "There's no way of knowing how much cash walked out of the place," said Dino Marino, the Casino Control Commission official overseeing the opening.

On the second day Trump had stood around the casino floor preening, telling Marino, "Isn't this going great?"

"No, Donald, it isn't. It's a disaster," Marino said.

"What do you mean? My people say everything's great."

"That's because they don't want to lose their jobs, Donald. They're telling you what you want to hear," Marino said, hoping to make Trump an ally in solving problems and not simply to ignite his fiery temper. When a few of Trump's people acquiesced to Marino's ideas about how to solve the problems, Marino figured he had done well.

The grand opening, the night of April 5, was supposed to be a gala, high-tech affair, but it was as much a disaster as the night it rained on the opening of Bugsy Siegel's Flamingo. Trump promised a load of celebs, but produced only the building's one-day owner, Merv Griffin, and model Elle MacPherson. He didn't have the loot to pay for more. Siegel had wanted his Hollywood pals like Cary Grant, Spencer Tracy and Joan Crawford, but got only George Raft and Georgie Jessel.

Trump promised high-tech wonders, but Fabu called Steve Perskie, the governor's chief of staff, "Steve Persico" and the green laser beams that were supposed to cut the giant ribbon wrapping the hotel tower didn't do so. Siegel had built a giant fountain with colored lights that was supposed to be visible a mile away, but then left it off because a cat had six kittens in the sump pump and he feared bad luck. Trump couldn't count the money straight, keeping the regulators on him, and eventually he had to take the Taj to Bankruptcy Court, giving up half his ownership. Siegel couldn't count the money straight, but the only regulators he dealt with enforced their rules with a gun.

While Trump advertised the Taj on television as his "billion-dollar dream come true," an ad which explained his dreams but not why anyone would want to gamble there, he took a very different position with the taxman. Trump insisted that the Taj was not worth a penny more than $400 million and its property taxes should be based on an assessment even lower than that.

During the second week, when the Taj still had not qualified for a full license, Trump promoted Ed Tracy from head of the Castle to Hyde's old job. Teams from the Plaza and the Castle, meanwhile, came to help straighten out the money. Marino regarded the Castle team as heroes, especially Barbara Primavera. Other problems grew, however.

Soon the *Inquirer* revealed that the contractors had not been paid; more than two hundred of them were due $72 million in all, money that Haybert had predicted would not be there. Add up all the vendors who said the Taj was behind and the bills came to nearly $90 million.

Tobman, the minaret salesman, complained that "on March 25 we were supposed to get paid for February. But then they told us there was a 'slight glitch' and to keep working and we would get paid April 5, the day of the grand opening. Then we were told we could get our checks late on April 6, which was a Friday so we knew that meant Trump wanted to keep the money over the weekend to earn the interest, which was fine. Then we were told we'd be paid on April 13 and then April 20.

"Next Perini Construction [Trump's general contractor] says they have not received the money from Trump and they don't know when we will get even a partial payment. I feel, and so do some of the others, that Trump has gone through all the money he raised from selling bonds and that we will be paid through cash flows from the casinos and not from monies he has already borrowed," Tobman said.

He was right. One internal estimate put the cost overruns and the cost of the abandoned work at $180 million above Trump's construction budget of almost $400 million. In the end the contractors would get about twenty cents on each dollar owed.

Meanwhile, the *Wall Street Journal*'s Barsky arrived late for his monthly poker game. A banker greeted him with this line: "Donald Trump's headed for a brick wall at a hundred miles per hour with no brakes." Barsky started to shrug off the story, since by then everybody knew Trump was in trouble. The *Philadelphia Inquirer*, followed a day later by *Forbes*, had recently obtained Trump's confidential net worth statement, which showed he was no billionaire, and Barsky's own stories had poked holes in Trump's Midas touch claims. But from the snickers in the room, Barsky discerned that his poker pals knew something was up and the next day he started working his banking sources. The result was a June 4 front-page lead story revealing that Trump and his bankers were negotiating from dawn to dusk in what amounted to a private bankruptcy proceeding. Trump the Invincible was suddenly at the mercy of his bankers, unable to make the June 15 interest and principal payments on the Castle or to pay many other bills as they came due. He had boasted in April that he would soon be the king of cash, but just then he looked a lot more like the duke of debt.

The bankers eventually agreed to loan Trump $65 million, of which the last $17 million was never advanced. It was such a complex deal that John Robbins, the Kenneth Leventhal & Company accountant brought in to value Trump's assets, quipped that "every lawyer in New York has come by for coffee, cookies and two billable hours." The legal fees at that point were $10.75 million and rising.

The banks agreed to slash interest payments and reschedule loan dates in a package that saved Trump at least $64 million a year for five years. They also put him on an allowance, though a very fine one worth $5.4 million in the first year. Within two years, though, the temporary patch job on his finances would be over, he would give up much of his real estate, his *Trump Princess* yacht, his Boeing 727 and his Super Puma helicopter.

The bankers' analysis of Trump's worth can be summed up easily: You are probably worth more than Donald Trump. By Trump's own analysis he was worth $1.4 billion. Leventhal figured he was worth one third to one half that much, while the bankers figured Trump was $295 million under water. The bankers' estimates included some generous calculations. Trump, Leventhal and the bankers all valued his yacht at $70 million, even though it eventually was taken back by Boston Bank & Trust for the $42 million Trump owed on it. They valued his Super Puma helicopter at the $10 million it would cost to replicate it, not the $2 million it was worth on the market. And the banks valued many assets at what Trump had borrowed against them, even if they were worth far less.

The banks did one more thing. They required Trump to hire a chief financial officer, someone acceptable to them. Trump's choice was Stephen F. Bollenbach, who was the CFO at Promus Companies and who on his first day on the job there, when it was still the Holiday Corporation, had helped put together a plan to ward off a raid by Donald Trump. Bollenbach proved to be a skilled negotiator. He also charged a stiff price. For ten dollars Trump sold Bollenbach a Trump Parc condo overlooking Central Park that was listed in the sales brochure at almost $5 million. Bollenbach also got a seven-figure salary with the banks guaranteeing his pay for two years.

By August the Casino Control Commission was drawn into the matter not because of its obligation to insure that casinos, their owners and those who work in them are financially stable and can pay their bills as they come due, but because the bailout gave the banks liens on the casinos. The commission had to approve the deal. When the commission balked at being rushed into a decision before its staff had analyzed the deal, it was not Trump's gaming lawyer, Nick Ribis, who took up the cause, but Thomas Auriemma, the deputy attorney general from the

230

Division of Gaming Enforcement. Auriemma asked another Trump lawyer, Thomas Cerabino, what would happen if the commission did not act that day. "The banks will move apart and take whatever steps they think are appropriate to protect their interests," Cerabino said. That threat of imminent and uncontrolled bankruptcy persuaded the commission to set a vote after the weekend. The commission then approved the bailout.

During this hearing, and during those that followed through the fall of 1990 and throughout 1991, the Casino Control Commission never looked at its own role in allowing Trump to get into trouble and in creating the illusion of his casinos' financial stability, a fiction maintained only by avoiding asking certain questions.

Anthony J. Parrillo, the enforcement division director, did tell his staff to go look at Trump's tax returns, which he conceded had not been reviewed since Trump was first licensed in 1981. Parrillo said that, like many others, he just believed Trump had bundles of money. Certainly a lot of money passed through his hands. During the thirty months before the bank bailout, Trump had a cash income of $375.2 million, or more than $1.6 million per week, nearly $10,000 an hour around the clock. Where had it all gone? Some had gone into propping up bad deals, covering stock market losses, and maintaining the Trump lifestyle, with its trophy mistress and a private army of security guards, some of whom carried MAC-10 automatic pistols under their suit coats. And a lot of it had gone to pay interest.

Not once did the Casino Control Commission exercise its broad powers of "strict regulation" to ask about the $90.5 million in capital withdrawals that Trump took from Trump Plaza and Trump Castle, money which would have allowed those casinos to make their mortgage payments without difficulty. Nor did the commissioners question the high-roller strategy at the Castle, which had led to huge cost overruns on the Crystal Tower and the purchase of the *Trump Princess,* both of which drained cash and reflected on business ability.

What the commissioners did do was approve the promotion of Tony Calandra from a casino salesman in charge of bringing in outer-borough high rollers to president of the Castle, a promotion Trump made one night on the spur of the moment in the baccarat pit when Calandra asked for the job and four Trump yes-men said he would be great at it.

231

Under Calandra the Castle's revenues declined while costs rose, which was predictable, since Calandra had no management experience whatsoever and thus could not have shown "by clear and convincing evidence" that he had the necessary business ability to run the Castle.

The commissioners also continued a policy of making sure that people seeking licenses as blackjack dealers and change makers were personally financially stable. Investigations were conducted to learn if applicants had unpaid debts, unpaid student loans or had collected excess unemployment benefits and not paid them back. When Steve Perskie, the 1977 sponsor of the Casino Control Act, was fired as Governor Florio's chief of staff in 1990 and named commission chairman, he lectured one man on his unpaid debts and then ordered a casino to deduct fifty dollars a week to help the man pay them.

Donald Trump was treated differently. His personal cash flow statement showed that, including the $10 million cash he paid Ivana in their divorce, he had $54.7 million in bills coming due in 1991 and an anticipated income of $1.6 million. Owing nearly thirty-five times one's income would not on its face seem to suggest financial stability, but Perskie brushed this matter aside even though Trump's solution to his problems was simply to stop paying his bills as they came due, but without seeking refuge in Bankruptcy Court as the Atlantis and Resorts had done because his bailout agreement would not allow that without dire consequences.

In April 1991, when the time came to renew Trump's qualifications and those of his three casinos, Perskie approved Trump personally, the Trump Organization and Trump Plaza. Auriemma, with help from Robert Latimer, who had ferreted out numbers for the Atlantis closing, filed a sixty-seven-page report which declared that "the Trump Organization will be insolvent in the near future, if it is not already, and if judged on that basis would not be financially stable" and "more worrisome is the financial health" of Trump personally.

But having laid the facts out in the record Auriemma opened a new escape from the financial stability requirement by suggesting that if Trump has a deal in the works that would make him stable once completed, that should be considered, too. Perskie immediately seized on Auriemma's initiative to help Trump. "It is obvious," Perskie said, "that neither Trump, the Trump Organization nor the Taj can satisfy the mandate of the Casino Control Act that they establish their financial stability by clear and convincing evidence." However, Perskie said he would vote to relicense because "substantial progress has been made" toward a new deal with the banks to settle their claims and that deal "may result in a financially stable" situation. Commissioners James Hurley and Pat Dodd, both former state senate colleagues of Perskie, agreed with this impromptu interpretation of the law Perskie had sponsored fourteen years earlier.

Commissioner W. David Waters said he could find no reason to deviate from the Casino Control Act's requirements. Waters believed that if Trump was unfit it was of his own making and that government should not intervene to protect him. Some predicted chaos if Trump lost his licenses, but Waters figured that the bondholders would step forward, propose that they take over as the real owners and hire competent managers. Besides, he figured, in the long run giving the commission's backing to owners when they could not pay bondholders would make it harder to raise money in the marketplace.

Since Trump needed four votes to keep his license that left his fate up to Valerie Armstrong, who longed for an appointment as a Superior Court judge. Armstrong said she wanted to avoid casting a no vote and she literally called out from the dais for help in finding some way to justify renewing Trump's qualification. Once again it was Auriemma of the Division of Gaming Enforcement, not Trump's own lawyers, who took up Trump's cause. Auriemma said the commission had broad powers and was obligated to look at many interests in making decisions. He said Trump could achieve financial stability by filing for Bankruptcy Court protection, but added "we should not necessarily, as regulators, be forcing" Trump to do that when "perhaps, the same result as a bankruptcy proceeding" can be reached through negotiation.

Martin Greenberg, the former Golden Nugget executive who represented Taj bondholders, supported Auriemma and said that financial stability, when he voted on the bill in the state senate, was intended to insure that casino owners were not tempted to break the law if they were in a squeeze for money. In what turned out to be a prescient observation, Greenberg said: "If financial stability were viewed as a component of integrity," then the fact that Trump may be a million dollars or so short, even after the bankers stop requiring payments, is not significant. "You have all the authority you need to monitor the financial condition and Donald Trump on a periodic basis so that you can assure yourself of that stability to avoid the temptation that would give rise to the loss of integrity."

Unbeknownst to the commissioners, events had already transpired—and been kept from them—which would test whether that authority would be exercised.

Before that issue arose, however, Trump would lose both of his biggest customers—for very different reasons.

24

The Warrior Returns

Akio Kashiwagi was a crafty soul. He wheeled and dealed for rebates and credit on a scale available only to those willing to risk millions of dollars on each trek to the tables. He also seemed to have all sorts of side deals going with casino hosts, like cashing in chips obtained on credit, which turned the paper risk of a marker into real exposure for the casino because the gambler had obtained hard dollars. And he tried to buy chips with instruments that some casinos found were not readily convertible into cash, ones that could only be cashed at a particular bank and only if Kashiwagi was standing there. Still, every casino executive worth his comping privileges wanted Kashiwagi, wanted to bag his wallet and have as their own trophy a story of how they had faced, and bested, the world's most fearless gambler. They wanted to tell stories like Dennis Gomes's favorite tale.

Gomes was a straight-laced regulator with an extraordinary reputation among others in law enforcement and among reporters, to whom he leaked some of the best crime stories to come out of Las Vegas. He came to New Jersey before it started casino gambling to show how regulation could be done. But his precise, unannounced raid on Resorts' Bahamas operation, which turned up file drawers full of evidence tying Resorts to Meyer Lansky's gang, and his insistence on following the letter of the law were rewarded by orders chaining him to his desk. Gomes quit and returned to Nevada, where he eventually ran the Dunes, which he leased from its Japanese owner. Gomes had most of his money, a million dollars, sunk in the Dunes, a broken-down excuse for a casino located on the incredibly valuable fourth corner where Caesars Palace, the Barbary Coast and Bally's Grand meet on the Strip. One week he lured Akio Kashiwagi to his table. For hours Gomes watched the play from his television monitor in his office, sweating as Kashiwagi's bankroll grew and grew by one hundred thousand dollars per bet.

When Kashiwagi was $5 million ahead he got up, stretched, and announced it was time to return to Kashiwagi Palace, his $80 million home near the foot of Mount Fuji, the home Japanese tourists kept mistaking for a temple because it was built with huge Japanese cypress logs common to Shinto shrines.

If Kashiwagi left the Dunes would close, because the cash he would demand would wipe the place out. Even if Gomes had the slot machines emptied of their winnings, the Dunes might not be able to cover all its outstanding bills. No matter what, Gomes told his Asian marketing guy, don't let that guy get away.

When the limo brought Kashiwagi and his host to the private jet at McCarran Airport, the pilot came back to say that he felt unlucky and did not want to fly.

"You're just trying to get me to come back so I'll lose," Kashiwagi replied to his host in Japanese.

"Well, you can fly, but I'm not going to die," the host said, heading for the door.

That did it. Kashiwagi said he would fly commercial. Inside the terminal he was taken to the Delta gate and told that the only remaining flight to Los Angeles would arrive too late for him to connect to the plane for Japan. That was sort of true. It was the last Delta flight that night. Kashiwagi, who did not read English, did not ask about other airlines.

The host recommended that Kashiwagi return to the Dunes and fly out the next morning.

"No, you're just trying to get me back to gamble," Kashiwagi said.

"Go to Los Angeles and it's going to cost you two thousand dollars for rooms and food for you and your companions," the host told Kashiwagi, knowing he was a tightwad when it came to expenses. That did it. Kashiwagi agreed to stay the night at the Dunes for free.

On the short limousine ride back the host suggested they have dinner together and then go see one of Norbert Alemain's naked girl revues. They shared a bottle of wine at dinner, but it was empty long before the late show would start so the host suggested that Kashiwagi gamble to fill the time.

"No," Kashiwagi said, "you just want me to lose my money."

"Not at all," the host said. "Just bet ten thousand dollars."

Kashiwagi sat down, put out ten thousand dollars and won. Gomes knew he had him. "He was thinking that he had shorted himself ninety thousand dollars because if he had bet his usual hundred thousand dollars that's how much more he would have won."

On the next hand Kashiwagi bet $100,000 and he stayed for hours chasing that $90,000. By dawn he had lost the $5 million cash and had signed markers for $5 million more. Gomes not only escaped ruin, he was a multimillionaire, even after giving Kashiwagi a 30 percent discount on his marker.

Stories like this abounded about Kashiwagi, stories about how he had broken or made careers, how he had negotiated for credit and discounts, how he wanted the best suites and then ate bacon, lettuce and tomato sandwiches. How he made deals governing how long he would play in return for credit and broke them. How he would quit when he was ahead. Stories about where he got all that money.

Kashiwagi appeared to have limitless wealth and yet he was not among the top thirty taxpayers in his prefecture. His Tokyo office was modest, with an apartment upstairs, though luxury cars filled the parking spaces out front. A business research firm showed that Kashiwagi's company had just five employees and sales of $15 million, yet Kashiwagi told casino executives he was a billionaire with an income of $100 million a year. Gomes and other casino executives figured he was a *sarakin*, a Japanese loan shark, with connections to the *yakuza*, the Japanese mob. That Kashiwagi was said to be part Korean, a serious detriment to business success in Japan, added to these suspicions.

Kashiwagi's reputation for craftiness, for working side deals and for quitting while he was ahead, weighed on the mind of Ed Tracy, who had just taken charge of all three Trump casinos when Kashiwagi returned to Trump Plaza. In February, Kashiwagi had beaten Trump Plaza for $6 million, a pittance compared to the $19 million that Kashiwagi won that month at the Diamond Beach Casino in Darwin, Australia, breaking its bank.

In May, Kashiwagi had been playing at Trump Plaza for five days and was insisting he should get more credit, that he had been promised more credit. Tracy met Kashiwagi in the Plaza Club, a lounge reserved for high rollers, and they sat near a large bronze Buddha that Trump Plaza had won away from another high roller, Bob Libutti. Tracy explained that he was a simple man, not familiar with Japanese social graces, but confident that he and Kashiwagi could talk amicably as businessmen.

"You obviously have enough money to stay here and gamble forever," Tracy said, "but frankly, I don't want you to. I apologize if someone failed to fully negotiate the terms of the game, but our agreement stands." Kashiwagi, under that agreement, was not supposed to quit until he had either gone bust or doubled his bankroll to $24 million.

Then Tracy dropped his bombshell: the $6 million credit line extended by Trump Plaza, matched by the $6 million check Kashiwagi left at the cage, would not be increased. After this game to the death ended, however, Mr. Trump would be honored to have his very best customer come up the Boardwalk to the new Taj Mahal, and if that was of interest, there could be discussions about how much cash and how much credit would make for a worthwhile game there. At the Taj, though, Tracy hinted, the maximum bet might be just one hundred thousand dollars, half what Trump Plaza allowed, depending on what kind of checks or other instruments the gambler had with him.

Kashiwagi kept his counsel to himself. In an elevator reserved for him and his entourage he descended to the baccarat table and resumed playing. At one point his $12 million stake had grown to nearly $19 million. But now he was down, way down, having lost all the chips he had bought for cash. He was playing on chips bought with credit, displaying the bold style and ferociousness that caused Al Glasgow to call him The Warrior. Kashiwagi never varied his bet of two hundred thousand dollars on each hand.

Jess Marcum, the little old mathematician, watched, too, knowing that time and the house advantage were on Trump's side, knowing luck was just so much hokum. In a temple full of believers in the capricious god Chance, Jess Marcum was a lonely infidel. A knowing smile decorated the little old man's face as he stood in his tired tweed coat, arms folded across his wheezing chest, watching the cards come out of the shoe. Marcum smiled because he had studied Kashiwagi. He knew what would happen if patience prevailed.

Trump had paid Marcum five thousand dollars plus expenses to tell him if Kashiwagi somehow had rigged the February game. Marcum and Glasgow watched videotapes made by cameras hidden in the smoky gray domes dotting the casino ceiling. Marcum quickly determined that Kashiwagi was no cheat. What fascinated Marcum were the subtle changes in Kashiwagi's face when he lost and how he kept coming at the house. "Turn off the machine. I know how to beat him," Marcum said. "This guy loves a challenge. He's a natural for the freeze-out proposition."

The freeze out, the double or nothing game, would have solved the problem back in February when Kashiwagi quit after just seven hours when he had won $6 million of Trump's money. Double or nothing would appeal to Kashiwagi's need for a challenge, Marcum figured, and to his sense of honor, and it would require him to stay until the end or something close to it. In New Jersey the casinos had to close for a few hours each day and Marcum knew that if Kashiwagi were down, but not out, he might contrive a reason not to return and blow the rest of his bankroll.

On the sixth night of Kashiwagi's visit, when The Warrior had played for nearly seventy hours, Marcum stood anonymously in the crowd of gamblers peering over the low marble wall. Kashiwagi was down to six rows of five-thousand-dollar chips, a bankroll worth $4.2 million bought on credit. Just after midnight Kashiwagi lost one bet. Then another. And another and another until he had lost eleven in a row, not counting the ties, on which Kashiwagi shrewdly made no bets. In less than ten minutes $2.2 million moved from Kashiwagi's side of the table to Trump's. Marcum, who had invented the tie bet, admired Kashiwagi for ignoring it because it showed that Kashiwagi understood Marcum's only god, probability. Soon Kashiwagi won some money back, but just before the 4 A.M. closing time, when Kashiwagi was down to $2 million and change, he rose, bowed to the dealers, and accompanied by a woman, a host, two casino security guards and his aide Daryl Yong, he left for the best suite in the house.

Glasgow sauntered to a telephone on the casino wall and called Trump with the news about Kashiwagi's bad luck. "Isn't he great," Trump exulted. "He is really the greatest."

On the seventh day Kashiwagi rested.

Glasgow went home and just before dawn fell into a brief, fitful sleep. Waking up, he dragged his spent fifty-six-year-old body into his kitchen. Glasgow kept thinking about the stacks of chips and hearing the words of the author, who the night before kept insisting that he and all the casino executives were wrong in their calculations on how much Kashiwagi was ahead or behind because their numbers did not match the value of all those chips in the baccarat pit. Could everyone be off by $480,000? Glasgow started asking himself. Glasgow lit a cigarette, pulled out a pencil and, looking around for something to make notes on, grabbed a paper sack his wife had left on the counter. He began adding up the numbers and realized that, indeed, they did not work out. Kashiwagi should have had almost a half million dollars more in chips at the table.

Glasgow grabbed the phone and called the Trump Plaza cage. "Anyone been cashing in five-thousand-dollar cheques?" he asked, using the casino term for such high denomination chips that they bore serial numbers.

Daryl Yong had, yes, the clerk replied. Yong had cashed in $474,000 worth of them during the week. Yong was Kashiwagi's translator and aide. At the table he wagered some of Kashiwagi's chips. Glasgow was astounded because the cash-ins meant that Kashiwagi had converted nearly 10 percent of the credit chips into cash, money Trump Plaza would have a hard time getting back if Kashiwagi played until he went bust.

When Kashiwagi awoke that morning he proposed that Trump extend him another $4 million credit. He needed more bullets to fire at his adversary. No, said Tracy, who knew from Marcum's pages of handmade calculations that the odds were 87 to 1 against Kashiwagi coming back from his current state to double his original bankroll. Tracy said no because while the world still thought Donald Trump was the modern

240

Midas, Tracy knew his boss had built a house of cards that could collapse if Kashiwagi were to win millions from the casino, just as Kashiwagi had nearly bankrupted Dennis Gomes a few months earlier.

Kashiwagi was furious. Trump lacked honor, Yong told casino reporter Dan Heneghan. Kashiwagi had come all the way from Japan after Trump presented him with a signed copy of *The Art of the Deal* and now Trump was not honoring his word that he would be delighted to extend Kashiwagi credit. But the aide said Kashiwagi would get his revenge. Trump's published life story would have a new use, Yong said. "We plan to burn it soon."

Kashiwagi called Caesars, which provided him a limousine to depart. While Trump would later propose that Kashiwagi return, that he come to the Taj on Pearl Harbor Day, that was just hot air. Kashiwagi had no intention of paying his marker. The word was spreading among casino executives that Kashiwagi was in hock deeply to the *yakuza*.

Kashiwagi continued to play and seek deals. Steve Wynn had him to the Mirage, though he was especially careful to make sure Kashiwagi did not use Mirage credit to put the house at risk.

As Christmas 1990 approached Kashiwagi asked the Sands in Atlantic City to let him play at two hundred thousand dollars a hand. While the Sands had taken enormous risks with José Joaquín Gonzáles Gorondona's money at the Aruba Concorde, it was much more cautious with its own tiny bankroll. Its corporate parent, Pratt Hotel, appeared to be in the black, but that was largely because it listed as an asset a $14 million unpaid arbitration award from a contractor. Take away this accounting equivalent of smoke and mirrors and Pratt Hotel's foundation was built on shifting sands. Marketing executive Rob Goldstein, who oversaw the Aruba operation, recommended that the Las Vegas Hilton take Kashiwagi's action. It did, and soon a Hilton exec called Goldstein to say thanks for the $15 million Christmas gift.

Kashiwagi continued to play, but not always pay, around the world. Then came January 3, 1992, the middle of the week-long celebration of the New Year in Japan, a time for families. Kashiwagi gathered his wife Meiko, his daughter and son-in-law to the palace, which was built with fine wood, polished stone and a sprawling kitchen filled with every modern convenience. That day Meiko and the next generation left to get strawberries, a trip that lasted more than six hours.

241

Just before dark someone entered by a side door. When the family returned much later they found the living room furniture overturned and blood everywhere. The fifty-five-year-old master of the house lay on the kitchen floor in a pool of blood, his face hacked beyond recognition by a samurai sword, a ritual murder weapon employed by the *yakuza* when dealing with deadbeats. The Japanese police soon arrested a *yakuza* who had checked himself out of the hospital that day, a man who had entrusted Kashiwagi to sell a luxury car for him and was displeased with the price it brought. They also arrested a companion of his, a nurse whose car retained traces of Kashiwagi's blood even after being run through a car wash. Eventually the police let them go, saying there were problems with the evidence.

Kashiwagi died owing Trump $6 million. With the money he won in February and the chips Yong cashed in, plus the expenses of bringing the player and his entourage from Japan twice, the experience was a loser for Trump, who was out about $1 million in cash. The Hilton held a $5 million marker from the Christmas 1990 visit. Casinos in Macao and elsewhere also held final markers.

Glasgow, ever the wit, heard the news of Kashiwagi's murder over the telephone. He looked up, relayed what he had just heard and instantly observed: "See what happens when you don't pay your markers?"

25

Stealing the Buddha

Fear spread through the dealers' lounge at Caesars on the Boardwalk even before table eight at pit three was roped off with red velvet. The dealers, as well as the boxmen, stickmen and floor persons, and everyone else who worked in the casino, knew who was coming to that table and what a disaster he could be for their careers, how failing to book a bet in the second or so while the dice were flying or calling a cocked die against him or even unknowingly igniting one of his countless superstitions could get them written up by the suits or disciplined, perhaps even squeezed out of their job.

The craps shooter who evoked these fears was a squat man in his fifties with a dome head, a big nose and the fast-talking style of a con man. He said his name was Robert Libutti, though over the years investigations by the racehorse industry and by Congress found that he had used other names, including Robert Presti and Nicholas Spadea.

Among all the 33 million people who played in Atlantic City each year he held one major distinction. Bob Libutti was the biggest loser of them all. He had made a name for himself as a big loser at Steve Wynn's old Golden Nugget, and when Steve Hyde left there to run Trump Plaza he persuaded his best player to come along. Casino records showed that Libutti had lost $12 million in less than three years. No one knew how deep his pockets were, but no one believed he had felt the seams yet. Caesars wanted that kind of action; that was why it had marketing agents in cities like Medellín. Now that Caesars had a shot at Libutti the dealers anxiously repeating rumors in the employee lounge knew that management would do whatever it took to get Libutti's action and that their careers, their jobs and even their human dignity meant nothing.

Caesars reserved its best suite, its Emperor's penthouse, for Libutti, setting before him a table piled high with lobster, potato chips and his other favorites. Dom Pérignon rosé champagne, Libutti's favorite, was chilled to just the right temperature and kept both in his suite and near his reserved craps table. Caesars even sent one of its staff out to find the particular Lalique crystal flutes he preferred.

These subtle touches, and every other action Caesars took that day, came on the recommendation of Lynden Stockton, a man who regarded himself as Libutti's friend, his very good friend. Stockton was a "senior marketing executive" with Caesars and he knew to the minute when Libutti would walk out of Trump Plaza and stroll the thirty or so paces along the Boardwalk to Caesars, where Stockton would be waiting, along with a security guard so that everyone would know this was a special player. For two years Libutti had gambled every other day at Trump Plaza, where he wagered as much as twenty thousand dollars on a roll of the dice and his average bet was nearly twelve thousand dollars. Stockton knew these closely guarded Trump Plaza secrets because, until the day before, Stockton had worked at Trump Plaza as a casino host.

When Bob Libutti made his numbers, his charm and generosity spread across the gaming floor and, to those who met his eccentric needs, he tipped lavishly. When it was time for his heart pills, any cocktail waitress who promptly brought just the right water in just the right glass and presented her tray in just the right way, could be rewarded with a black chip worth $100. If he saw someone who looked down and out, he was known to hand them a crisp $100 bill or a chip, perhaps an orange one worth $1,000 if their story seemed especially compelling. In addition to whatever bankroll he brought to the table, Libutti usually started each day with 50 crisp $100 bills in his pocket, under the money clip his sainted mother had given him before she died, a money clip made from a $5 gold piece minted in 1932, the year he was

244

born. Libutti said he always kept a last $1,000 in his pocket to tip the helicopter pilots and anyone else he needed to reward for their service.

When Libutti crapped out, though, the charming and generous spirit disappeared in less time than it took a dealer to call the dice. Libutti's superstitions joined with his fury at losing to bring forth a vile magma of denunciations at the poor devils who caused his loss because they looked at the dice the wrong way or spoke at the wrong moment. It was as if a human Mount St. Helens blew its top, scattering burning words everywhere. The poor devils assigned to Libutti's table ceased to be employees or servants or even human beings. They became bitches and cunts, motherfuckers and cocksuckers, niggers and ugly people, Jew cunts and kikes, spooks and gooks, chinks and slant-eyed pieces of shit.

"Who the fuck do you think you are?" Libutti would rail, sometimes threatening to punch a dealer or use his influence with Steve Hyde or even The Donald to get the offender fired. No accusation was too absurd when Libutti's temper took hold. A cocktail waitress who adjusted the hem of her costume was accused of running her finger over her clitoris and rimming the glass.

To kill the evil jinns that made the dice land seven-up Libutti would squeeze the red cubes in his stubby-fingered fists. When his human strength failed to crush the evil spirits he would hurl them at the chandelier or the floor or even at the dealer who had picked these goddamn, no-good thieving dice. Once he grabbed the stick and snapped it, breaking its unlucky influence.

Anger consumed Libutti until he seemed ready to kill those around him, anger fueled by the self-hatred that consumed him when he lost because losing was a sign of how he stood in God's eyes and because he could not bring himself to quit when he was ahead and he could not stop when he was losing until all the money was gone—except for the last thousand. In these moments, when he felt so loathsome he knew the dogs would hide in the farthest corner of the mansion rather than sleep on the covers with their master, the murderous tone of his voice reflected an inner desire to kill himself, a thought that worsened his misery because the church taught that suicide was an unpardonable sin.

The casino workers knew that whatever streamed from Libutti's mouth, whatever he called them, the suits expected them to stand there smiling and to say, "Yes sir, Mr. Libutti," so he would stay at the cra·

245

table until the wad of cash he brought that day belonged to the casino. Nothing was to interfere with his compulsion to gamble.

The rules in this most highly regulated of industries did not apply to Bob Libutti. Cocktail waitresses were forbidden to accompany players up to their rooms, but if Libutti wanted five or six of them to come along and giggle and sip the best champagne, then Hyde would send them right up. If Libutti insisted that some stupid motherfucking dealer had called a cocked die wrong, that it was really leaning to a hard six and not a seven, then management would interrogate the entire team working the table and let Libutti throw the dice again on his next visit.

The knowledge that Libutti was above the rules was no secret. Everyone who worked in the Trump casino knew it and so did plenty of others. At Duke Mack's, Graybel's and other watering holes where the dealers eased the strain of their jobs over whiskey and beer, the best way to top the tales of player foolishness and outrages was to recount the latest story about Bob the Monster.

Bob Libutti said and did whatever the fuck he felt like, right down to ordering Jim Gwathney, a Casino Control Commission inspector whom Libutti felt stood too close to his game, to get lost. Finally Libutti threw several dozen black chips into the air, shouting "free chips." Later Gwathney's bosses told him to stop hawking the game, not to be so aggressive, in effect not to do his job. Another inspector, Greg Stroemmel, who has only one arm, was invited outside by Libutti, who vowed to break his arm because he, too, had "hawked" his game. The state did nothing about the threat. Stroemmel got the message: "This guy's losing millions and the casino wants his money and the state wants its cut of the win."

With Stockton's help Caesars had everything in perfect order to satisfy Libutti's whims and to show him how people who really knew how to run a casino, as opposed to what Caesars regarded as the amateur act at Trump Plaza, could treat a man of Mr. Libutti's stature. Yet this visit was about to turn into the worst day of Bob Libutti's gambling life, one that eventually would end the perks like the ten thousand dollars in cash that Trump Plaza funneled to him each month and the round-the-clock limo and driver. Before it was all over government agents wearing flak jackets would raid Libutti's home, poking through his wife's underwear drawer. Trump Plaza and Caesars would not escape this maelstrom, though they would fare better than the customer they most desired.

Libutti, a man ruled by superstitions, was about to get confirmation of his beliefs. Had he consulted the calendar Bob Libutti might have realized this was a bad day to gamble, that he should have stayed home.

It was Friday the thirteenth.

But the compulsion that led Libutti to Caesars was too deeply ingrained for him to stay home. That compulsion had been constantly reinforced since it had first surfaced when he was fifteen years old and a relative took him to the track.

"I'm a no good degenerate gambler," Libutti later said of his life, examining his fourth twenty-five-dollar cigar of the day. His short frame sunk into a feathery sofa, one of only six pieces of furniture in a living room the size of many houses, each wall more than thirty feet long. The windows along one side afforded a view of the expanse of greensward that led to a wood lot. A stone fireplace along another wall rose twenty feet in the room before the chimney broke through the ceiling. All around were bronze statues of famous horses: Man o' War, Seattle Slew, Secretariat.

He had grown up impoverished in Union City, in a neighborhood of immigrants from Italy who worked hard jobs digging ditches, hauling crates and breathing in deadly fumes while they rubbed varnish on coffins. He saw how well his wife's brother, the singer Jimmy Roselli, had done and he vowed to escape poverty. Now he lived in a modern manse, a few blocks from Richard Nixon's place in the multimillionaire's town of Saddle River, New Jersey, though the house belonged to his daughter, Edie. So, too, he said, did Buck Chance Farm, a great name for a gambler's stable, even if it existed only on paper.

Three decades ago, when he was just old enough to drink, he had owned a couple of bars in North Jersey, joints known for lots of action. He also worked some soft jobs, like driving gangs of workmen to Brooklyn waterfront job sites and then getting paid for a full shift with no work. "It was like a honeymoon," he said wistfully of that job. But gambling soaked up all this easy money until in 1967 he went bust. Joan and the two kids went to live with one set of relatives while he slept on the floor at cousin Vincent Presti's one-bedroom apartment and argued with his hosts every night. He started using the name Bob Presti, he said, because the mailman would not leave his letters in the Presti box otherwise.

Then he got a bright idea, one that would get him out of poverty and on the road to Atlantic City. He decided to become a racehorse consultant. "I knew nothing of the business, but I had the desire," he said. "If you're a good judge of women's legs you can judge racehorses. It's a gift."

Libutti worked the angles. He needed a nice house, probably a mansion, to make himself look prosperous. In the newspaper he saw an ad for a furnished house, in an exclusive Long Island community, owned by an academic whose family was going to Italy. It was perfect. "We're going to do a lot of entertainment. My game plan is, I'm going to invite Ralph Wilson, who owns the Buffalo Bills, and the George Steinbrenners and all these people. This is a game, what it's all about."

Libutti asked his mother for five hundred dollars to get him started. He invited the homeowners to dinner at a fine restaurant, showing up in a limousine he rented with part of his mother's money. "I made a good impression on them because that was going to be important—you've got to remember, the people are leaving their house and their furnishings to people that they don't know." It worked. But the dinner and the limo had used up the five hundred dollars. Libutti needed cash to pay the rent.

"I go to the liquor store in town and I said to the guy: 'I just bought twelve Tall Tree Court, the house. I'm going to be doing a lot of entertainment and I'm going to be running up big liquor bills. There's two things that will be required of you if you want my business. Number one, I would want bills on everything so that they could be written off and you're going to have to give me a thirty-day trust.' He says, 'Well what do you mean by that?'

"I said, 'Well, I want to give you a liquor order and I want to round it off to whatever it's going to come to; I want some cash from you because I don't have any cash for about three weeks from closing the house.' Now I just moved in, okay? I gave him a three-thousand-dollar liquor order and I gave him a check, a postdated check for sixty days and he gave me two thousand dollars cash and three thousand dollars in booze. That was going to be our eating money—remember we didn't make the horse order yet. This was the very first day I'm there. Now we've got money, we've got liquor, we've got a mansion of a house."

What Libutti doesn't have yet is a racehorse. He learned that could be accomplished on a promise with no cash.

"I bought two shitty little horses for thirteen thousand dollars at an auction and you have thirty days to pay for them. In them days anybody got credit, you didn't even have to be a horseman. They give you the credit. After I bought the horses, I found it was very hard to sell.

"So now I said the only way that I can find anybody with money is, let me look at the *New York Times* and see who's got a Rolls-Royce— who's got a Rolls-Royce has got to have money. And if they've got money, and if I can't sell them a horse, then this is wrong and I can't stay in this business. So I looked and this guy's got a Corniche convertible, Rolls-Royce, 1971 Rolls-Royce—no, it was a 1969 Rolls Corniche convertible for sale for twenty thousand dollars. I called up a Rolls-Royce dealer, I said, 'What would you pay for a Rolls-Royce convertible?' and I described the car the way it was in the paper. The guys says we'll pay around fourteen thousand dollars for the car.

"So now if I can talk this guy who bought the newspaper ad into taking a horse for the car, I got my first deal made. So what I did, I called up this guy, it turns out he's a doctor, multi-, multimillionaire." Libutti said it went like this:

"I see you have a car for sale."

"Yes, I have it for sale for twenty thousand dollars."

"I see it in the paper two weeks in a row. I have maybe a deal for you and you may find it ridiculous. I have a horse that for tax reasons I couldn't sell."

Libutti picked up his fifth cigar, lit it, and explained that he had concocted the tax story because "you have to have an excuse, right—tax reasons. Now this is a cliché in racing, anybody wants to sell a horse, you don't want to sell a bad one, you want to sell it for tax reasons."

The doctor bought the deal. Libutti was in business, though not before Joan spent three days trying to fly to the doctor's home, getting diverted to another airport and getting lost driving the big British vehicle back to Long Island.

Soon Libutti was trading horses back and forth, including a promising young winner named Jim French. Libutti had a hidden interest in Jim French, a fact that got him banned from horse racing in New York and that made his name mud. The Thoroughbred Racing Protective Bureau said following its tracking of Libutti's horse trades: "The entire thread was of organized crime influence."

That's when Libutti started wheeling and dealing through his wife Joan and through Edie. Libutti made lots of money in those years and life was better than he ever imagined until his only son died. Libutti blamed himself for the drugs.

One day in 1986, a bank president who was Libutti's good friend, the kind of banker who would loan him one hundred thousand dollars on a telephone call, came by in his limo. "You need to get your mind onto something else," the banker said and off they went to a Manhattan whorehouse. Libutti said he looked at the place, said he was too old for this shit, and sulked in the limo until his banker returned after a few hours, grinning and telling the driver to head for Atlantic City. Outside the Golden Nugget, Libutti said, his banker pal handed him ten thousand dollars.

"As soon as I started gambling I forgot about my son, completely forgot about it," he said. It was the first relief he had felt. It cost him the $10,000, but the next day Libutti was back with $50,000 of his own money. When Hyde left for Trump Plaza, Libutti followed, which fit perfectly with Trump's desire to have only the biggest, only the best, in his joint.

When the maze of tall columns in Trump Plaza, which were needed to support its thirty-eight stories, were stripped of their mirrors and fabric and covered with marble, along with the walls and the floor, some took to calling the lobby Libutti Forest because it was his losings that paid for it all.

Libutti never asked for credit, not for himself. But he often took over the credit office on the casino floor, where he would eat hot dogs and drink champagne while the helicopter was being repaired. Eventually he asked for his own limo and driver around the clock and Hyde gave it to him.

Libutti played with cash, which meant the casino was not obligated to investigate the source of his money and could accept his statement that people like Steinbrenner paid him as much as a quarter million dollars for his opinion on a yearling's chances of becoming a Triple Crown winner, a multimillion-dollar stud.

Sometimes, though, other players came and bought chips on credit and then passed them to Libutti at the table, players like a horse trainer who had a two-hundred-thousand-dollar credit line at Trump Plaza. While Trump Plaza kept such detailed records of Libutti's play that it could determine that his average 1987 bet was precisely $13,929.52, no one knew how many hundreds of thousands, or even millions, Libutti gambled and lost with chips obtained on other players' credit.

To keep gambling Libutti said he had certain needs. They were all satisfied, including his need for a predictable ten thousand dollars each month so he could cover his nut, pay his electric bill and the like. Each month he would get show tickets from Trump Plaza and trade them to a broker for ten thousand dollars cash.

The creative minds at Trump Plaza also gave Libutti cars. Ferraris. Rolls-Royces. Whatever he wanted. The rules required that the casinos buy the cars, but Libutti could instantly sell the cars back to the dealership, which would deduct a commission and then give him cash. Trump Plaza did not bother to arrange title to the cars—the casino and the car dealer simply exchanged checks, giving Libutti the cash, $1.6 million, with which to gamble. And when Libutti lost the money his temper would explode and Hyde would have to calm him down.

When he was ahead and decided to quit, which wasn't often, Libutti said there was always a problem leaving. "The helicopter always had some fucking mechanical problem and it would be fixed in a few hours or whatever other goddamn lie they could tell to keep me there. But if I ran out of money I'd turn to Rollo, my chauffeur, and I tell him to take the helicopter out to my house and get the attaché case with the seventy thousand dollars so I could keep playing and the helicopter was always ready for that."

To keep this lucrative business Hyde extended Libutti every privilege he could imagine. Libutti flew with Donald Trump in his black Super Puma helicopter and he sat between Donald and Ivana at Wrestlemania IV until one of the wrestlers threw a snake toward them. Libutti jumped up as if to block the creature while Ivana left in a huff. He even arranged a horse for Trump, to be called DJTrump, but then Trump ordered the horse run on a day when a sickness was sweeping the track where it was kept, ruining the animal. Trump refused to pay, so Hyde stepped in to pick up part of the loss.

When Edie turned thirty-five, Trump Plaza threw a lavish party and made a professional videotape of it. Donald Trump gave Edie a cream-colored Mercedes-Benz convertible.

Joan was given free vacations. "They sent me to Paris on the Concorde to get me out of town. They sent my grandson and I to China, to Japan, to Thailand. They offered me first class on the QE 2, but I'm not a boat person," she said.

Joan got gifts, too, especially when she began complaining that her husband was spending too much time and too much money gambling and especially after the Buddha disappeared.

"They had me so entranced that they got me to the point where I started taking artifacts, antiques from the house, down there to gamble," said Libutti. "The jade Buddha that's in the chairman's suite at Trump Plaza cost me one hundred eighty-five thousand dollars. There's another Buddha, the bronze one that cost me forty-five thousand dollars," Libutti recalled, Joan watching his every word, her eyes afire. Trump Plaza arranged for a liquor vendor to buy the Buddhas and then sell them to the casino, Libutti said. "I got fifty some thousand for them. I went to the table, made two bets and lost it."

One time Hyde called Libutti to invite him down and Libutti balked, saying Joan was furious at his gambling.

"Bob you gotta get down here, guys are beating our brains out," Hyde said.

"I can't," Libutti answered.

"Last night we were beaten for eighty-five thousand dollars and there's another guy down there right now beating our brains out. Luck is really going against us today. You should be down here."

"Eighty-five thousand dollars? Who? Who won that?" Libutti said.

Hyde named the player and filled in more details, working to close the sale. Then Libutti stopped him.

"I can't, Steve. Joan'll kill me. She will fucking kill me if I come down there today."

"You want to come?"

"Of course I want to come. Guy beats you for eighty-five thousand dollars, of course I want to come."

"Go to the office. We'll pick you up at one thirty."

"What about Joan?"

"I'll take care of her. Don't worry. She'll be glad you came. Just get the cash."

Joan said a limo soon showed up at her door with two women from Trump Plaza, who said they had come to take her on a shopping spree in Manhattan. Anything her heart desired at Tiffany's or wherever, Donald would be glad to pay.

"They'll do anything to get your money," Joan said. "They'll wreck your marriage if it will get them money."

The truth in Joan Libutti's observation emerged on Friday the thirteenth of May in 1988. It happened in a way that showed how one person can make a difference.

Joel Respes was a craps floor-person, a foreman in a suit who supervised the stickmen and boxmen and rated players to determine the level of comps they would get. When he came back from his break he was told he would not be working pit three, but would be sent on to handle other tables. The reason, he was told, was that he was black and Mr. Libutti preferred white males on his game.

Respes, who had started out as a dealer the day Caesars opened and had made floor person at age thirty-five, did his job quietly and when his shift ended he walked out the door to his car. But he could hear his late father's voice telling him about how his dream of being an engineer died in the fifties when the engineering schools turned him away even though he qualified. And he could see his children losing respect for him because he said one thing about standing up for your rights and then did not stand up for his own. He had gone two blocks when he pulled over and got out.

Respes walked back into Caesars and headed for the Casino Control Commission booth. There he made out a complaint accusing Caesars of racial discrimination.

"I felt like Caesars had put up a sign that said 'For Whites Only' and I felt angry that Caesars wanted the player's money so badly that they did not care at all about the feelings of their employees," Respes said. "I could not believe that Caesars would treat its employees as inhumanely as they did."

The complaint reached Fred Gushin, the Division of Gaming En-

forcement lawyer who had pursued the case against the cocktail waitress who found a chip on the floor and who had brushed aside Bob
Signore's complaints that Trump Castle played by a different set of rules
than it gave players. Gushin cared passionately about civil rights issues
and the moment he saw Respes' complaint he knew he had a case.
While the enforcement division sometimes delayed for years and years
deciding whether to issue a permanent license, Gushin filed this complaint in just six weeks. Respes was not the only employee the complaint named as having had his civil rights trashed in a manner "repugnant" to state policy. On orders from casino manager Nick Niglio and
shift manager Rachel Bogatin, the enforcement division showed, Respes
and two women dealers had been replaced with white men.

The recommendation to remove blacks, women and, had any been
around, Asians came from Lynden Stockton, the casino host hired away
from Trump Plaza by Caesars marketing operation. An internal Caesars
memo said Stockton told Caesars that Libutti "did not want Blacks or
Orientals dealing on his game; he had no problem with females, but
preferred males."

When the complaint was filed Libutti screamed loudly that he was
being wronged by the state. "I never, ever said I wanted only white
males," Libutti said, a point Gushin was always careful to acknowledge.
The decision to remove Respes and the women came because of Stockton's perception of what Libutti wanted, a perception lent credence in
large part because Stockton is black.

Libutti said he harbors no hatred of any group, that the language he
used is the language of the streets where he grew up, and that he abhors
racial discrimination. "The way I speak is vulgar, in the sense of common," he said. Besides, he added, if he was a racist, why did Mike
Tyson give him the gloves he wore in one of his championship bouts?

Maryann Egli, who was replaced by a white male during another
Libutti visit to Caesars, later testified at an administrative hearing that
she never complained about being ousted to accommodate Libutti. "You
learn not to say too much . . . so I would like to keep my job . . . so I
didn't say anything," she testified. Later an administrative law judge
found that Caesars conduct was "insensitive, bizarre and traumatic" to
Respes and the other wronged employees. The judge recommended fining Caesars $15,600, the amount Libutti lost at Caesars.

In late 1989, the Casino Control Commission took a much bolder step, fining Caesars a quarter million dollars, the second-largest fine ever imposed against an Atlantic City casino up to that time. Caesars attorney Jeffrey Parliman said that once a lawsuit against Caesars by Respes and the women was settled the casino would be taking disciplinary action against employees whom he would not identify by name. Respes listened to Parliman's observations and felt he had a good idea who Parliman had in mind. Respes was gratified by the fine, feeling that the rightness of his action and the immoral conduct of Caesars had been established beyond all doubt, but he also said that when the time came for promotions "I am sure that my name will be overlooked."

Director Anthony J. Parrillo said his enforcement division's pursuit of the case was significant because "players cannot come in and dictate the rules."

But Libutti had been dictating the rules for some time and the Casino Control Commission knew about it. Inspectors like Gwathney and Stroemmel had written up Libutti's conduct, only to be slapped down by their superiors for doing their jobs.

Libutti had his own interpretation of what the state was doing, an interpretation both cynical and biting, but one that gained credence as events unfolded. Libutti's view was that the state wanted him to play and lose so it could collect its 9.25 percent take and that once he went broke the state would move against him.

It did.

Steve Perskie, who as a state legislator championed bringing casinos to Atlantic City and sponsored the Casino Control Act, served nine months as chief of staff to Jim Florio after the Democratic congressman was elected New Jersey governor in 1989. When Perskie's arrogant style, and his championing of the biggest tax rate hike in state history, made him a liability, Florio made him chairman of the Casino Control Commission.

At one of his first meetings Perskie said he wanted the enforcement division to file a petition banning Libutti from the casinos because of his sexist and racist language, a curious position for Perskie, a former judge, since it amounted to a direct assault on Libutti's First Amendment right of free speech. It would also be the first time anyone had been banned from a casino in New Jersey or Nevada for anything other than being a mobster. Commissioner Valerie Armstrong alone protested that Perskie's approach was improper, saying the casinos that did not throw Libutti out for being unruly should be disciplined. But Perskie prevailed on a 4 to 1 vote.

Mitch Schwefel, the enforcement division attorney assigned to make Libutti the one hundred and fifty-second person banned from the Atlantic City casinos, knew he would have a tough time defending an exclusion in court if Libutti fought it. But he had other information.

Leonard "Leo" Cortellino and Charles Ricciardi, Sr., had told Robert Walker, a state police detective working undercover, about a bookmaking operation they ran in Atlantic City for an associate of the Gambino family headed by John Gotti, the dapper don who used murder as a management tool to weed out both superiors and subordinates.

The pair told Walker that they knew Libutti and his brother-in-law, singer Jimmy Roselli. Later Cortellino and his pal Louis Lubrano told Walker that Libutti "was in Donald Trump's pockets," explaining that Libutti had obtained a lucrative contract for Roselli at Trump Plaza for "big money." They also said Libutti was known to have run a number of scams with horses.

Libutti, meanwhile, went to see Ed Tracy, who was then head of all three Trump casinos, about getting $375,000 he felt Trump owed him. In the course of the discussion Libutti gratuitously dropped John Gotti's name. Tracy, a man of scrupulous honesty, smelled a shakedown and called the state police, who wired his office. At the time Trump was deep in negotiating his bailout with the banks.

When Libutti walked into Tracy's Taj Mahal office, Tracy got right down to business.

"The problem that's remaining is the, ah . . . two hundred and fifty number," Tracy said.

"Right," Libutti answered.

"No way can I make that happen. . . . My problem is a simple one. It's that the banks will see everything. Donald doesn't sneeze without them holding a handkerchief for him. . . . We cannot make a deal that on paper doesn't make economic sense. They'd just throw it back at us and say, 'What's this?' " Tracy explained.

Their talk veered off to other subjects until Tracy steered it back to the payment Libutti wanted.

"So tell me how you want to structure this again?" Tracy asked.

"We'll take the money off Roselli's contract. . . . We'll say, listen, he wanted a thirty-thousand-dollar increase per show . . . so you got him to do the show for the same fifty-six thousand five hundred dollars, with a bonus if he signed for a year . . . and I get the bonus of a quarter million dollars," Libutti said.

During the conversation Libutti explained how John Gotti offered to deal with Frank Sinatra because of how the Chairman of the Board had treated Roselli, who grew up on the same block in Hoboken as Sinatra. The two singers had been feuding for two decades and the latest development was when both were to sing in Atlantic City, Old Blue Eyes at the Sands and Roselli at Trump Plaza, where both were sought after because of the crowds of free-spending wise guys they drew to the tables. Sinatra hired away several of Roselli's musicians.

"We sat in front of John Gotti about six weeks ago, seven weeks ago, and John said, 'You want me to handle it for you right now Jim? Fuck him?' "

Later in the conversation Libutti brought up Gotti again, saying "Gotti wants me to find out if he can come" gamble in the Trump casinos. "He said he never got a letter [banning him from the casinos], that means he's not barred."

Libutti insisted then and later that he was "only puffing" and had never met Gotti, though he added, "he's the kind of guy I should like to be around. I admire the guy."

Later Trump would tell the *Philadelphia Inquirer* that he had heard the name Libutti, but could not even remember what the guy looked like because they met, maybe, once. Libutti went ballistic at this distancing by Trump. "He's a liar," Libutti said, taking off into another angry tirade filled with four- and seven- and thirteen-letter denunciations of Trump and his integrity.

Libutti also said he was aware of all sorts of serious rules violations at Trump Plaza that would be of interest to the casino regulators. He said he and Trump had a deal for an "elaborate marketing scheme" designed to inflate the table drop—the amount of chips reported sold—because Trump wanted to report a higher figure than Caesars. He told one story of Donald Trump coming to him on the casino floor and personally handing him a check.

"Now you tell that one to Sweeney," Libutti said, referring to Jack Sweeney, whom Perskie had handpicked to succeed Parrillo as enforcement director, a job that is supposed to be independent of the commission. "And when Sweeney hears it you know what he'll say. He'll say, 'Bob Libutti doesn't have any credibility and we're not going to look into it.' Well, he doesn't need Bob Libutti because when Donald gave me that check there was a whole casino full of witnesses. There was the pit boss and the floor guy and the dealers and the stickman and my driver and bopidy bopidy bop, a whole fucking room full of people who have licenses and Sweeney's got this power that he can sit anyone who works in a casino down and tell them, 'You answer these questions or we ruin you.' He can make 'em empty their goddamn pockets and if they don't they lose their fucking licenses. So you tell him there's plenty of witnesses to that and to a hell of a lot more shit they pulled that ought to cost Donald his goddamn license."

Sweeney was advised of Libutti's claim that Trump personally handed him a check.

"Well, if that was true it would be very serious," Sweeney said, "but Libutti's got no credibility."

Sweeney was then told that Libutti had anticipated that response and was told about the other witnesses.

"Well, that'll be thoroughly investigated," Sweeney said. It marked the first time that Donald Trump had ever personally been the subject of an enforcement division investigation. It did not last long. Several of the witnesses Libutti identified said they were never contacted, never questioned. But Sweeney's office did call in one witness and ask him under oath about the accusations. Donald Trump denied them. He said the check in question had been turned over, but in a perfectly legitimate way. Sweeney took his word for it.

Libutti, whom the commission banned from the casinos because of his Gotti remarks, soon had new problems. At noon one day Edie kissed her mother good-bye in the kitchen and climbed into the Mercedes-Benz convertible Trump had given her. Moments later Joan Libutti noticed people in dark clothing with guns rushing her house. They were IRS agents and local police, wearing riot suits and flack jackets, come to serve a search warrant, wanting to know where her husband got all the money for gambling.

The regulators, the high-up ones who did not want to see either Libutti's conduct or the casinos' until Joel Respes stepped forward, ultimately fined Trump Plaza for discriminating against its own workers and for deceiving the commission with fake-gift cars that were meant to help Libutti get cash.

Trump Plaza was fined $200,000 for discriminating against its female and minority employees. For the sham car deals the fine was $450,000.

26

FlopWorld

A week after the Miss America Pageant marked the end of the busy 1988 summer gambling spree and the start of the long, hard off-season, a massive expansion of the Atlantic City Tropicana was finally finished, giving it the largest casino in town, doubling its hotel rooms to more than one thousand and providing a new name: TropWorld Casino and Entertainment Center. Ramada had sunk more than $600 million into the joint (before counting depreciation). By contrast, the Holiday Inn chain had just $255 million invested before depreciation in Harrah's Marina, its fabulously profitable Atlantic City casino.

TropWorld's most touted feature was Tivoli Pier—a two-acre indoor amusement park that featured attractions such as a mini–roller coaster, a Ferris wheel and a small theater with robotic dogs doing impressions of entertainers, with Elvis as a hound dog and Joan Rivers as a sleek grey-hound bitch. The roller coaster had only one dip capable of scaring a six-year-old. The Ferris wheel, which dominated the lobby, could not carry people because of fire safety concerns. The robot dogs all clicked mechanically when their mouths moved.

Tivoli Pier cost $19 million, the company said. Paul E. Rubeli, who was then head of Ramada's gaming operations in both Atlantic City and Nevada and later would be promoted to president, insisted this money was wisely spent. After all, he reasoned, an animatronic theater does not require huge fees charged by name performers for live appearances. This did not explain why, conversely, TropWorld had just spent even more than $19 million to build the largest live theater in town, with seventeen hundred seats and an optional nine hundred bleacher seats.

In Rubeli's mind Tivoli Pier could keep a visitor entertained and fed for two hours for about twenty-five dollars. Compared to what a wife or girlfriend might spend in boutiques and jewelry stores—money her gambler companion might otherwise blow at the craps tables—it seemed to Rubeli like a smart investment.

"Tivoli Pier is not meant for the frequent visitor," Rubeli said. "It is to solve the problem of what to do with your spouse, with your girlfriend, with your friends when you want to say 'Get off my back. I want to shoot craps.'"

The trouble with that theory was that Atlantic City depends on frequent visitors. The city boasted it was the number one tourist destination in America with more than 33 million visitors that year, 10 million more than saw Disney World in Florida. But that was misleading because in reality, Atlantic City lived on frequent repeat visits. "Atlantic City's really got two million people who come here sixteen times a year," Claridge president Roger Wagner often observed.

The next year's numbers proved TropWorld was a disastrous error in judgment. Its casino had grown nearly 82 percent larger and its hotel rooms doubled, but the amount players lost rose just 22 percent, from $233 million in 1988 to $284 million in 1989. The following year the amount players lost shrank back to $277 million, further evidence that the expansion strategy failed to benefit shareholders.

A revealing test of how well shareholder money was invested compared the amount won in each casino to the gross amount invested in the property. In 1990, TropWorld's casino won about forty-five cents for each dollar its building cost. Harrah's won $1.08.

The promised big profits that would have justified the $210 million spent expanding TropWorld turned out to be huge losses. The megafacility, as management liked to call it, lost $11.3 million in 1989. The smaller Harrah's earned $80 million that year.

In 1990, competition grew fierce as Donald Trump's Taj Mahal opened. Massive layoffs and other cost-cutting reduced TropWorld's loss to $3.7 million. In 1991, it lost money again. Since the day it opened in 1981 as the Atlantic City Tropicana the property had never once earned enough in its few profitable years to put its cumulative performance in the black. As 1992 began TropWorld's cumulative loss over its eleven years totaled almost $20 million.

As Rubeli kept insisting that fine-tuning by management and an improved economy would put luster on TropWorld, employees devised their own name for Ramada's crown jewel. They called it *Flop*World.

The Las Vegas Tropicana was faring poorly, too, under Ramada management. The company poured $70 million into building a new hotel tower and decorating the entire complex with a South Seas Islands theme, including fake bamboo frames for the kaleidoscopic mirrors over each bed. An inner courtyard of the nineteen-hundred-room Island of Las Vegas was transformed into a water park, with fountains, hillocks dotted with palm trees, and free-form swimming pools, one featuring blackjack tables at which gamblers in swimsuits could wager while their legs dangled in the water. Players could swim up to slot machines, too. All in all it was one of Ramada's few smart moves, although events would soon show that the company failed to take advantage of the investment.

In the main casino saltwater fish tanks straddled banks of video poker slot machines like watery fences. But few gamblers seeking the rush of gambling chose these tranquil spots. Despite the huge investment in expansion and refurbishing, two entrances to the casino required gamblers to walk down long corridors with battered wallpaper past guest rooms where room service trays sat on the floor. By 10:30 on Saturday nights, often the busiest time for a casino, most Trop restaurants had shut down. Hungry gamblers had their choice of the coffee shop or El Gaucho, an Argentinian steak house that was at odds with the tropical theme but that did feature a panoramic view of a white gravel roof.

The stated purpose of the $70 million investment was to take advantage of the giant Excalibur casino then being built directly across the Strip by Circus Circus Enterprises, a firm that rewarded shareholders richly by earning 45 percent on its common equity in 1991. With four thousand rooms Excalibur was slated to become the largest hotel in the world.

When Excalibur opened in June 1990, drawing huge crowds to the Strip's normally deserted south end, Ramada's executives had an extraordinary opportunity to showcase the renovations and enhancements at the Island of Las Vegas. Out front new landscaping would create an attractive entrance with palm trees and a pair of giant Aku-Aku statues beckoning visitors. But instead of maximizing this opportunity, Ramada executives seemed to do their best to make sure none of the gamblers filling the Excalibur wandered across the Strip to try their luck at the Trop. The week the Excalibur opened the landscaping project was not finished and an ugly assemblage of wood and wire barricaded the Trop's main entrance. Ramada literally fenced players out.

Ramada management also blew $5 million in just two years on Eddie's Fabulous Fifties, a Reno casino it closed in 1989.

In Laughlin, the booming new casino town where Nevada, Arizona and California meet at the Colorado River, the Ramada Express also lost money. It was the only casino in Laughlin not on the banks of the Colorado River. Bill Paulos, who oversaw the two profitable Circus Circus casinos there, figured Ramada Express was on the fast track to nowhere. "Not only are they not on the water, but what kind of management themes a casino like a train station?" Paulos said. "Have you ever felt comfortable in a train station?"

Ramada chairman Richard Snell did not see it that way. In his mind the location was terrific. True, it was not on the water, but it was right at the center of town, the center of the action in Laughlin.

Nevertheless, two years later Rubeli, who had succeeded Snell as chief executive officer, stood before securities analysts and conceded that Ramada Express's track record showed continued losses.

The extraordinary ability of Ramada management to make ledgers run red was not a skill limited to casinos. Ramada squandered millions more in an attempt to get Sun Belt residents to indulge in calories just as the fitness and healthy eating movements caught fire. In 1985, Ramada acquired the Marie Callendar Pie Shops chain in California and a few nearby states for $56 million cash and slightly more than 6 percent of Ramada's stock, then worth about $15 million.

For Don Callendar, the Southern California entrepreneur who grew his mother's pin money idea into a chain and then sold it to the profit-starved executives at Ramada, the deal was sweeter than his rum raisin pie. In addition to all that cash and stock—making him Ramada's largest single shareholder—Callendar got a fat consulting contract and Ramada picked up all the costs of his Canadair jet.

Soon even Ramada's executives could see they had made a bad deal and started looking for a way out. One day they asked to use the jet, as the contract with Callendar allowed. He refused. Ramada said Callendar had breached his duties, cut off his consulting fees, quit paying for the jet and told Callendar future talks would best be held in court.

In May 1988, Ramada sold the pie shops for $54.5 million. For more than a year Ramada refused to specify how much of its shareholders' money was lost in the pie shops fiasco. But finally, in the back pages of a report filed with the Securities and Exchange Commission in Washington, Ramada management put in the record just how much its pie binge lost—a whopping $60.8 million.

Ramada's namesake lodging business was not healthy either. The hotel group lost $7.8 million in 1988 after years of earning modest profits.

All these miscalculations created a company with a very dim future. The entire Ramada empire had not earned a profit from continuing operations since 1984, when it eeked out one half million dollars in earnings on revenues of $334 million. Each year that followed operations showed losses, although asset sales and other devices produced modest net profits until 1988, when the bottom line was a loss of more than $5 million. Like a gambler at the tables who has fallen behind, Ramada had stayed too long in a game where it lacked the skill to be a successful player.

Luck, however, is a fickle mistress and in the middle of all this waste and mismanagement, she smiled on Ramada in the persons of Hong Kong billionaire Cheng Yu-tung Henry and his son, K. S. Cheng.

Outwardly they were very different men, but worked closely together in business—and they both loved gambling. In his sixties, Cheng Yu-tung was so tight-fisted that he rode the subway to meetings, the *Wall Street Journal* reported. The younger Cheng, in his forties, liked sports cars and nightclubbing with celebrities. Together they controlled the New World Development Company. The father owned more than 40 percent of New World, a stake then valued at more than $5 billion based on Hong Kong Stock Exchange trading. He also owned many private ventures that made the pair flush with cash.

New World offered $540 million cash for Ramada's lodging empire—the thirty-five hotels and motels Ramada owned plus franchising rights to nearly eight hundred more hostelries—in April 1989. In all Ramada had more than 144,400 rooms under its brand name.

New World's offer was an incredible price, three times what Ramada valued the assets on its books and probably twice what most investors would pay—and all in cash. But father and son Cheng were not typical investors; they were fabulously rich men anxious to transfer their vast wealth to the safe haven of the United States. In 1997, then just eight years away, the British crown colony where they lived was scheduled to return to Chinese rule. Just two months after the Chengs struck their deal with Ramada the Chinese government massacred prodemocracy demonstrators in Beijing, a communist atrocity that certainly struck fear in laissez-faire capitalists like the Chengs.

The riches the Chengs offered could cover up for a lot of mistakes in Phoenix. News of the deal drew attention away from the harsh reality that the first quarter of 1989 was another disaster for Ramada. Ramada's gambling operations suffered a net loss of $18.6 million in the first three months. Nevada law allows casino owners there to operate in such extraordinary secrecy that an annual report to legislators on casino winnings lists casinos without names. But Ramada's books showed that baccarat players from the Far East had beaten the house so badly that the entire casino win at the Las Vegas Trop plummeted 30 percent, causing a first quarter operating loss in Las Vegas of $3.9 million.

As much as they loved to gamble, especially during breaks in negotiations, the Chengs didn't want the casinos. They wanted only the Ramadas, Rodeways and related inns and hotels.

Ramada, which had not paid a dividend since 1981, had the Hong Kong money committed before the Cheng deal was announced. Chairman Snell proposed a cash distribution of seven dollars per share. He also proposed creating a new company composed only of Ramada's three casinos: TropWorld in Atlantic City, the Tropicana in Las Vegas and the Ramada Express in Laughlin.

Snell named the company Aztar, an invention derived from the *Az-*

Temples of Chance

tec heritage of the Western Hemisphere and the company's plans to be a Wall Street *star*. But even Snell admitted that things were going so badly that around the water coolers at Ramada's Phoenix headquarters he had overheard subordinates calling the new company *Ishtar*, a reference to the budget-busting Hollywood megaflop starring Dustin Hoffman and Warren Beatty.

The amazing part of Snell's plan to create Aztar was not that an entire company would rely on three badly located, poorly managed, money-losing casinos, but that management believed the new company could afford to pay a seven-dollar-per-share dividend and survive. Ramada had more than 40 million shares of stock outstanding, so the distribution would cost $284 million.

In addition to the $540 million from the Chengs, Snell wanted to sell $400 million of new junk bonds. The debt would help entrench management by making Aztar unattractive in a takeover, as would a plan that eventually would put about 10 percent of Aztar stock in management hands. In many ways this resembled what the rival Holiday Corporation had done earlier when it paid a sixty-five-dollar-per-share dividend financed with $2.6 billion of bank and junk debt that gave the firm a negative net worth, at least on paper. But this was Ramada, not Holiday. This was 1989, after Drexel Burnham Lambert had been indicted and after the junk bond market had started collapsing and the real estate market had become depressed. The last big casino junk deal, Merv Griffin's takeover of Resorts International from Donald Trump, was already in trouble and within weeks Griffin would declare an end to interest payments on Resorts' debt.

Even the almost-anything-goes-in-finance New Jersey Casino Control Commission could see problems with Snell's plan to create Aztar. While all the casinos sought headlines denouncing the commission for interfering in management decisions, the fact was that the commission usually went along with whatever the casinos wanted in the way of financial engineering.

Wall Street's merchants of casino junk and stock routinely told prospective investors the deals had to pass the scrupulous inspection of the New Jersey Casino Control Commission, that every deal had to be certified by the commission and meet a financial stability test. But in judging restructurings, the commission took a narrow view of its duties. It op-

266

posed provisions that permanently entrenched existing management. Beyond that it was willing to take a casino company's word about how swell a deal was almost at face value, as shown by its approval of the looniest deal of them all, Merv Griffin's debt-laden takeover of Resorts. The commission made it easy for casino owners to prove by clear and convincing evidence that they would possess financial stability through these deals by allowing owners from Ramada to Donald Trump to produce paid experts who expressed the opinions managements wanted, opinions that a few pointed questions, in many cases, could have shown to be outrageously optimistic fantasies. Rarely did the regulators produce their own experts and when they did their testimony was often discredited during intense cross-examination by lawyers for the casino owners.

In ruling on the proposal to create Aztar, Commission chairman Read observed in October 1989, that he was glad that he did not have to vote on the plan as a Ramada director. But then he declared that it was really not his concern because the New Jersey Casino Control Commission is not "disposed to act as guardians for shareholders."

One issue was whether Snell had been candid in advising other Ramada directors about plans to dispose of the lodging chain. When the day came to vote on the plan Read, a veteran real estate lawyer who favored half-glasses as he read his opinions so he could glance up and take the pulse of his audience, mused about whether Snell and other executives had misled Ramada directors. He decided to take Snell's word for it that his spoken words to Ramada directors revealed more than was apparent from the board's minutes.

Read did see a problem with the financial projections Ramada and its investment banker, Salomon Brothers, offered to support the deal. While Ramada characterized its projections as conservative, the commission chairman pointed out that "the record clearly demonstrates that Ramada's past performance record regarding the accuracy of forecasts is most unimpressive." One earlier Ramada projection had missed the mark by 275 percent.

Salomon's testimony was simply not to be believed, Read said, given its stake in a successful deal. Fees and expenses for the deal came to $35 million, the prospectus showed. Besides, Read mused in what turned out to be a prescient observation, what if all the millions of additional dollars that Ramada projected its players would lose at TropWorld, the Las Vegas Trop and the Ramada Express were never realized? What if there was no growth in casino revenue, which Read called a worst-case scenario. But even if there was no growth in revenues, Read decided, Aztar would have enough cash after the seven-dollar-per-share distribution to pay its bills as they came due.

Read had given no thought to a real worst-case scenario—an absolute decline in revenues. In so doing he again brought himself to grant Ramada the benefit of the doubt and without further debate the commission unanimously approved the restructuring.

There was just one problem. Wall Street wouldn't go along. Marvin B. Roffman, the analyst at the Janney Montgomery Scott securities brokerage in Philadelphia who had a stunningly successful track record in picking winners and losers in casino stocks and bonds, had recommended selling Ramada stock months earlier. Roffman did not expect the new Aztar would be able to achieve the significantly improved profit margins predicted in a three-hundred-page prospectus. "This year in Atlantic City, Ramada benefited from one casino (the Atlantis) closing," Roffman said, "while next year Donald Trump's Taj Mahal will open, and he is going to be trying to take business away from them. So if they can't show a material turnaround in the third quarter, how can they possibly do well next year?"

When the deal finally went through on December 29, 1989, the market, by refusing to buy the securities Salomon Brothers first tried to peddle, had slashed the seven-dollar dividend to just one buck per share. The changed deal launched Aztar with $100 million cash on hand. Even so, Aztar fared poorly. Its stock soon plummeted from fourteen dollars to around four dollars per share.

But Ramada's shareholders were not the only ones to suffer at the hands of its management. There was also Mitzi Briggs.

27

Mitzi's Misfortune

In the dark Carving Cart restaurant behind the failed El Morocco Casino on the Las Vegas Strip a white-haired hostess in a tasteful floral-print dress waited at her podium. She looked like Norman Rockwell's vision of the ideal grandmother with her big glasses and a serene smile that broadened when two customers, the first in many long minutes, appeared. After seating them in one of the dark booths covered with red Naugahyde, she recovered a Styrofoam cup from under her podium and strolled over to the lounge. Slipping her cup under the bartender's gun, she pressed the Coke button and watched it fizzle. "It's all gone," she said to no one in particular. "I sure know about that."

Indeed. Once upon a time Mitzi Briggs had $44 million. But that was before Las Vegas. Now her charming Gothic mansion on the San Francisco peninsula, the stone castle she called Camelot, has been sold off. So has her private Bahamian Island and yachts to sail to it, as well as thirty-five breathtaking acres on the Monterey Peninsula where the Carmel River flows into the Pacific Ocean.

Now she lives in an apartment in Las Vegas, working days as a Catholic parish secretary.

Briggs lost her fortune in a Strip casino. She didn't gamble at the

269

Tropicana; she bought it. She got taken twice, first by the Kansas City mob and then by the Ramada lodging chain. The mob shriveled her fortune, but it was Ramada that made her a pauper.

The FBI went after the mobsters, and the Nevada casino regulators followed their lead. But the casino regulators never looked into how Ramada emptied Briggs's pockets.

Briggs rarely talked to strangers. But between seating patrons one night at the Carving Cart she slipped over to the bar, puffed on Virginia Slims she ignited from an equally slender gold lighter, and spoke about her life.

When FBI wiretaps revealed that Nick Civella, the Kansas City mob boss, was getting money skimmed from the Trop, it was too much even for the laid-back Nevada gaming regulators, who told Briggs and her partners to find buyers fast or be thrown out. Ramada, which operated the world's third-largest lodging chain from its headquarters in Phoenix, was so anxious to get into a business in which it had no expertise, but was certain would produce phenomenal profits, that it agreed to terms that eventually would haunt it and play a major role in busting Briggs.

The Tropicana's books were such a shambles that a dozen Ramada auditors and managers were dispatched to Las Vegas. Instead of a fixed price both sides agreed on a formula based on profits over eighteen months. The contract gave one of Briggs's partners, Deil Gustafson, veto power over major operation decisions at the Trop so he could make sure Ramada maximized profits and thus paid the highest price under the formula.

Six months later Ramada, fearing Nevada regulators would object to Gustafson's role, insisted on removing any prospect of control by the sellers as a condition for closing the sale. Court records showed that while the written requirements were deleted at Ramada's behest, the company indicated that the spirit of the agreement to maximize profits would be followed.

Ramada also wanted to buy the *Folies Bergère*, but it did not want to deal directly with Joe Agosto, the Kansas City mob's man at the Trop, who controlled the show. Ramada insisted that Briggs and her partners buy the Follies and then resell it to Ramada as part of the Tropicana deal. They did, but they deferred final payment to Agosto's Productions

270

and Leasing Corporation until early 1981, after Ramada was to make an installment payment on the Trop. When Ramada failed to make the $2.7 million installment payment, Briggs and her partners did not pay Agosto's Productions and Leasing, which filed suit. Despite having prompted this litigation by its failure to make a promised payment, Ramada later cited Agosto's lawsuit as evidence that it might become a victim of the unpaid creditors of Briggs and her partners.

Ramada failed to make the installment payment because it didn't have the money. Its Atlantic City project was on the way to becoming the most expensive hotel in the world and cost overruns had eaten all of Ramada's cash and all it could raise by selling ninety hotels.

The honorable stance in such a situation is to ask a creditor, like Briggs and her partners, to accept a partial payment or to negotiate an extension. Ramada did not bother with such niceties. It simply did not pay the bill when it came due.

Briggs and her partners sued Ramada. Ramada's board considered ways to settle the dispute. Tom Martin, Ramada's chief financial officer and its key negotiator in the Trop deal, prepared a memo in June 1980 recommending that the directors replace the complex price formula with a fixed sum. He noted that among the reasons Briggs and her partners would want to go along was that "Briggs will get some cash, though severely discounted."

Martin had two major worries, the memo showed. While Ramada could benefit if the Las Vegas Tropicana showed little or no profit, which would lower the amount due Briggs and her partners, it would have to pay higher legal fees, management time would be diverted from more important issues, the news media might get wind of the ploy, and New Jersey casino regulators would start investigating allegations of wrong-doing by Briggs and her partners.

More worrisome, the memo warned, was the danger that people friendly to Briggs could walk into the Las Vegas Trop with a huge bank-roll the day before the earn-out period ended and lose it all, resulting in unexpectedly huge profits for the casino. Under the five-times-profits buy-out formula, the memo noted, "the net effect would be to multiply those losses by five and cost Ramada a great deal of money." The prospect of Briggs and her partners conniving to lose, say, $20 million so

271

they could collect $100 million struck real fear into the Ramada directors. They agreed with Martin's recommendation to settle with Briggs and her partners for monies already paid plus $14.2 million more. All that remained was for Briggs's lawyers to secure signed and notarized releases from about four hundred creditors, declaring they had been paid or that they would not sue Ramada. It looked like the end was at hand. It was not.

In December 1981, Tom Martin asked one of Briggs's partners, Ed Doumani, and his lawyer, Jay Brown, to defer for one year a third of the $6 million payment due him in a side deal. Ed Doumani agreed, but said as a condition he wanted the final $14.2 million payment to Briggs and her partners, including himself, made quickly. He said that any claims from creditors could be used to offset the balance due him.

Someone noted the payment was due the last day of 1981, when Martin planned to be on vacation. Martin told Doumani and Brown that he would call Lionel Sawyer & Collins, Ramada's Las Vegas lawyers, and tell them to draft an extension of the contract so the deal could close in early 1982.

Meanwhile, Briggs's lawyers began rushing to obtain all the releases from vendors, banks and others from the days when Briggs owned the Trop. The creditors ranged from a $4.96 bill from a typewriter repairman who could not be located to Briggs, who had loaned her own casino $5.7 million.

Ramada's recently appointed chairman, lawyer Richard Snell, was so busy dealing with the Atlantic City fiasco that he hardly had time to cope with the Las Vegas Trop. But as a deadline loomed to pay Ed Doumani and Briggs, Snell turned his attention to what he had regarded as a small-fish problem in Las Vegas. Snell knew that Ramada was in "dire straits" and that four days earlier Ramada had been unable to pay the $6 million to Doumani.

On the first business day of the new year Brown called Martin to discuss closing the deal and collecting the $14.2 million. The cooperative, agreeable Martin was a changed man, down in the dumps, his voice filled with apologies about how things had changed radically at Ramada. Brown demanded an immediate meeting with Snell.

The next day Snell and director Ed Carson held a Ramada directors' management committee meeting where Martin and other Ramada executives discussed the $14.2 million due Briggs, Doumani and others. Martin reported that the Las Vegas Trop had earned significantly less money than anticipated and, as a result, the fixed price that had been agreed to seven months earlier was no longer a bargain, especially since there was no longer any fear that Briggs or her partners might connive to lose millions to get their money back fivefold.

Snell did not like hearing that Ramada no longer had a great deal. He studied the sales agreement and focused on Briggs's obligation to get all four hundred Tropicana creditors to sign statements promising not to sue Ramada. He also focused on a deadline for completing the deal, a deadline that had passed five days earlier without the written extension that Martin had said he would take care of before leaving on vacation. Snell and Carson told Martin that they did not want any further extensions, a curious position in view of Ramada's inability to fork over the $14.2 million due.

The next morning Brown hopped a jet to Phoenix, meeting up at Sky Harbor Airport with Martin Kravitz, a junior associate in his law firm, who had flown down from Las Vegas lugging a box full of releases.

Years later Harold P. Gewerter, another lawyer representing Ed Doumani, would argue in court that what transpired that morning showed that "Ramada represents the ugly side of corporate America: Sit on your corporate assets. Don't honor obligations. Take advantage of the little guy who relied on you. Spend countless legal dollars to invent a way to break your promise, moral, legal or otherwise."

At Ramada's headquarters a beaten Martin took Brown aside for a private chat. As Brown recalled it, Martin said he was sorry for what was about to happen. "Jay, I hope this doesn't affect my friendship with you, but there has been a change of waters over here. I cannot live up to what we agreed to."

Silently the trio trudged down the hall into a corporate throne room, with Snell's large desk in the center and sofas along the walls. The atmosphere was icy. Snell got right to the point.

"Do you have each and every single release?" Snell asked, as Brown recalled it.

"No," Brown answered, "but I have most of the releases. Some of them are impossible to obtain." He was thinking of the $4.96 typewriter repair bill from some guy who had disappeared. Others had sent the

273

releases in signed but not notarized. Some people sent telexes saying they were not owed any money.

"Do you have each and every release?" Snell demanded. "Is there one missing?"

"There's more than one missing, but not many," Brown replied.

"If one is missing then the deal is off," Snell announced.

By this Snell did not mean Ramada would walk away and Brown's clients could take their casino back. What Snell meant was that Ramada would keep the casino and not pay another penny.

Brown was dumbfounded. He implored Snell to remember all that had been accomplished, to think of poor Mitzi Briggs who was in desperate straits. He heard Snell tell him, "we made a bad deal for ourselves. I'm looking for a technicality to get out of it." Later, under oath, Snell denied making any such remark.

Kravitz concluded that Snell was looking for an excuse, any excuse, to get out of paying the money. "It was a bad deal," Kravitz heard Snell say. "If you were sitting in my chair would you go through with this deal?"

When Brown made his plea for some consideration for Mitzi Briggs, Snell again turned to the releases, asking, "Are all the releases there? Are you missing any?"

That ended it. Brown and Kravitz flew back to Las Vegas to spread the bad news.

More than eight years later the lawsuit Mitzi Briggs and Ed Doumani brought because of what Snell did that day was heard by Nevada District Judge Earle W. White. In its reports to shareholders over the years Ramada had asserted again and again that it was confident it would prevail.

Ramada hired the most powerful law firm in Nevada, Lionel, Sawyer & Collins, one of whose partners is Grant Sawyer, the former governor whose administration created the Black Book barring mobsters from the casinos. Against this legal powerhouse stood Harold P. Gewerter, a baker's son from Los Angeles, a young lawyer unknown to most of the figures who rule Las Vegas.

On the witness stand Snell denied the most damaging testimony by Brown and Kravitz. He said the sellers had simply failed to fulfill their duty to provide the signed and notarized releases from the creditors by the deadline.

Then, one by one, Gewerter walked Snell through a list of the major creditors from whom releases had not been obtained, which formed the basis for Snell's decision to keep the Las Vegas Tropicana without paying for it as promised.

"I haven't the slightest idea what this document is," Snell complained, referring to the list.

It was a report prepared by Ramada's legal department.

First Gewerter focused on the biggest release that Ramada said had not been obtained. It was a $5.7 million claim for a loan to the Tropicana by none other than Mitzi Briggs.

Was Mitzi Briggs's release one of those that Ramada said it had to have and that was missing? "I have no personal knowledge," Snell answered.

Next came a release sought from one of Briggs's partners, Deil Gustafson, for $2.1 million, followed by $2 million from the late Joe Agosto's Productions and Leasing for the *Folies Bergère*. All Snell could say was that he had no personal knowledge. By the time Gewerter had finished he had accounted for nearly all the necessary releases. Most of the money was due either to people like Briggs who were parties to the agreement or who had agreed to sign a release simultaneously with being paid. None of the others, some of whom were listed by mistake, had come forward to claim a cent.

When Judge White ruled in May 1989, nearly a decade after the case began, he awarded Briggs and her partners every penny they sought plus interest at 14 percent, a total of more than $34 million. He called Ramada's executives "jerks."

The judge made fifty-four findings of fact, including one that at the meeting in the throne room Snell had "insisted on having each and every release, which was in violation of the intent and understanding of the parties. Defendants by this action displayed corporate arrogance."

Ramada cried foul. Snell insisted that Judge White's ruling would not withstand an appeal. Ramada took the case to the Nevada Supreme Court, which expressed its unanimous view of Ramada's claim with two words: we disagree.

275

Courtesy of Gewerter's work Briggs and her partners had won the largest judgment in the history of the Nevada state courts.

The ruling by Judge White and the Nevada Supreme Court would seem to go directly to the integrity and business ability clauses in the New Jersey Casino Control Act. Gewerter thought so and so did Ed Doumani and Mitzi Briggs. But Division of Gaming Enforcement attorneys made—but never kept—any of several appointments with Gewerter to see his files.

While Ramada finally paid in full, for Briggs justice delayed was justice denied. "I won't see a penny of it," she said.

Briggs had pledged her last $10 million in Stauffer stock as security for a loan she had intended to repay with the final payment from Ramada. When Ramada didn't pay, and the value of her stock fell below the loan margin, the stock was sold to cover the debt and she lost everything. Briggs then signed over her interest in Hotel Conquistador, the firm through which she had owned the Tropicana, to Ed and Fred Doumani, who were investors with her in the Tropicana and who often helped her out financially, including giving her the hostess job in their Carving Cart restaurant until it closed.

The lure of money that brought Briggs and Ramada to Las Vegas was beginning to spread. The nation's heartland was adopting a new attitude toward the business of its native sons a generation after Benny Binion, Ross Miller and Moe Dalitz.

28

Rust Belt Renaissance

Through the booming eighties the Quad Cities became one of the sorest spots in the Rust Belt. Six factories closed and twenty thousand good-paying jobs disappeared, many permanently as machine tools were wrenched from the floor and shipped away on the same railroad cars and barges that for years carried off the tractors and combines and other farm machinery made first by John Deere and later by International Harvester, J. I. Case and Caterpillar in the big factories lining the Upper Mississippi River.

The Quad Cities—there are five, actually, Moline, East Moline and Rock Island on the Illinois side, Davenport and Bettendorf on the Iowa side—called themselves the Detroit of farm machinery. In the late thirties the United Auto Workers sent agents from Detroit to organize, and after many bitter strikes they, too, began thriving. By the eighties their contracts were so fat that a bathroom cleaner could make fifteen dollars an hour in wages and fringe benefits. The companies paid because they wanted no interruption in the hefty profits they pulled out of the plants. No one got rich working the factory floor, but many prospered from their labor.

Around the same time that the Japanese targeted Detroit, they also targeted the Quad Cities. As with Detroit, the Quad Cities factories we old, the production methods outdated and the innovation that made Deere flourish decades ago no longer drove the companies. Year by year the Japanese tinkered with their designs, improved quality and ate away at the Quad Cities' market. Caterpillar vowed to fight, building the world's most modern tractor-engine plant so it could win back old customers and attract new ones. But the price management demanded for this investment was more cooperation from the work force and a focus on the long term. When the workers struck for more money, the company moved the manufacturing equipment to a nonunion plant in Wisconsin.

Bob Arnould could feel the hurt of Davenport's people, and he wanted to help. Arnould was a creature of reform, one of those handsome young men who came along in the seventies when part-time citizen legislatures were giving way to full-time professional lawmakers. The people of Davenport elected Arnould to the Iowa House of Representatives in 1977 when he was twenty-four years old. Making laws for other people is the only career he has known.

In the midst of the factory closings and layoffs, in what Arnould calls Davenport's darkest days, he took a vacation to Montana that would soon change Davenport. Arnould played blackjack at a bar in Kalispell. In most of America playing cards for money is a crime, often a felony, even when it is among friends. Montana's part-time lawmakers had drawn a distinction between social betting and commercial gambling, a distinction recommended by the National Commission on the Review of the National Policy Toward Gambling in its 1976 report to President Ford. In Montana, so long as players put up the money and do not bet against the house—that is, so long as no one operates a casino—card games are legal.

Returning to Davenport, Arnould visited another young career lawmaker, fellow Democrat Tom Fey. Over lemonades on Fey's back deck, Arnould talked about his romantic views of riverboat gamblers. Many Americans shared those images of men in satin vests who smoked cheroots, mustachioed dandies with hearts of gold, because the Hollywood dream merchants had once created television series like *Maverick* and *Yancy Derringer,* the latter starring an actor from Davenport named Jock Mahoney. Riverboat gambling was no stranger to the Quad Cities. Older folks used to ride the *Quinlan,* a wooden ship that ferried people between Moline and Davenport and also gave fun cruises—the main deck for dancing, the top deck filled with slot machines—until an ambitious Moline prosecutor raided her almost a half century earlier and ordered the one-armed bandits tossed into the Big Muddy. How wonderful to bring that era back, Arnould thought, pondering all the new jobs gambling tourists could create among his constituents.

For two years Arnould and Fey prepared the legislative soil in Des Moines. They proposed small-stakes gambling, limited to five dollars per bet and a two-hundred-dollar loss per trip. Their bill had barely sprouted in April 1987 when a Republican chill hit. The Democrats needed 51 votes. Their party held 58 seats, but only 42 Democrats voted for riverboat casinos. Del Stromer, the House Minority Leader, insisted his party members refuse to support the bill because "one of the responsibilities of the Republican party leader is to not make the majority party look good." Besides, Stromer said, he doubted many more people would vacation in Iowa and if they did, "instead of going to dinner or going shopping, they will lose the money." When the bill came up for another vote, Stromer said the price for Republican support was limiting product liability claims to ten years after purchase, a change sought by farm machinery firms and other Iowa manufacturers.

Two veteran Republican lawmakers from Scott County (home to Davenport and Bettendorf), Don Hermann and Hugo Schnekloth, fought gambling. They denounced it as folly, saying it offered a false hope that would enrich a few casino owners by draining money that would otherwise go to buy cars and toasters and to build retirement nest eggs. If you don't believe us, they would say, just look at the study that the city won't hand out. Go down to the public library and read it.

The single photocopy of the KPMG Peat Marwick analysis at the library indicated that riverboat casinos would create few jobs. Adding up all the hours of part-time work and counting them as full-time equivalents showed just 250 new jobs would be created. If the riverboat operators built hotels and retail shopping bazaars, the study estimated twenty-one hundred more jobs would be created—equal to one tenth of the lost factory jobs. Significantly, the study found that 450,000 people already took a riverboat cruise each year—a number that would grow to only 490,000 with the addition of casinos. But more significantly the study estimated that one in three gamblers would be locals and in win-

279

ter, when the river sometimes freezes over and the riverboats would be tied to the docks, virtually everyone who gambled would be a local. The study made no effort to determine how many dollars would be diverted from local merchants selling cars and toasters and mutual funds.

"Riverboat casinos won't create the kind of jobs we want, the kind you can raise a family on and build a life," Hermann told everyone who would listen. "These riverboats will be just four-dollar-, five-dollar-, maybe six-dollar-an-hour jobs. And what will the gambling interests invest here? Next to nothing. They'll build a dock and a restaurant and pave for parking, but the real business floats. When Illinois passes gambling those riverboats will just float on out of here to be closer to Chicago."

Schnekloth, a farmer who with his sons raises corn and soybeans and feeds them to cattle, decided that moral arguments would appeal only to a narrow band of citizens so he focused on economics. He spoke of how working the land had made Iowa a place everyone there loved, how taking iron ore and processing it into machinery created value. "Gambling is an awful poor foundation to build an economic system on," he argued. "Casinos don't make anything. They just take money from a lot of people and give it to a few."

Together the pair tried in vain to remind their constituents of the history that had made the Quad Cities prosper. In the 1830s, when nine of every ten Americans lived on a farm, the pioneers who crossed the Mississippi River into Iowa thought they had found heaven on earth. They had earned their bread from the sandy soils along the eastern seaboard or the only partially tamed expanse from the Appalachians to the Mississippi, land thick with trees that had to be hewn down by hand and boulders lurking just a furrow's depth beneath the surface. But in Iowa and nearby parts of Illinois the dirt was so rich it was black, a fertile cover sixteen feet deep in places, enough to ensure eternal harvests.

Once the yeoman farmers put their plows to the land, though, it seemed nature had played a cruel trick. The iron blades cut the surface, but the rich gumbo clogged the moldboards instead of falling aside in neat rows. Many quit the land in despair. Then in 1837, an Illinois blacksmith named John Deere, who had come from Vermont looking for a better life, took an old steel saw from his barn and beat it into a plowshare. He tinkered with the design until, finally, the thick dirt that jammed on rough iron flowed smoothly across the slick steel surface.

Farmers rushed to buy Deere's improved plow. In 1847 the prosperous blacksmith moved from Grand Detour to Moline, beside the rapids that interfered with commerce on the Upper Mississippi, but that meant he could ship his products up river or down. Throughout his life Deere refined his products and developed new ones and soon others came to compete, helping to develop an agricultural system so efficient that by the time Kemmons Wilson opened his first Holiday Inn only one American in eleven still lived on a farm. That's how to create wealth, Hermann and Schnekloth said, by turning rocks into machines, not by tossing dice.

But most people did not want to listen, especially those without jobs or who knew someone who had moved away from family and friends in search of work, which meant just about everyone in town. The local newspaper, the Quad City *Times*, criticized Schnekloth and Hermann for standing in the way of a better future for their communities.

In 1989, Arnould and Fey again planted their bill in Des Moines. This time it took root because some of the men who stood to profit from its passage helped work for it. Lobbyists employed by riverboat owners emphasized all the millions of dollars that they said would be invested.

The lobbyists also focused on the small stakes that they favored, saying this would protect people from betting over their heads. The Quad City *Times* and other newspapers praised these limits as consumer protections. But the gambling interests loved the small stakes provisions because they understood numbers—and these numbers worked *against* consumers. The reason is "gambler's ruin." At five dollars per bet each player begins with forty opportunities to wager while the casino's bankroll is virtually unlimited. "With these rules the odds that you will double your bankroll at craps are twenty-five percent—and that you will go broke before that are seventy-five percent," noted I. Nelson Rose, a California law school professor who specializes in gambling issues. In any casino, the house advantage will eventually consume a player's bankroll if he doesn't quit the game. But a player is much more vulnerable to a losing streak if he or she has only forty opportunities to wager. It is this limited ability to withstand a losing streak that creates "gambler's ruin."

281

The odds for roulette players were even worse, especially since the Iowa riverboats help themselves by adding two zeros to the wheel instead of one. Double-zero roulette gives the casino a hefty 5.3 percent advantage on each spin, which at sixty or seventy spins per hour quickly erodes players' bankrolls. As Rose calculated it, the likelihood that a roulette player would double his $200 before going bust was just 4 percent, while the house had a 96 percent chance of busting each player. Rose could hardly believe any state would consider rules so unfair to the public. This kind of blatantly anticonsumer law was precisely what the seventies reformers claimed would disappear once the citizen lawmakers were replaced by professionals.

Further, the two-hundred-dollar limit would pose few obstacles for obsessive and compulsive players bent on wagering more. First off, they could sign up for more than one trip a day and they could also have a friend buy in and then leave, especially in winter when the cost of a ticket to get on board would be about two dollars. Rose predicted a black market would develop in chips, with some people pocketing and then selling them to serious gamblers at a price slightly above their face value.

To a casino owner a two-hundred-dollar loss limit could be a godsend. The average visitor to Atlantic City lost less than eighty dollars of his or her own money.

These numbers were well understood by John E. Connelly, an obese man with a ruddy face, a shock of white hair and stubby hands who dug coal in his youth before building a fortune that *Business Week* estimated at $125 million in 1989. He owned hotels, restaurants, his own Lockheed Jet Star and thirty-four riverboats, every one of them profitable without a casino, though he wanted all the casinos he could get on his boats. "If I'd had slot machines on them I wouldn't be here today talking to you," he told one reporter much later, "because I'd have so much money I'd have something better to do."

This time Arnould and Fey had cultivated more support for the bill, and the news media, especially the Quad City *Times*, made their work easy by becoming champions of the cause. In April, after Fey's bill had passed both houses in Des Moines, he credited the bill's success to "a long, hard effort by individuals and interest groups." Connelly, too, praised the legislature's sagacity, saying, "Iowa in its wisdom has bro-

282

ken the monopoly of Las Vegas and Atlantic City. And I see it growing, because it's bringing gaming right into the heartland of America."

Illinois lawmakers soon followed Iowa, just as Hermann and Schnekloth had predicted, except that the statute placed no limits on bets. Later Mississippi and Louisiana, where the 1890 lottery scandal ended America's second wave of legalized gambling, passed similar laws. Missouri scheduled a popular vote on legalizing gambling for November 1992.

On April 26, 1989, the Iowa casino bill was signed into law by Terry E. Branstad, the Hawkeye State's popular young Republican governor, who said gambling would give "a shot in the arm" to river towns. Hermann and Schnekloth, devastated that the leader of their own party had signed the bill, decided to retire. Both insisted they would have won new terms easily, but on the streets of Davenport and Bettendorf most folks viewed the lawmakers' retirement as a polite way of avoiding defeat in the next election. So successfully did the gambling advocates stir the sentiments of the people that every public official who opposed gambling in Scott County failed to win at the polls in 1989 and 1990.

With casino boats approved, Iowa established a distinction for itself as the state that offered the most varied forms of gambling. Iowans could wager on a state lottery, on dogs, on horses, at church bingo and at casinos. Even Nevada did not offer so many types of gambling because its constitution forbade a lottery and it had no operating dog or horse tracks.

Once floating casinos became a local option in Iowa, Scott County voters quickly approved them, as did voters in five other counties on the Mississippi and Missouri rivers that give Iowa east and west coasts. The next issue was who would get the licenses.

John Connelly wanted to sail from Davenport. He found himself pitted against Bernard Goldstein, a local scrap-metal dealer and barge operator whose family, some thought, was the richest in the area. Connelly promised to invest $76 million, Goldstein $32 million.

Connelly's proposal included building a $30 million hotel, an elevated riverfront promenade that would cost more than $3 million and modest public park improvements. But his shrewdest move was to take over the Black Hawk Hotel, a downtown dowager that had been unable to support a mortgage obtained with help from the Small Business Administration. Taking over the loan payments on the underlying first mortgage made Connelly immensely popular with the Davenport Bank, regarded by many as the most important power center in town. In return for this the city agreed to exempt his new hotel and any Black Hawk improvements from taxes for three years; to build him a nine-hundred-space parking garage with a skywalk to his new hotel; and to grant other lucrative concessions. Eventually Connelly sweetened his proposal until he was talking about investing $90 million, a figure he justified by claiming 789,000 gamblers would come each year, far more than projected by the Peat Marwick study.

Goldstein's proposal was modest. He said that $40 million was the most anyone could expect the business to support. In November, seven months after Branstad signed the casino bill, Goldstein bowed out, announcing that he would focus on his plans for Bettendorf, a few miles up the river, where an old J. I. Case factory would provide parking and perhaps land-based development for his *Diamond Lady* riverboat casino.

Free to proceed, Connelly refurbished the *President*, a 1926 tour boat he had used for excursions in St. Louis. But the land-based development he promised Davenport kept being delayed. After Donald Trump's troubles became household knowledge Connelly said Trump was partly to blame for his difficulty raising financing and there was nothing he could do. Meanwhile, the scheduled start of riverboat gambling in 1991 approached.

On April Fool's Day, one minute before the sun began rising over Bettendorf, a velvet rope came down and a throng in heavy coats, the women in high heels, surged onto the *Diamond Lady*, the first legal riverboat casino in America.

Iowa law required the boats to recall the era of wooden paddle wheelers that belched black smoke from their coal engines. The Goldsteins tried. Their $8 million ship had a steel hull with white paint, gingerbread and exhausts for the diesel fumes designed to resemble nineteenth-century smokestacks. A bright red paddle wheel on the back added to the illusion, but the paddles were for show; a small electric motor churned a wispy white froth on cue for ABC's *Good Morning America* broadcast.

On board a pair of sweet-looking blondes with parasols, their shoulders bare despite the chill air, mingled and posed for pictures. Inside gamblers could choose from two casinos. The main-deck casino, packed tight with table games, had only tiny windows high above the slot machines lining the plain gray walls. The Texas deck two flights up contained mostly slots, but featured picture windows.

A few minutes past dawn actor Howard Keel, who played the gambler in the 1951 film *Show Boat*, set a five-dollar chip on the virgin green table, took a pair of red-and-white dice from Goldstein and tossed them, becoming the first person to gamble legally on a riverboat in America. The dice came up eight. Four rolls later Keel landed another eight and the dealer paid him with a five-dollar chip. Keel shook the dice in his left hand a second time, rolling a five. But before another five came up he rolled seven, crapping out and losing his bet. Keel grinned as the dealer took his chip, then left the table to shake hands with visitors.

A few hours later in Davenport, under a bright sun that took the chill out of the gentle breeze, several thousand gathered beside the *President*, a few crowding onto the freshly poured sidewalks that bordered fields of bare earth. A high school band played as a giant American flag waved under the cloudless spring sky. One after another speakers at the rostrum praised small-stakes gambling as the savior of Davenport's economy. The priest who prayed over the ship compared it favorably to Noah's ark. Mayor Thom Hart, oblivious to the dirt field where most of his audience stood, said that because of the casino ship "this ugly parking lot has been transformed into a festival place." But the most effusive encomium came from L. C. Pike, the Iowa racing commission chairman, who wore a plaid polyester sport coat and waved the ship's casino license, declaring, "this may be as important to Davenport as the Bill of Rights and the Magna Carta."

When the throng swarmed up the gangplank, a dime-store Mark Twain motioned them into a vision in which Victorian England meets Las Vegas on Old Man River. The *President*'s main casino stretches one hundred and eighty feet from bow to stern. The main floor is fifty feet wide, its ivory walls trimmed with gold-painted filigree, its ceiling fake tin except where smoky gray half-balls holding television surveillance cameras poke through. Above the thirty-four green-felt tables huge bowls of faux alabaster, slung from chains, provide extra lighting.

285

Twenty-two oval mirrors in gold frames ring the room. From the promenade other gamblers could lean on brass rails and watch the action below. Arnould had promised family entertainment and the *President* had a place for kids to stay while their parents played, a large room just above water level with a gray metal floor, banks of arcade games—and no place to sit during the two-hour cruise. Outside, any resemblance to a nineteenth-century paddle wheeler was hard to find. There was a half circle on one side intended perhaps to suggest the idea of a side wheel on the sixty-seven-year-old *President.*

Connelly, Governor Branstad and Arnould, who has since become Speaker of the Iowa House, climbed to the top deck for the television cameras, the Black Hawk Hotel visible in the distance. No one asked about the *Quinlan*'s slots buried in the river mud under the *President*'s keel.

Arnould, sipping free champagne in the sun after the cameras had moved on, said he knew nothing about gambler's ruin. He didn't know about the hated riverboat sharpers called blacklegs, like the ones they hung in Vicksburg in 1835, either. "I can't say I ever read a serious history of gambling," he said. "By the way, isn't this a great day?"

Meanwhile, Connelly had gone back down to the casino where he sat on a stool, his back to one of his six hundred and eighty slot machines, all built by International Game Technology of Reno. All around him people pumped in coins and sipped free champagne in flutes. Connelly greeted a steady stream of admirers with the polished small talk of a successful salesman; flirted with the women; thanked those who praised him; and offered a chip from his pocket to one sore loser.

Connelly told those who circled around that more states would follow Iowa's lead, states like Missouri and Pennsylvania, where he operated tour boats. Soon, he said, his casino riverboats would sail from historic Penn's Landing on the Delaware River in Philadelphia and on the Allegheny and Ohio rivers in Pittsburgh. Pennsylvania governor Bob Casey had said he would veto a bill if it passed, but Connelly said in time Casey's opposition would erode, just as the opposition had lost in Iowa. All Connelly had to do was to follow John Deere's example, tinkering with the details until he could plow through the opposition.

Everywhere, the casino advocates promised regulation to ensure the law would be obeyed. None, though, wanted the "strict regulation" that New Jersey voters were promised. Neither, as it turns out, did New Jersey's top regulators.

29

Looking the Other Way

> An integral and essential element of allowing
> casinos in New Jersey rests in public confidence and
> trust in the credibility and integrity of the
> regulatory process and casino operations. . . . It is
> in the public interest that [casinos] be strictly
> regulated and controlled . . .
>
> —From the preamble to the
> New Jersey Casino Control Act

Jim Gwathney had just come on duty as a Casino Control Commission inspector at Trump Castle on December 17 when one of the gambling hall's security guards furtively offered a bit of news. "Someone just bought three million dollars worth of chips, but left without playing," the guard whispered.

Strange, Gwathney thought, since he knew nothing about it and yet large chip purchases were routinely monitored to catch money laundering and other illegalities. Gwathney, a man who took his inspection duties as seriously as the weight-lifting that made him look like a muscle-beach regular, told his supervisor, Bob Lagg, that he was going to find out who bought the chips. "Don't worry about it," Lagg told him.

Gwathney thought that was strange, too, although he knew that while the inspectors were the "eyes and ears of the commission," paid to nose around to keep the system honest, it was a charade. The inspectors had no power. When Robert Libutti was losing some of his $12 million and he complained that Gwathney was watching his game too closely, Gwathney's bosses ordered him to watch the play on a television monitor. "Our job is to create the appearance of regulation," Gwathney and many of his colleagues said.

Being told to look the other way, though, was more than Gwathney

288

could stomach and he fumed until his shift ended after midnight. Gwathney rose early and telephoned Chris Best, the commission's principal inspector at Trump Castle, and started talking about the $3 million deal. Best had no idea what Gwathney was talking about. "Look on the shift summary," Gwathney said, assuming the chip purchase had been routinely logged. It wasn't.

That afternoon, when Gwathney returned to duty, he again told Lagg he was going to investigate. "Don't even mess with it, leave it alone," Lagg told him, adding that orders had come from Jack Julian, the chief inspector.

What the hell is going on? wondered Gwathney, who had been notified he was being laid off. Later he and others would sue Chairman Steve Perskie, saying he targeted them for layoffs under pressure from the industry because they did their jobs and would not look the other way.

A few days later, Principal Inspector Chris Best shared with Gwathney the reason he was told to look the other way. "Keep this confidential," she said, explaining that Chairman Perskie and Jack Sweeney, who was supposed to be the independent enforcement division director but was in fact a crony handpicked by Perskie, knew all about the chip purchase in advance and had approved it.

What Gwathney had stumbled onto, and what his bosses wanted to make sure he did not investigate, was an illegal loan to Trump Castle, a loan made in the form of chips purchased but not played because it provided the lender with absolute security and would not violate the terms of Trump's bailout deal with his bankers.

The chip buyer was Fred Trump, who was giving his son an advance on his inheritance so he could make the December 1990 mortgage payment on the Castle.

Harvey I. Freeman, Trump's closest aide, thought up the chip deal as a ruse to get around the Casino Control Act's strict controls on who can put money into a casino or take it out. When the Casino Control Act was adopted in 1977 its promise was that no one would be allowed to put money into the casinos or take it out without a license, without having their background investigated. This principle was the bedrock of the entire regulatory system and the promise that gambling could be a good industry for New Jersey. But now the law had become a hindrance to

Donald Trump and the man who as an assemblyman had sponsored the law, Perskie, was doing his best to help Trump get around it.

The ruse prompted an extraordinary response by a law enforcement agency: even though the law-breaking was deliberate and planned, enforcement division director Jack Sweeney's office worked closely with Trump lawyers to help Donald Trump escape the penalties mandated by law for illegally loaning money to a casino. The penalty was forced return of the loaned money, something Trump Castle could not do because the very day the chips were bought the proceeds went out to help make the $18.4 million mortgage interest payment to bondholders. The Castle was so pressed for funds that it ended the year with just $770,000 in cash, a tiny sum for a business with annual revenues of $260 million.

Sweeney did indeed know about the illegal loan in advance, but he did not share his knowledge with Tom Auriemma, the deputy attorney general assigned to the Trump casinos. When Auriemma learned of it—because Trump Castle suddenly had enough cash to make the mortgage payment instead of falling a few million short—he went to Sweeney for permission to file a complaint. What for? Sweeney asked, saying he saw nothing wrong and, besides, Trump casino lawyer Nick Ribis had told him in advance about the chip purchase.

Auriemma felt strongly that a complaint had to be filed, but the best he could wheedle from Sweeney was permission to negotiate with Trump's lawyers and to ask their advice on what to do since the law plainly made the loan illegal and mandated return of the money as well as barring Fred Trump from the casino industry. By spring Trump Castle had admitted the loan was illegal and agreed to pay a thirty-thousand-dollar fine, less than half what a bank would have charged in fees to arrange a proper loan, assuming any bank would have loaned Trump a penny more at that point.

Reporters, meanwhile, began asking Sweeney about rumors that he had advance knowledge of the loan. Each time he said plainly and clearly that he did not. Much later he would explain that while he was told in advance of what was planned, that was not really advance knowledge since nothing had happened yet and thus his statements were not lies.

Since Section 95 of the Casino Control Act mandated return of the illegal loan proceeds, a way around this had to be found if the ruse was to help prop up Trump and help him maintain an advantage with the bondholders he would eventually have to face in Bankruptcy Court. Perskie, who had championed the 1976 casino initiative and had sponsored the Casino Control Act with the reassuring words in its preamble, knew how to take care of this problem. He broke the matter into two issues. He ordered that Fred Trump's fitness to lend money to a casino be heard first. While the illegal loan made Trump unqualified—some casino lawyers felt it barred him forever from the industry—that issue was not yet before the commission. Thus, lacking any reason *on the record* to deny Fred Trump, he was licensed. Fred Trump, however, did not loan any more money to the Castle and in June 1991, the mortgage went unpaid.

When the commission met one week later Perskie brought up the illegal loan and the negotiated thirty-thousand-dollar fine, a pittance compared to the significance of the loan to Trump and compared to penalties imposed in the past for far less serious offenses such as false and misleading advertising. Two of the commissioners, W. David Waters and Valerie Armstrong, would not go along quietly. They challenged the official version of events and accused the enforcement division of showing favoritism to Trump. They even began to say publicly what little people and their lawyers, people like cocktail waitress Diane Pussehl and lawyer Gregory Imperiale, had said for years: that casino regulation relied on two standards of justice, separate and unequal.

Armstrong said she was "mystified by this settlement." Armstrong noted that during earlier hearings on Donald Trump's financial stability, "I was rather concerned about the situation" involving Fred Trump, "but I didn't want to prejudge at that time since all of the facts were not before me. I guess to put it quite simply, I still don't feel that all the facts are before me. This, to me, is a really serious situation."

Armstrong noted that in the Trump hearings she was repeatedly told "that integrity questions are not an issue, everything is on the up and up, and it seems to me a financially distressed casino should not be deliberately violating the Casino Control Act."

She said in addition "the settlement itself bothers me because we have not been told who concocted this scheme, who participated in it . . . or why it was perceived to be necessary for the transaction to take the form it did. And I guess what really bothers me here is the next time

291

something like this happens it may not be between father and son. . . . I think we are sending the wrong message and I guess my basic question to both counsel here is why do we have a settlement that is so sparse?"

Armstrong, aware of well-circulated talk among casino inspectors that Sweeney had advance notice, asked Auriemma a direct question: was the Division of Gaming Enforcement notified in advance that the transaction was going to take place?

"No, the division was not," Auriemma replied. Later, Auriemma would insist that his response was neither a lie nor misleading because the call from Nick Ribis was not advance notice, but "contemporaneous notice." He said he regarded the entire day's events—from arranging the transfer of funds in Fred Trump's New York bank account to the nearly three hours that Fred's attorney, George Snyder, spent traveling to Atlantic City as well as the actual chip purchase—as the transaction. By this reasoning there was no advance notice even though hours passed between the Ribis call to Sweeney and the chip purchase, even though Sweeney had plenty of time to study the law and to tell Ribis the law was to be obeyed.

Waters was more explicit than Armstrong. "You have two standards for determining what the penalty is going to be," he said, one for run-of-the-mill employees who get named and punished and another for Trump casino executives who go unnamed and unpunished.

Chairman Perskie, anxious to shut down this line of official comment, proposed raising the fine to sixty-five thousand dollars and delaying a vote until after the commissioners could talk in private. At the next commission meeting Auriemma and Trump attorney Joseph Fusco presented the commissioners with a written statement naming three Trump executives as the responsible parties. Neither Harvey Freeman, who concocted the ruse, nor Nick Ribis, who had tipped Sweeney, was named. Castle president Tony Calandra was named, but everyone knew he was a figurehead without real power. What the commissioners did not know was that the other two executives named as the responsible parties—Ed Tracy, who headed all three Trump casinos, and Pat McCoy, the Trump Castle chief financial officer—had fought to stop the illegal loan. Tracy had been forced out of his job soon after that. McCoy resigned under pressure. It was the rankest kind of lie, but because both the enforcement division and Trump's lawyer certified its truthfulness no one questioned the stipulation.

Even without the knowledge of Tracy and McCoy's failed efforts to enforce lawful behavior, Armstrong believed the settlement was an insult. "There are fifty thousand employees in this industry that we hold to the highest standards, and the way this entire matter was handled, as far as the settlement, is I think an affront to those fifty thousand employees. It is an affront to the service worker who is caught in the employee locker room smoking a joint and who gets his license revoked or suspended, to the cage cashier who steals five dollars. Those people are accountable to us and they are accountable to us in detail to tell us what happened and to acknowledge it. I look at the deliberateness of the violations here as being an extremely aggravating factor."

Waters concurred on the double standard, saying that when a rule is violated "if it's just an average employee a complaint is filed very quickly" and the individual is held responsible and fined or suspended. "This instance, where we are climbing higher into the corporate hierarchy, it's pretty evident, and I don't know why, that there is a reluctance on the part of the division to follow that same standard . . . it's greater than a disappointment to me, it's an outrage that the Division of Gaming Enforcement would take this position and fail to carry out what I understand to be its responsibility to enforce the provisions of the Casino Control Act."

There it was, on the record, in a public meeting, two of the commissioners saying that when it came to owners, or at least to Donald Trump, there was a double standard.

The commission did not enforce the law mandating return of the money because despite these words, Perskie was assured of at least three of the four votes he needed to get the sixty-five-thousand-dollar fine approved, ending the matter. Waters dissented. The key vote was Armstrong, who gave Trump what he needed, saying she did so reluctantly and only because there was no hint of mob involvement. Nick Ribis knew she would clear it back when he called Sweeney to boldly announce the illegal loan plan. "Valerie always goes along in the end," he had said four months earlier when asked to predict if the commission might force return of the illegally loaned money.

Two days after the vote Waters received an anonymous letter charging that Sweeney and Perskie "approved" the illegal loan in advance. He sent it on to Florio's attorney general, Robert J. Del Tufo, who in turn ordered his executive assistant, Frederick DeVesa, to conduct an internal affairs investigation.

DeVesa's probe took a broader view of the issues than just the anonymous writer's charge of advance approval because Del Tufo would not continence untruthful statements by Sweeney or other subordinates nor would he allow subordinates to wink at the law. DeVesa said what he learned from the inquiry satisfied him that Sweeney "did not go light" on the illegal loan or those involved and that he found nothing indicating that Sweeney had treated the matter outside policy bounds acceptable to Del Tufo. He added that in reviewing Sweeney's conduct he gave considerable weight to Sweeney's having taken over as division director only weeks before and his lack of familiarity with the nuances of the Casino Control Act.

DeVesa never asked the central question in the affair, though. He never asked why Sweeney did not simply enforce Section 95 of the Casino Control Act and direct Trump Castle to return the illegally loaned money. That was the issue that prompted Ribis to call Sweeney in advance, because if the money were loaned, and then had to be given back, Trump Castle would have had to close its doors. The only way to repay Fred would have been to do what Dennis Gomes pondered the night Akio Kashiwagi almost got away: raiding the casino cage and emptying the slot machines. Why wasn't the central issue explored?

"Frankly," DeVesa said, "I never thought of it."

DeVesa did write to Waters when the probe ended. "We found no evidence to substantiate the allegations contained in the anonymous letter." How could that be, since Sweeney admitted he was tipped in advance? DeVesa focused on the anonymous letter writer's charge that Sweeney had "approved" the illegal loan. By law only the commission could approve the loan, so DeVesa found nothing wrong. DeVesa's letter said nothing about the contradiction between Sweeney's repeated statements to reporters that he learned of the loan after the fact and his admission that he knew in advance. Likewise, the report was silent about the contrast between what Auriemma told the Casino Control Commission and the truth.

Even before DeVesa's report was finished Armstrong, a Republican, was named to the Superior Court bench by Perskie's patron, Governor James Florio, a Democrat. Waters's term expired that fall and Florio replaced him with a lobbyist for the school teachers unions who had worked closely with Perskie when he was the governor's chief of staff.

The two commissioners who dared point out that the emperor had no clothes were gone and with them went the last pretense of "strict regulation," the vow that obedience to the law would always prevail over economic interests. "Strict regulation" had been just another politician's promise, torn apart piece by piece and finally swept into the dust bin of history.

Afterword:
Coming Soon to a
Neighborhood Near You

The spread of commercial gambling is inevitable. By the end of this century almost every place in America where it has not already arrived will join the trend.

In Chicago, plans for a $2 billion gambling zone were endorsed by Mayor Richard M. Daley. Caesars World, Hilton Hotels and Circus Circus, three of the strongest operators, proposed the development, saying it would create forty thousand new jobs. Their proposal was made just a few months after the television networks opened their nightly newscasts with videotape of thousands of jobless people lined up in freezing temperatures for a chance to get nine hundred jobs offered by a Loop hotel. If the Illinois legislature approves the plan it would put pressure on every city with substantial convention business to approve casinos.

Many Americans want to gamble and the few who object on moral grounds cannot sway elections anymore except in places like Utah. Anyone who doubts this truth need only look at the stock market, which the brokerages say is always looking forward. The single stock that rose the most in value in 1991 on the New York Stock Exchange was International Game Technology, the leading manufacturer of video slot machines. The 441 percent explosion in IGT's price per share occurred because the company expects to see its market expand vastly as state after state legalizes versions of the machines in neighborhood bars and other locations—and the market believes IGT is right.

The only impediment to this trend will be a scandal, a major one that captures the public's interest, a repeat of 1890 when the Louisiana Lottery tried to buy the legislature in Baton Rouge wholesale.

The issue is how to deal with this third wave of gambling fever. Gambling will always be with us, legal or not. To make wagers among friends a crime is to create vice. But to make the noblest expression of our civility, the democratic state, a partner in wagering is to encourage pathologies to enrich the state's coffers, a Faustian bargain.

Bad as the mob is, having Corporate America dominate the casino business is worse. The mob was limited to Nevada, and its own incompetence at managing a business as complex as casinos limited its profits. Most of those murdered were themselves mobsters or their associates. Many people who now play on credit at corporate-owned casinos would never have signed a marker in the days when the mob sent enforcers to collect them.

Corporate America has access to skilled managers and it can employ the same marketing clout that sells dandruff shampoo to push casinos and create an appearance of respectability. But licensing an enterprise does not change its nature.

Gambling cannot build America. Iowa taxpayers have already learned that retired lawmakers Don Hermann and Hugo Schnekloth were right about the folly of relying on floating casinos for economic revival. In July 1992 the *Diamond Lady* and its sister ship, the *Emerald Lady*, sailed south to Biloxi, Mississippi, which had approved riverboat gambling without limits on how much players could lose. Both ships lost money in their first year of operation. Bettendorf City Council authorized a lawsuit to recover what it said were $661,000 in subsidies to Goldstein, a sum equal to $28 for each man, woman and child in town. Down in Fort Madison, where the *Emerald Lady* docked, taxpayers were left with a bill for $2.6 million in improvements they built to attract the gambling ship. A few people soon started drawing comparisons between Bernard Goldstein and Professor Henry Hill, the fictional *Music Man* who duped Iowans out of their money.

No turn of the cards, however slickly packaged, can create wealth as John Deere's smooth steel blade did when he found a way to plow the heavy soil of Iowa. But trying to prohibit gambling is also doomed to failure because taking risks is part of our nature. Gambling can be a source of enjoyment and entertainment. How then to control the rapacious nature of casinos?

In considering when, where and how to allow gambling it is essential to keep in mind that what most people do is social gambling and what the gaming industry wants is commercial gambling.

A bet between friends over who will win a round of golf, an office World Series pool or a weekly poker game poses little or no risk to the social fabric. Such social bets should not be a crime, much less a felony.

Commercial gambling is different. It can quickly and easily bring economic ruin, inducing instability that threatens the social fabric. In minutes an uncontrolled casino can turn a millionaire at a craps table into a pauper.

The forces that motivate casino owners and their marketing staffs cause them to go beyond entertaining those in control of their pocketbooks and to prey on the foolish, the compulsive and the weak, as the stories in this book have shown. A democratic state has a legitimate interest in devising laws that restrict and control casinos, just as laws compel drivers to slow near schools, require meat packers to sell only safe food, and limit liquor to adults. The promise made in the New Jersey Casino Control Act—that casinos would be strictly regulated—was a sound one and should be a model for the rest of the nation.

But the execution of New Jersey's laws significantly sold the lofty promise short, as the first licensing hearings demonstrated. The men and women who operate the Casino Control Commission and the Division of Gaming Enforcement have, with the rarest of exceptions, been honest, dedicated servants working in the fray. Their errors in judgment stem partly from human frailties and partly from the strictures of the system they swore to serve.

By coming down hard on little people the casino regulators created an appearance of being tough. But from Resorts International's mob ties through Donald Trump's illegal loan, the regulators treated casino owners by a different standard than they did everyone else, as two commissioners ultimately came to acknowledge publicly. It is a natural human tendency to use a heavier hand against the weak and powerless than against the powerful, but it is also a practice repugnant to both the U.S. and New Jersey constitutions that each of the commissioners swore to uphold.

Beyond letting economic considerations shape their judgments about the fitness of casino owners and executives, the commissioners allowed themselves to hear what they wanted and to screen out undesired facts, another natural tendency. Nowhere was this theme more clear than when the Casino Control Commission certified as financially stable junk bond deals that any careful reader of the prospectuses could tell were doomed to failure. The Atlantis mortgage bonds turned to junk less than six months after Drexel Burnham Lambert sold them. Merv Griffin's deal to buy Resorts was in trouble just three weeks after Drexel wrote him a check for $325 million and the bondholders got just one interest payment before watching their investment axed to pieces in Bankruptcy Court. Trump made only three interest payments on his Taj Mahal Casino-Hotel, and two of those were made with the bondholders' own money before filing Chapter 11. The commission found Bally Manufacturing financially stable in 1990, but six weeks later Bally began missing payments to banks and bondholders it owed more than a billion dollars.

Kaye Handley, a sharp-eyed securities analyst whose specialty is the stocks and bonds of companies on the edge of collapse, followed how the Casino Control Commission and the financial markets dealt with the Trump and Griffin borrowing binges and their aftermath. Those who focused on whether that particular deal involved fraudulent conveyance —cheating investors by wrongly transferring their property to someone else—missed the larger point, she said. The Atlantis, Resorts, Trump and Bally cases all fit a pattern.

"What has gone on in Atlantic City," Handley concluded, "is a global fraudulent conveyance presided over by the New Jersey Casino Control Commission."

Every time a casino owner borrowed money and could not pay it back the commission signaled that it would stand by the casino and take its side against the creditors, unless the casino would have to fold anyway as the Atlantis did. In the long run the policies followed in New Jersey should hurt the casinos in trying to raise debt capital. Who is going to lend money to a business that, if it is unable to pay the money

299

back, can run to a government agency that will shield it from the natural consequences of its own misjudgments?

Requiring the construction of megacasinos that incorporate hotel rooms and cost several hundred million dollars undermines strict regulation because the economic consequences of revoking a casino license are enormous for the affected workers, for investors, for lenders and for the government expecting a stream of revenues. A smarter strategy would be to lower the cost of entry into the market by allowing free-standing casinos so that the impact of suspending or revoking a license falls mostly on the owners and their managers who flouted the law.

W. David Waters, the Casino Control commissioner most hated by the casino owners and their executives because he resisted the sirens of economic interest, believes it is also critical to enforce the integrity requirement and to define that term clearly. As the Trump casinos drifted into bankruptcy and he heard more and more complaints of rules violations, culminating in the illegal Trump loan, he realized that integrity was whatever the commission said it was. "Having integrity has come to mean that you haven't been convicted of a felony, and that's just plain offensive to me," Waters said.

Perhaps one reason that Waters remained so unswayed by the passions of the moment was that he came to the commission after he retired. The appointment of people whose career and personal financial interests stretch out before them invites a natural unwillingness to take unpopular stands and to buck powerful interests.

The trend, however, is not toward efforts to define integrity or toward stricter regulation, but toward elimination of as much regulation as possible in New Jersey—and the avoidance of rigorous regulation where commercial gambling is being introduced.

Just consider the Pequot Indians' Foxwoods casino, which opened in 1992. The chairman of the Pequot regulatory board is attorney G. Michael Brown, who once headed New Jersey's Division of Gaming Enforcement. Brown is also the attorney who raised the money to finance construction of Foxwoods. He also recruited the president of the casino, Al Luciani, who used a desk at Brown's law firm when he was out of work after being fired as president of Merv Griffin's Resorts casino in Atlantic City. The investigator who reports to Brown, George Henigson, works in the same suite of offices at Foxwoods as the executives who run it.

Other basic requirements for effective casino regulation include:

1. Ban credit gambling. In Iowa today players can charge their chips to their bank card and lose money that will cost them 19.8 percent interest. New Jersey casinos charge no interest, but again and again they have used credit to lure people into playing way beyond their means.

2. Make gaming debts uncollectable and make any attempt to collect such a debt a crime.

3. Ban advertising. Not just television advertising, but any kind of advertising, including direct mail to customers. People who want to gamble should have the opportunity to do so. But stimulating demand encourages all of the social problems that accompany gambling.

4. Require casinos to close for at least a few hours on weekdays so that an individual can get a grip on his pocketbook before the casinos thoroughly clean it out.

5. Ban free alcoholic drinks, which serve only to loosen wallets and, at blackjack and other games involving skill, to reduce the likelihood that the player will make smart decisions.

6. Fine, suspend and ultimately revoke the license of any casino that allows juveniles to gamble. The mere presence of a minor on a casino floor should cause an automatic fine.

7. Destroy old slot machines, just as dice and cards are altered after use. The New Jersey Commission on Investigation found that when casinos finish with a slot machine it can be sold anywhere—and many end up owned by mob-controlled outfits that place them, illegally, in bars.

8. Send auditors, unannounced, to examine casino invoices and transactions to lessen the likelihood of money laundering.

9. Make casinos liable for the return of embezzled money lost by any rated player who received extensive complimentaries.

10. Finally, casino laws should be drafted not to *legalize* gambling, but to carve out an exemption from the criminal law.

These ideas can be useful tools to limit and control commercial gambling, but adoption of even the most carefully written laws alone is not enough. A citizenry, and a news media, that actively examine and criticize those entrusted with the duty to regulate casinos are essential. As the history of the New Jersey Casino Control Commission has shown, no law can make officials see problems and wrongs they do not want to see.

Acknowledgments

For nearly four years I investigated and reported on the casino industry for the *Philadelphia Inquirer*, a newspaper led by men and women whose reputations for integrity and tenacity are richly deserved. While many dailies become *oldspapers*, regurgitating the official version of events along with the official criticisms, the spirit of investigative reporting thrives in every section of the *Inquirer*. This spirit enabled me to look deeply into the inner workings of the casino industry and to understand its impact on our lives.

Sources are the mother's milk of journalism and in the world of gambling I found several hundred people willing, often anxious, to share their knowledge of the casinos and the agencies assigned to regulate them, as well as the world's biggest gamblers, whose names and habits had been the industry's most closely guarded secrets.

A few helped only briefly, but provided critical information. Many gave freely of their time, devoting countless hours to repeated interviews. Others pointed to little-known public records or provided access to secret files. To those sources not named in the text, and particularly to those who asked that their names not be mentioned, I express my gratitude and my hope that after reading this work they will feel that their time was well spent whether or not they concur with the conclusions I have drawn.

I especially appreciate the irrepressible Alice Martell, my agent, and Joel E. Fishman, my editor (as well as Joel's assistant, Wendy Goldman), because before the explosion of casinos across the land began they could see that it was coming and that the story behind this needed to be told.

Many fellow reporters generously shared materials from their files, provided critical introductions to sources and offered valuable advice. I am especially indebted to George Anastasia, Barbara Demick, Mark Fazlollah, William K. Marimow, Arlene Morgan, Jim Naughton, Jonathan Neumann, Bob Samsot, Mike Schurman, Steve Seplow, William H. Sokolic and Craig Stock of the *Philadelphia Inquirer*; David Crook, Steve Christensen, Al Delugach, Dennis McDougal, Betty Lukas, Mark Pinsky and Bob Sipchen of the *Los Angeles Times*; Dan Heneghan of the *Press* of Atlantic City; Kathleen M. Berry of the *New York Times*; Neil Barsky of the *Wall Street Journal*; Allan Sloan of *New York Newsday*; Howard Stutz of the Las Vegas *Review-Journal*; Wayne Barrett of the *Village Voice*; Harry Hurt III, Wes Mills of WQAD-TV and my Japanese translator, Rosemary Morrison.

I especially wish to thank these individuals, not named in the text, for their insights: in Atlantic City, Vicki Abt, Gil Brooks, John Donnelly, Noel Eisenstat, Captain Joseph Guzzardo of the New Jersey State Police, Warren Kasdan, Hersh Kozlov, Harry Jay Levin, George Miller, Marilyn Morris, Alyce Parker, Roberto Rivera-Soto, Gary Selesner, Kaleem Shabazz, Ed Tracy, Jim Wise and Jack Wolf; in Las Vegas, Mark Atkinson, Shannon Bybee, Chick Goodwill, Mike Rumbolz, Glen Schaeffer and Bob Stupak; on Wall Street, Warren Foss, Charles M. Masson and Wilbur L. Ross.

Three of my eight children—Mark, Andrew and Amy—helped with clerical tasks and library research, their youthful eyes adding unexpected insights. Throughout the writing of this book my wife and fellow writer, Jennifer Leonard, gave freely of her criticism and affection.

—David Johnston
Cheltenham, Pennsylvania
March 1992

About the Author

David Johnston has won two national prizes for investigative reporting, one of them a George Polk Award for exposing brutality and intelligence-gathering abuses by the Los Angeles Police Department. He joined the *San Jose Mercury-News* in 1968, becoming at nineteen its youngest staff writer, and has since been an investigative reporter at the *Detroit Free Press, Los Angeles Times* and the *Philadelphia Inquirer,* where he covered the casino industry for four years and now covers business news. He lives in suburban Philadelphia with his wife, Jennifer Leonard, and their two daughters.

Index

Index

307

Index

Index

Index